The
Georgia–
South Carolina
Boundary

Financial assistance for the research represented in this book was provided through the Office of Coastal Zone Management, National Oceanic and Atmospheric Administration, from funds made available under the Coastal Zone Management Act of 1972. Financial assistance was also provided by the State of Georgia Department of Natural Resources and Office of Planning and Budget.

LOUIS DE VORSEY, JR.

The Georgia–South Carolina Boundary

A PROBLEM
IN HISTORICAL
GEOGRAPHY

The University of Georgia Press
Athens, Georgia

© 1982 by the Board of Regents of the University
System of Georgia
Paperback edition published in 2008 by
The University of Georgia Press
Athens, Georgia 30602
www.ugapress.org
All rights reserved
Designed by Sandra Strother Hudson
Set in 10 on 13 Baskerville
Printed digitally in the United States of America

The Library of Congress has cataloged the hardcover
edition of this book as follows:
Library of Congress Cataloging-in-Publication Data

De Vorsey, Louis.
The Georgia-South Carolina boundary : a problem in
historical geography / Louis De Vorsey, Jr.
xii, 219 p., [2] folded leaves : ill. ; 24 cm.
ISBN 0-8203-0591-X

Includes index.
Bibliography: p. 209-214.
1. Georgia—Boundaries—South Carolina. 2. South
Carolina—Boundaries—Georgia. 3. Georgia—
Historical geography. 4. South Carolina—Historical
geography. I. Title.
F292.B7 D45   1982
911'.758 19   81-10441

Paperback ISBN-13: 978-0-8203-3242-0
ISBN-10: 0-8203-3242-9

CONTENTS

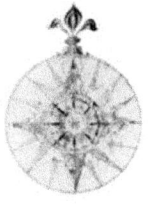

Maps and Tables   vii

Acknowledgments   xi

Introduction   1

21
PART I: The Georgia–South Carolina Boundary as Determined by the Treaty of Beaufort, April 28, 1787

51
PART II: The Lower Savannah River and Mouth Area in the Eighteenth Century

81
PART III: Changes in the Morphology of the Lower Savannah River Area, 1787–1900

161
PART IV: Concluding Observations

Epilogue   205

Bibliography   209

Index   215

MAPS AND TABLES

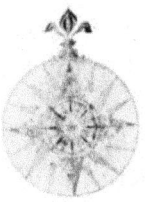

MAPS

1. U.S. Geological Survey Quadrangles showing Savannah Area, 1955 *follows page 16*

2. U.S. Geological Survey Quadrangles showing Savannah Area, 1971 *follows page 16*

3. Section of "A Map of the British Empire in America with the French and Spanish Settlements adjacent thereto, by Henry Popple, 1733" *page 25*

4. Disputed territory described in the Beaufort Convention Preamble *page 37*

5. Section of "An Accurate Map of North and South Carolina with Their Indian Frontiers, Shewing in a distinct manner all the Mountains, Rivers, Swamps, Marshes, Bays, Creeks, Harbours, Sandbanks and Soundings on the Coasts; with the Roads and Indian Paths; as well as The Boundary or Provincial Lines, The Several Townships and other divisions of the Land In Both The Provinces; the whole from Actual Surveys By Henry Mouzon and Others, 1775" *page 39*

6. Section of "The Coast, Rivers and Inlets of the Province of Georgia, Surveyed by Joseph Avery and others. Published by Command of Government, by J. F. W. Des Barres. 1st Feby. 1780" *page 42*

7. U.S. Coast Survey Preliminary Chart, 1855, overlaid on the Avery Map, 1780 *page 44*

8. "A View of Savannah as it Stood the 29th of March 1734," by Peter Gordon *page 60*

9. "Chart of the Savannah Sound," by William De Brahm *page 65*

viii Maps and Tables

10. "Plan and Profile of Fort George, on Coxpur Island," by William De Brahm   *page 67*

11. "A Plan of the Inlets and Rivers of Savannah and Warsaw in the Province of Georgia. Performed by order of the President and Assistants this 1st June Ano Dom 1751 per Henry Yonge Surv."   *page 70*

12. "Plan of the French and American Sieg of Savannah in Georgia in South America under Command of the French Gener. Count d'Estaing The Britt: Commander in the Town was General August Prevost, 1779"   *page 78*

13. "Savannah River, From Its Mouth to the City of Savannah By John Le Conte, Topr. Engr., 1821" [Redrawn from original]   *page 102*

14A. "Chart of Part of the Savannah River, 1833, Surveyed & Drawn by Lieut. John Mackay, 2d Regt. Arty."   *page 106*

14B. Same as above   *page 108*

15. "Chart of a Portion of the Savannah River," by M. L. Smith, 1849   *page 114*

16. U.S. Coast Survey, Preliminary Chart of Savannah River, Georgia, 1855 [Redrawn from original]   *page 124*

17. "Savannah Harbor, Ga., Showing Progress of Improvement to June 30, 1888"   *page 134*

18. Index Map, Savannah River, Georgia, showing works constructed from 1804 to 1896 [Redrawn from original]   *page 148*

19. Section of U.S. Coast Survey, Preliminary Chart of Savannah River, Georgia, 1855, overlaid on a 1976 U.S. Department of Commerce Map of Savannah River [Redrawn from original]   *page 164*

20. Plat of two marsh islands about 3 miles below Savannah, surveyed May 12, 1760 by H. Yonge S.G. for Edmund Tannatt Esqr.   *page 168*

21. Plat of 2,060 acres of land granted to James Oglethorpe, Esqr., for the use of the Trustees of Georgia, certified January 20, 1733/4   *page 170*

22. Plat showing three marsh islands granted to Archibald Smith, surveyed March 24, 1813   *page 172*

23. Plat of Noble Jones, Esqr.'s 800 acres marsh land, surveyed March 9, 1768   *page 183*

TABLES

1. Barnwell Islands: Cartographic Analysis Summary *page 174*
2. Jones Island–Mud River: Cartographic Analysis Summary *page 185*
3. Oyster Bed Island Area: Cartographic Analysis Summary *page 191*

ACKNOWLEDGMENTS

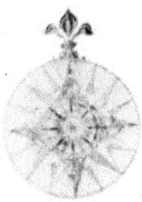

THIS BOOK grew out of research undertaken at the request of Assistant Attorney General Patricia T. Barmeyer. I owe her, her colleagues Sarah Evans Lockwood and Don A. Langham, and staff personnel at the Georgia Department of Law, my deepest thanks for their willing help and constant encouragement as I prepared my research report, trial testimony, and finally this book dealing with the Georgia–South Carolina boundary controversy.

Also deserving of my heartfelt thanks are a host of archivists and librarians in this country and in England. Particularly helpful on an almost day-to-day basis have been Marion R. Hemperley, the deputy surveyor general of Georgia, and Robert M. Willingham, Jr., the librarian in charge of the University of Georgia's special collections of documents and historical maps.

Farther afield, Richard W. Stephenson and John A. Wolter of the Library of Congress Geography and Map Division and Ronald E. Grim and Gary L. Morgan of the National Archives Cartographic Archives Division were unstinting in their responses to my frequent calls for assistance. Personnel at the Georgia Historical Society; Savannah District Corps of Engineers; South Carolina Historical Society; Georgia Department of Archives and History; South Carolina Department of Archives and History; the Navy Department Library; Duke University Library; British Library; British Public Record Office; National Maritime Museum, Hydrographic Department; and William L. Clements Library, are all deserving of my thanks.

James O. Wheeler, head of the Department of Geography, is thanked for his unflagging support through the several years I have devoted to this problem. So too is Robert C. Anderson, vice president for research, who aided in obtaining the funds necessary to allow the full-color maps included in the book. Those funds were provided by the University of Georgia Research Foundation, Inc., whose support is greatly appreciated. So too was the constant administrative and logistical support provided by the Institute of Community and Area Development. Albert F. Ike, associate director of that organization, is singled out for particular thanks for frequently "going an extra mile" on my behalf in an administrative sense.

Finally, I thank Rosalyn, Megan, Kirsteen, and Kevin for being patient and understanding during those many weekends and evenings when I was preoccupied with my research and the preparation of my testimony and this book.

*We enjoy the fruits of the plains
and of the mountains, the rivers and
the lakes are ours, we sow corn,
we plant trees, we fertilize the soil by
irrigation, we confine the rivers and
straighten or divert their courses.
In fine, by means of our hands we essay
to create as it were a second world
within the world of nature.*
CICERO, De Natura Deorum

INTRODUCTION

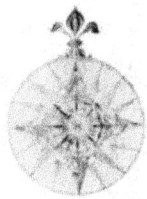

THIS BOOK EXAMINES the historical geography of Georgia's boundary line with South Carolina in the Savannah River from the city of Savannah to the sea. The need for such a study was first made known to me at a meeting in the State Judicial Building on December 9, 1975, at which conflicting opinions concerning the location of the boundary between the two states, particularly in the area known as the Barnwell islands, Jones Island, and Oyster Bed Island, were outlined.

In the weeks following that conference I began to look into the history of the Georgia–South Carolina boundary line, flew over the contested area, and examined the complex geography of the river channel and islands from a motor launch. One of the most vivid impressions to come out of these firsthand experiences was the extent to which the lowermost Savannah River has been altered by human actions. Particularly dramatic were the works of the United States Army Corps of Engineers, which has been operating in the area for more than a century. So effective had been their efforts to tame the forces of nature and provide a secure deep-water channel for oceangoing vessels that it seemed no exaggeration to call the lowermost Savannah a man-made river.

There could be little doubt that trying to understand descriptions of the boundary as they had been written in eighteenth-century documents would be difficult or impossible if one referred only to the modern maps of the engineer-altered river. A major effort in historical-geographical reconstruction was needed—an effort that would recreate the geographic conditions and perceptions that prevailed when crucial documents such as the Colonial Charter of Georgia of 1732 or the Beaufort Treaty of 1787 were written.

Interest in the lower Savannah River began to heighten as the subject of lateral seaward boundaries for the seaboard states came to a head in 1976. In that year President Gerald Ford signed and made effective amendments to the Coastal Zone Management Act of 1972. Under the terms of the amended act, very large sums of federal money were to be made available to assist coastal states and local communities that might be affected by new or expanded energy facilities. Secretary of Commerce Elliot L. Richardson made this point clear in a letter to coastal state governors. In his letter the secretary mentioned that $1.2 billion in financial assistance had been provided for in the legislation (Elliot L. Richardson, letter to Honorable George Busbee, undated, marked received October 10, 1976).

The disbursement of this money was to be made according to a formula outlined in the act. The sums granted would depend upon the amount of newly leased outer continental shelf acreage adjacent to a particular state as well as the amount of oil and gas ultimately produced from leases located there. Also important in the formula was the amount of oil and gas actually first landed in the state and the amount of new employment that would result from the expanded outer continental shelf energy activity. As a result, it became vitally important to know just which states held legal claim to the area of any particular outer continental shelf energy development.

For the purpose of calculating the formula for payments, the legal claim of a state to the outer continental shelf acreage was to be determined by extending existing state lateral seaward boundaries for approximately two hundred miles to the limit of the outer continental shelf. In the mid-1970s, however, few if any of the Atlantic seaboard states had clearly defined lateral seaward boundaries, a condition that remains largely unchanged into the 1980s.

There seemed to be general agreement that the termination point of the Savannah River boundary—wherever that might be—would be the logical beginning for any lateral seaward boundary between Georgia and South Carolina. The end of the river boundary would serve as the beginning point for a lateral boundary that would reach out to the three-mile limit. Beyond the state-controlled three-mile limit, seabed resources are controlled by the government of the United States. The revenue-sharing formula outlined in the Coastal Zone Management Act amendments was to be applied over this vast area, out to the limits of the outer continental shelf. Thus the position from which such a line would originate could result in the inclusion of a potentially lucrative area of seabed in the formula of one state and its loss to the other.

At about the same time that the provisions of the Coastal Zone Management Act and offshore drilling right leasing were stimulating a heightened interest in the seabed, the actions of another federal agency served to focus attention squarely on the boundary in the Savannah River. The agency concerned was the United States Geological Survey (USGS), which has the primary responsibility for producing large-scale topographic maps of the United States.

In addition to their task of making maps of the unmapped areas of the United States, the Geological Survey must also "maintain" or bring up to date existing maps. As the Savannah area began to reflect the impact of accelerating economic development in the late 1960s, the existing 1955 edition large-scale topographic quadrangles (as the USGS maps are called) became outmoded. Because the production of entirely new maps is a costly and time-consuming task, it is sometimes avoided by the revision of existing maps. For the rapidly developing Savannah area, the Geological Survey decided to produce an interim map revision based on aerial photographs taken in 1971. On these photo-revised map sheets of 1971, changed or altered features were shown in purple ink. A note included with the marginal information printed on the maps stated, "Revisions shown in purple compiled from aerial photographs taken in 1971. This information not field checked." Thus the users of the maps were made aware of their interim status.

The 1971 photo-revised maps showed a change in the state boundary between Georgia and South Carolina in the vicinity of Savannah. On the 1955 map sheets, the boundary was drawn to follow the approximate center of the main navigation channel from Fort Jackson to a point just to the east of the protective jetties near Fort Pulaski National Monument (Maps 1 and 2). As a result, the whole of the Savannah River's South Channel and intervening Elba, Bird, and Cockspur islands were shown to be within the Georgia limits. The Tybee National Wildlife Refuge, located on areas identified as Oyster Bed Island and Jones Island, as well as an area identified as Barnwell Island and Barnwell Island No. 2, were shown to be entirely within the limits of South Carolina. Thus it was that the most definitive and widely available detailed topographic maps showed the Georgia–South Carolina boundary through a crucial sixteen-year period which saw the Savannah region move into an era of unparalleled economic growth and land development.

When the photo-revised maps of 1971 were issued, they soon

caught the attention of those with any interest in the lower Savannah River's marshy islands and banks. Of particular note was the greatly altered placement of the Georgia–South Carolina boundary. Instead of following the middle of the main navigation channel and passing through the protective jetties, it was shown to make some sharp swings northward to the South Carolina side and embrace the Barnwell islands and Oyster Bed Island within the limits of Georgia. No longer did the boundary pass through the jetties near Fort Pulaski; rather, it was shown to swing away in a wide arc about a mile and three-quarters to the north.

The U.S. Geological Survey was careful to show these boundary line alterations in the distinctive purple ink reserved for non-field-checked revisions made from 1971 aerial photographs. They printed the caption "Indefinite Boundary" along the altered segments. No other explanation of this significant change in the major political boundary included on the Savannah area topographic maps was provided.

The Geological Survey does not, of course, have the authority to make decisions as to the legality of any given boundary. It is their policy to position boundaries on their maps as accurately as possible by employing all the evidence available. As a result, boundary positions shown on USGS maps are not, in themselves, legally binding.

A USGS Information Office release dated April 4, 1977, stressed this point and went on to note that in drawing the topographic quadrangle maps of the Savannah area, they had taken into account "the interstate agreements, court decisions and cartographic evidence as indicated on maps prepared as early as 1780" (United States Department of the Interior, Geological Survey, Information Office, Reston, Virginia, "State Boundary Disputes," April 4, 1977).

The Geological Survey's photo-revised topographic maps were to play a major role in stimulating the boundary dispute that complicated relations between Georgia and South Carolina in the mid-1970s. The new boundary line, once drafted and issued, could not be withdrawn. It served to influence attitudes and opinions on both sides of the Savannah River.

The Georgia legislature, acting on a tentative agreement with South Carolina, passed a law in 1969 that drew further attention to the boundary shift shown on the Geological Survey's 1971 maps. Briefly, the law amended the Georgia Code relating to the boundary to ensure that the lateral seaward boundary between the two states would be legally extended out to any distance on the seabed which the government of the United States might ultimately grant to the seaboard states. At that time most of the Atlantic seaboard states were joined in litigation with the United States to decide whether the states or the federal government would control continental shelf resources beyond the three-mile limit. In effect, the Georgia legislature was making sure that the state's claim was clearly defined. With that motive looming large in their minds, the legislators appear to have been unaware of any controversy, actual or potential, concerning the boundary in the lower Savannah River. Although not stated in the 1969 act, the Georgia legislators were responding to what they doubtless perceived as a need arising from the litigation known as *United States v. Maine et al.*

Georgia's 1969 law provided for the due east seaward extension of the lateral boundary with South Carolina. Such an extension created no problem in itself. The point in the Savannah River from which the seaward extension began did, however, contribute to the boundary dispute that arose in the 1970s. That point was designated as the center of the "hypothetical line connecting the seawardmost end points of the existing protective jetties" (Georgia Laws 1969 Session, p. 677). This is precisely where the old 1955 Geological Survey maps had shown the boundary to be, but it was a significant distance to the south of where the "indefinite" boundary had been drawn on the 1971 Geological Survey map. To an interested South Carolinian, this was an important fact. Fortunately for Georgia, the 1969 law had required that the lateral boundary it described receive congressional approval within a stipulated period of time. Congress did not act within that period, and the law never became operative.

A major construction development by the Georgia Ports Authority, which was undertaken at the outset of the 1970s, ensured that widespread attention would be focused on the area immediately adjacent to the same protective jetties that had been referred to in the 1969 law. In their continuing effort to keep Georgia's port and cargo handling facilities abreast of international technological progress, the Port Authority began the construction of a facility known as a LASH terminal (Lighter Aboard Ship Handling). LASH ships carry their cargo packed in barges (lighters) that can be easily and quickly offloaded to continue to a destination by water while the ship resumes its oceanic voyage.

To be effective a LASH facility must be easily accessible to large oceangoing vessels. For Savannah, this requirement was best met by building several miles downstream from the city's existing port facilities. The site chosen was immediately upstream of the protective jetties adjacent to the area known as Oyster Bed Island. This location placed the line of breasting dolphins and other facilities comprising LASH along the northern side of the main navigation channel adjacent to the southern flank of the peninsula known as Oyster Bed Island.

On the 1955 Geological Survey maps this area was shown to be in South Carolina, whereas in 1971 the "Indefinite Boundary" was drawn across the neck of the Oyster Bed Island peninsula to place it in Georgia. Thus, misunderstandings concerning the construction of LASH could easily have arisen to contribute to the burgeoning boundary dispute.

In the mid-1970s the Geological Survey began to prepare a new edition of their topographic quadrangles showing the Savannah–Savannah River area from aerial photographs taken in 1974. Colored proof copies of these new maps showed the boundary in the same position as in the 1971 photo-revised maps that were being replaced. Not unexpectedly, this caused consternation in South Carolina. On February 23, 1977, South Carolina State Senators James M. Waddell, Jr., and William Howell introduced a Concurrent Resolution "To Declare that the United States Geological Survey Should Immediately Begin Consultation with the Authorized Representatives of Both South Carolina and Georgia in Order to Correct the Erroneous Delineation of the Boundary Line Between South Carolina and Georgia."

Eager to maintain good relations with state and local agencies, the Geological Survey sent senior staff members to make a formal presentation explaining their rationale for delineating the state boundary. Early in the April 1977 proceedings, South Carolina Senator Waddell read the following summary of that state's position:

> This delegation is here on a fact-finding mission. For many years U.S.G.S. has published quadrangle sheets depicting the Savannah River boundary between Georgia and South Carolina as it is drawn on the 1955 quadrangle sheets. South Carolina believes this boundary, as depicted on the 1955 quadrangle sheet is in accord with the Convention of Beaufort of 1787, the historical document which set the boundary between the two States.
>
> Now the latest U.S.G.S. maps, revised in 1971, show that this boundary has been redrawn for no apparent reason. Realizing that this 1971 revision was not an arbitrary decision, the South Carolina General Assembly

has, by concurrent resolution, requested this meeting between U.S.G.S. and South Carolina for purposes of discovering the basis for the boundary revision. This delegation is here in a spirit of cooperation in an attempt to correct this improper boundary delineation.

South Carolinians are deeply concerned over the new boundary delineation since this questionable shift could possibly have a detrimental effect on the natural and economic resources of the State of South Carolina.

We are concerned further by the fact that a change in the South Carolina border was drawn on a map without any consultation with the proper offices of our State. We realize that maps are subject to change; but any change must be a justified one.

We feel that the boundary, as shown on the 1971 quad sheet, is in error. In fairness to all concerned parties we feel that now is the time to explain thoroughly and completely the basis for this change. The attainment of this explanation is our sole mission at this time. [Senator James M. Waddell, Jr., Statement read at USGS Georgia–South Carolina Boundary Presentation, Atlanta, Ga., April 4, 1977]

In the introduction to their presentation, Geological Survey personnel made a number of general points concerning boundary disagreements between states. These seem worthy of inclusion here in light of the dispute outlined by Senator Waddell. By means of a projected visual graphic the Geological Survey personnel reviewed several key background matters relevant to the general topic of state boundary conflicts. Among these was the important role of Congress, which must consent to and approve boundary settlements or changes between states. It was also pointed out that the U.S. Supreme Court was the tribunal charged with settling state boundary disputes that could not be settled by the parties themselves. In concluding this portion of their presentation, USGS representatives vigorously stressed the fact that "the U.S. Geological Survey does not establish boundaries nor does it adjudicate boundary disputes" (USGS, Georgia–South Carolina Boundary Presentation, Atlanta, Ga., April 4, 1977). A large number of relevant early maps showing the lower Savannah area were then projected and discussed. These maps varied widely in scale and date, with the earliest being from the year 1780. Throughout the presentation, Geological Survey personnel stressed that their agency "had no ax to grind" in the matter of the boundary's location and that they felt the placement shown on the 1971 map and proof sheets in 1977 was based on a reasonably correct interpretation of historical document and map evidence.

After their explanatory analysis of the many maps projected, the Geological Survey representatives outlined several ways of indicating a disputed boundary on the forthcoming Savannah area maps. They emphasized that any cartographic technique or caption employed to show the disputed boundary would have to be satisfactory to both states before it was adopted and printed.

On May 3, 1977, Senator Waddell, as chairman of the South Carolina Boundary Commission, wrote to the assistant director of the Geological Survey's Eastern Region outlining his state's position in the matter of the depiction of the disputed boundary: "Any maps printed by U.S.G.S. should show the boundary as it had been depicted in virtually all U.S.G.S. maps printed prior to 1971. Specifically, the line should be depicted in the same manner and location as it appeared on the 1955 7½ minute U.S.G.S. quadrangles depicting the area of concern. Further, the line should be in accordance with the laws passed by both the South Carolina and Georgia Legislatures in 1969 and 1970, which are in accordance with the 1955 U.S.G.S. 7½ minute quadrangles" (James M. Waddell, Jr., letter to William B. Overstreet, assistant director, Eastern Region USGS, May 3, 1977).

To add weight to his contentions, Senator Waddell further indicated that South Carolina was ready to "take whatever steps are necessary, including seeking injunctive relief through the courts," to protect what it saw as its interests in the matter of maps showing its boundary as depicted on the 1971 sheets. Obviously, none of the compromise methods of depicting the boundary suggested at the Geological Survey's presentation of the previous month was found satisfactory in South Carolina.

A further meeting between Geological Survey personnel and South Carolina representatives led to a compromise on May 10, 1977. South Carolina agreed to allow the Savannah area maps to be printed with no boundary lines shown in the disputed Barnwell Island and Oyster Bed areas. A caption was to be included stating: "Portions of Georgia–South Carolina boundary in dispute. Boundary omitted in approximate area of dispute."

Although this solution satisfied South Carolina, it met with objection in Georgia. In a letter written on May 20, 1977, the attorney general of Georgia, Arthur K. Bolton, reacted to the compromise that had been worked out between the Geological Survey and South Carolina. He wrote that "Georgia feels that U.S.G.S. would be unnecessarily yielding to pressure and would be disserving the public" were it to adopt the South Carolina position (Arthur K. Bolton, letter to William B. Overstreet, assistant director, Eastern Region USGS, May 20, 1977).

Faced with a dilemma, the Geological Survey ultimately published the 1978 edition of the Savannah area maps with no boundary line at all. Each map carried the caption "Georgia–South Carolina boundary in dispute, not shown" in small print off the lower left-hand margin. In the absence of any state boundary whatsoever, serious confusion on the part of people with an interest in the disputed area and resources seemed inevitable.

In addition to its significance as a major artery of commerce, the lower Savannah River forms a broad and extensive estuary within which commercial fishing has long been established. In recent years, commercial shrimping has become the most important single part of the fishing activity there. As uncertainty grew concerning the location of the Georgia–South Carolina boundary through the waters of the fishery in the mid-1970s, commercial shrimp fishermen could not help but become involved in the dispute, especially because the crucial laws controlling the seasons and times for commercial shrimping varied in the two states.

In July 1976 representatives from Georgia and South Carolina met at Belmont Plantation, South Carolina, in an effort to forestall serious problems and resolve differences concerning shrimp and other fishing in the lower Savannah River. Although Georgia proposed a line of demarcation for the control of shrimp fishing in the area of the boundary dispute, little except an agreement on shad fishing farther upstream resulted from that meeting.

By the spring of 1977 the problems surrounding the uncertain location of the boundary in the lowermost Savannah River had become so great that a meeting between the governors of the two states seemed necessary. Such a meeting was held on May 23, 1977, with an agenda that included the problem of commercial shrimp fishing. The governors agreed that representatives from their respective states should meet to arrive at detailed agreements that would minimize such problems until the boundary line dispute could be resolved.

A month after the governors' meeting, on June 20, 1977, Georgia's commissioner of natural resources, Joe D. Tanner, led his state's delegation to a meeting held at Columbia. Commissioner Tanner attempted to negotiate an agreement to resolve the existing differences in the fishing laws of the two states that were applicable in the dispute-clouded Savannah Sound shrimp fishery. The agreement, as proposed by Tanner, would have created a zone within which a license from either state would be considered valid by enforcement officers from either state. Northern and southern lines limiting this zone of reciprocity were designated as well as a prohibition against shrimping within the Savannah's protective jetties. There was also to be a Law Enforcement Demarcation Line to which the laws of each state would reach and at which law enforcement patrols from each would be terminated. This Law Enforcement Demarcation Line, although not identical with the "Indefinite Boundary" shown on the 1971 USGS map of the area, was close to it and definitely north of the 1955 USGS map line through the protective jetties which South Carolina claimed. Even though the last provision in the proposed reciprocal agreement specifically stated that it would "in no way be considered as an interpretation of the boundary line between Georgia and South Carolina," South Carolina officials rejected it, and the issue of fishing law enforcement in the Savannah estuary remained unresolved (Georgia Proposal Concerning a Reciprocal Agreement . . . in Area in Dispute . . . , Columbia, S.C., June 20, 1977). As Georgia's Governor Busbee wrote a week later, "the failure to arrive at an agreement concerning commercial shrimping [created] a state of law enforcement limbo in that disputed area" (George Busbee, letter to James B. Edwards, governor of South Carolina, June 28, 1977).

In an effort to avoid the problems that would inevitably result from such uncertainty, Governor Busbee urged that Governor James B. Edwards "personally" consider the proposal Commissioner Tanner had made at the meeting at Columbia the week before. Before Governor Busbee's letter had reached Governor Edwards, an event took place squarely within the disputed area that heightened the boundary controversy and brought it to the attention of the national news media. The event grew out of the attempt by Georgia rangers to arrest a South Carolina shrimp fisherman in the disputed waters on the day after Governor Busbee wrote his letter urging the adoption of a compromise agreement. A headline accompanying the story of the attempted arrest, which appeared in the *Washington Post* on July 12, 1977, read, "Fisherman Caught in Two States' Fight Over Border— and Right to U.S. Aid." The *Post* correspondent was clearly linking the arrest incident with the larger issue of state-federal seabed resource revenue sharing and lateral seaward boundaries. A map showing the disputed area and the boundaries claimed by each state accompanied the article to provide a clear idea of the dispute.

In the warrants that were sworn out against the shrimp-boat captain, he was charged with illegally fishing in Georgia waters without first obtaining a commercial saltwater fishing license from that state. Additionally, it was charged that after being arrested, he refused to obey the command of the boarding Georgia ranger and piloted his boat back to Hilton Head Island, South Carolina. In the documents associated with Georgia's request for the extradition of the fugitive shrimp-boat captain it was also stipulated that "the Defendant further committed a simple battery upon one of the rangers" (Andrew J. Ryan III, district attorney for the Eastern Judicial Circuit, Application for Governor's Requisition for the Extradition of James B. Saxon, Jr., Savannah, Georgia, July 11, 1977). It would appear that although guns were not drawn, conditions surrounding the boundary dispute had moved to a new level of tension. Pushing, grabbing, and flight to resist arrest could escalate easily to the level of a "fishing war" of the sort that had sometimes marred the tranquility of other coastal areas in the past.

Georgia's request for the extradition of the offending shrimp-boat captain was subsequently refused. Apparently, South Carolina state officials agreed with the logic of the captain, who had been quoted in the press as saying that if he were to be extradited, "there won't be a dispute any more over the boundary" (as quoted in *Washington Post*, July 12, 1977). Needless to say, the incident and subsequent developments only served to strengthen the resolve of Georgia authorities to seek a resolution for the boundary dispute in the Supreme Court of the United States. Governor Busbee had indicated this resolve in his letter to Governor Edwards on June 28, so both states were already moving toward a judicial resolution in the summer months of 1977.

In addition to the obvious problems connected with law enforcement in the disputed area, state authorities on both sides of the Savannah River had become concerned over such longer-term issues as future economic development, natural resource exploitation, and the resulting environmental alteration of the area. Clearly, the lower Savannah River boundary dispute had escalated to the dimensions of a major issue in the half-dozen years following the appearance of the Geological Survey's 1971 photo-revised map sheets. Although never claimed as "official" by any interested party, the boundary depiction on these maps acted as a catalyst to bring the two states to a point where litigation in the nation's highest court seemed to be the most advisable course of action.

On August 10, 1977, Attorney General Arthur K. Bolton publicly announced that he was filing "a motion for leave to file suit in the Supreme Court of the United States . . . in the name and behalf of the State of Georgia against the State of South Carolina in order to have the Court determine the boundary line in the Savannah River between the states of Georgia and South Carolina." The attorney general also noted: "The petition for the State of Georgia has been prepared by members of the staff of the State Law Department and amply sets forth the reason for this action" (The Department of Law, State of Georgia, "for release on Wednesday, August 10, 1977, from the Office of Attorney General Arthur K. Bolton").

After due consideration of Georgia's "Motion for Leave to File Complaint and Complaint" and its supporting brief, the Supreme Court placed the boundary line case on its docket for the October term, 1977, as case number 74, Original (indicating that the case originated in the Supreme Court rather than at a lower judicial level).

The full text of Georgia's Complaint, which was presented to the Supreme Court in August 1977, is printed below. The Geological Survey maps that were attached to the original document as Exhibits A and B appear here as Maps 1 and 2 and can be consulted as necessary.

In The

SUPREME COURT OF THE UNITED STATES

October Term, 1977

No. 74, Original

State of Georgia, Plaintiff,

v.

State of South Carolina, Defendant.

COMPLAINT

Comes now the State of Georgia, by and through its Attorney General, and brings this suit against the Defendant, the State of South Carolina, and for its cause of action states:

1.

The jurisdiction of this Court is invoked pursuant to Art. III, Sec. 2, Clause 2 of the Constitution of the United States, and 28 U.S.C. § 1251(a)(1).

2.

On June 9, 1732, George II, King of Great Britain, France and Ireland, issued letters patent establishing the Colony of Georgia, and describing the boundary between the Colony of Georgia and the Colony of South Carolina as "the most northern Stream of a River there, commonly called the Savannah."

3.

On April 28, 1787, commissioners appointed by the two states executed a convention resolving a dispute between the two states as to their common boundary, which convention is hereafter referred to as the Treaty of Beaufort, which was properly ratified by the two states and by the Congress of the United States.

4.

The Treaty of Beaufort, which established the boundary between the State of Georgia and the State of South Carolina, provides in pertinent part as follows:

"Article first, The most northern branch or stream of the River Savannah, from the Sea or mouth of such stream, to the fork or confluence of the Rivers now called Tugoloo and Keowee, and from thence the most northern branch or stream of the said River Tugoloo 'till it intersects the Northern boundary line of South Carolina, if the said branch or stream of Tugoloo extends so far North, reserving all the islands in the said Rivers Savannah and Tugoloo to Georgia; but if the head spring or source of any branch or stream of the said River Tugoloo does not extend to the north boundary line of South Carolina, then a west line to the Mississippi, to be drawn from the head spring or source of the said branch or stream of Tugoloo river, which extends to the highest northern latitude, Shall forever hereafter form the separation, limit, and boundary between the States of South Carolina and Georgia.

"Article the second. The navigation of the River Savannah, at and from the bar, and mouth, along the Northeast side of Cockspur Island, and up the direct course of the main northern channel, along the northern side of Hutchinson's Island opposite the town of Savannah, to the upper end of the said Island, and from thence up the bed or principal stream of the said River to the confluence of the Rivers Tugoloo and Keowee and from the confluence up the Channel of the most northern stream of Tugoloo River to its source; And back again, by the same channel to the Atlantick Ocean, Is hereby declared to be henceforth equally free to the citizens of both States, and exempt from all duties, tolls, hindrance, interruption, or molestation whatsoever, attempted to be enforced by one State on the Citizens of the other; And all the rest of the river Savannah, to the southward of the foregoing description, is acknowledged to be the exclusive right of the State of Georgia."

5.

By the terms of the Treaty of Beaufort, all islands in the Savannah River are specifically reserved to Georgia. In addition, the Treaty of Beaufort, as construed by this Court in *Georgia v. South Carolina*, 257 U.S. 516 (1922), provides that the bed of the Savannah River, to the middle of the northernmost stream or branch thereof, is within the boundaries of the State of Georgia and subject to its jurisdiction.

6.

The State of South Carolina and the State of Georgia presently have a dispute concerning the location of the boundary between the two states in the lower reaches and mouth of the Savannah River, from approximately the City of Savannah, Georgia, downstream to the Atlantic Ocean. In addition, the parties are in dispute as to the location of the lateral seaward boundary between the two states.

7.

The boundary dispute between the State of Georgia and the State of South Carolina is illustrated generally by maps published by the United States Geological Survey, which are attached hereto as Exhibits A and B. Exhibit A is a reduction of a composite of the United States Geological Survey quadrangle sheets for Savannah, Ga.–S.C.; Fort Pulaski, S.C.–Ga.: and Savannah Beach North, S.C.–Ga., which quadrangle sheets were published by the United States Geological Survey in 1955. Exhibit B is a reduction of a composite of the 1971 revisions of the same three quadrangle sheets. Exhibit A, published in 1955, shows the boundary line in the location argued for the State of South Carolina. Exhibit B, published in 1971, correctly relocates the boundary in certain areas.

8.

The lower reaches and mouth of the Savannah River, from the City of Savannah to the Atlantic Ocean, have been extensively altered by the actions of the United States Army Corps of Engineers in improving the Savannah River for navigation. The topographical changes resulting from actions of the United States Army Corps of Engineers are avulsive changes in the river and do not change the location of the boundary line between Georgia and South Carolina.

9.

By operation of the Treaty of Beaufort, all islands and former islands in the Savannah River, such as Pennyworth Island, Barnwell Island(s), Jones Island, Oyster Bed Island, and several unnamed islands, are within the boundaries of the State of Georgia and are subject to the jurisdiction of the State of Georgia, even though these islands may now be affixed to the mainland of South Carolina as a result of artificial man-made changes. In addition, there are certain areas now located on the northern bank of the Savannah River which were originally located south of the middle of the northernmost stream or branch of the Savannah River; where the river has changed course because of artificial man-made changes, such areas remain within the boundaries of the State of Georgia.

10.

The boundary between Georgia and South Carolina runs north of the peninsula of land generally referred to as Oyster Bed Island, as shown on exhibit B, and continues in a northeasterly direction to a midpoint between Tybee Island, Georgia and Hilton Head Island, South Carolina, which is the middle of the mouth of the Savannah River.

11.

The lateral seaward boundary between Georgia and South Carolina runs from a midpoint between Tybee Island, Georgia and Hilton Head Island, South Carolina, which is the middle of the mouth of the Savannah River, easterly in a due east direction along a parallel of latitude to the three-mile limit.

12.

Since 1787 the State of Georgia has continuously claimed and asserted jurisdiction and sovereignty over all islands in the Savannah River, over the Savannah River and the bed thereof north to the middle of the northernmost stream or branch thereof, and over all waters and waterbottoms lying south of the middle of the mouth of the Savannah River.

13.

The State of South Carolina has acquiesced in the State of Georgia's exercise of jurisdiction and sovereignty over all islands in the Savannah River, over the Savannah River and the bed thereof north to the middle of the northernmost stream or branch thereof, and over all waters and waterbottoms lying south of the middle of the mouth of the Savannah River.

14.

The 1977 Session of the General Assembly of South Carolina passed a concurrent resolution, stating in pertinent part as follows:

"WHEREAS, the boundary between South Carolina and our sister state Georgia has for many years been in question; and

"WHEREAS, the location of the boundary is of importance regarding the management of natural resources, the location of industry and many other items of interest to both States; and

"WHEREAS, there exists no document or other historical record which would support the placement of the boundary as presently delineated by the United States Geological Survey; and

"WHEREAS, the General Assembly finds the United States Geological Survey to be in error regarding the agency's delineation of the boundary on the Fort Pulaski and Savannah topographic maps as updated in 1971 . . ."

15.

The Boundary Commission of South Carolina, established by the South Carolina General Assembly, has stated in correspondence with the United States Geological Survey that the State of South Carolina contends that the boundary is as shown on Exhibit A, and that the location of the boundary is presently in dispute in the areas of Barnwell Island and Oyster Bed Island.

16.

In the 1977 Session of the General Assembly of Georgia, the House of Representatives and the Georgia State Senate passed identical resolutions providing that the State of Georgia and the State of South Carolina presently are in dispute concerning the location of the boundary between the two states in the lower reaches and the mouth of the Savannah River and further stating in pertinent part as follows:

"1. That the Georgia House of Representatives [Senate] hereby expresses its desire that the boundary line between the State of Georgia and the State of South Carolina be precisely located in the lower reaches and in the mouth of the Savannah River;

"2. That such boundary line should be precisely located only as established by the Charter, the Convention of Beaufort and applicable principles of law;

"3. That the boundary line between the State of Georgia and the State of South Carolina in the lower reaches and in the mouth of the Savannah River is not the middle of the present navigational

SAVANNAH QUADRANGLE
GEORGIA–SOUTH CAROLINA

1. A reduced composite of the three 1955 United States Geological Survey topographic quadrangle maps covering the area of the Georgia–South Carolina boundary dispute. The state boundary is shown to follow the approximate middle of the main navigation

FORT PULASKI QUADRANGLE
SOUTH CAROLINA–GEORGIA

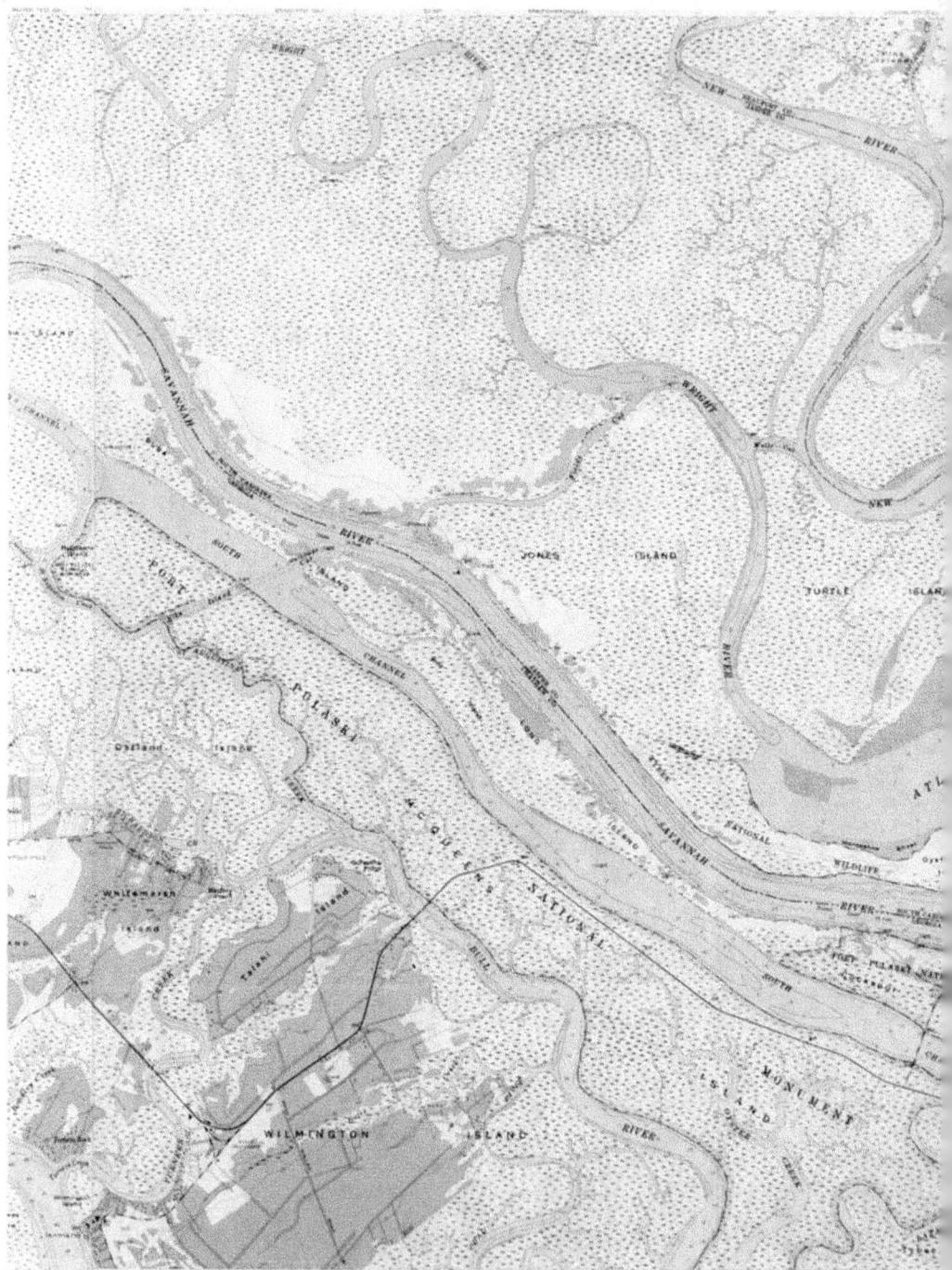

portion of the river from Fort Jackson through the rock jetties to a point north of T
Island. The Barnwell islands, Jones Island, and Oyster Bed Island all appear to be i
South Carolina. (Original map scale 1:24,000 has been reduced by 70%.)

SAVANNAH BEACH NORTH QUADRANGLE
SOUTH CAROLINA–GEORGIA

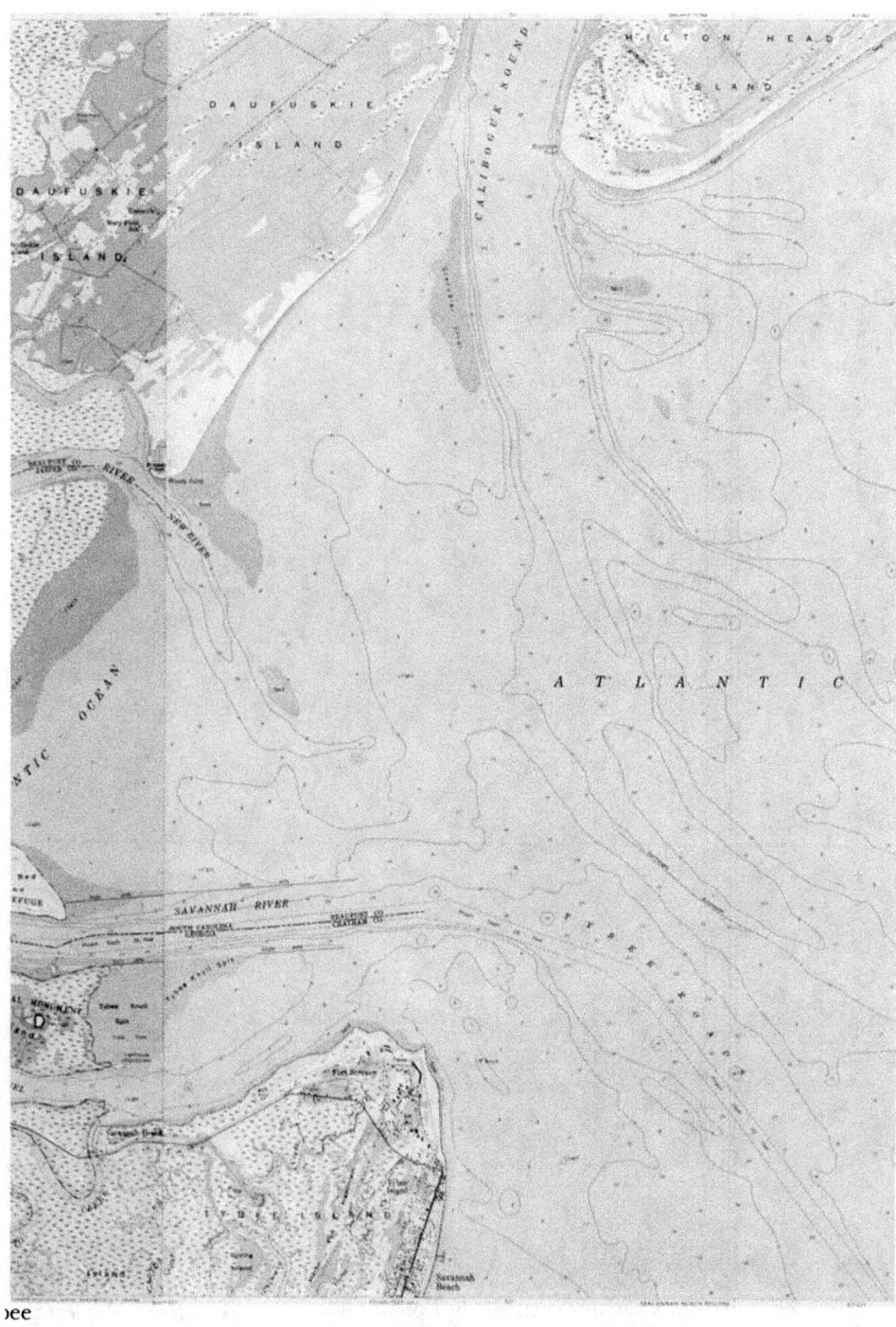

SAVANNAH QUADRANGLE
GEORGIA–SOUTH CAROLINA

2. A reduced composite of the three 1971 photorevised United States Geological Surve topographic quadrangle maps covering the area of the Georgia–South Carolina bound ary dispute. On these maps, portions of the state boundary line have been revised in th

FORT PULASKI QUADRANGLE
SOUTH CAROLINA–GEORGIA

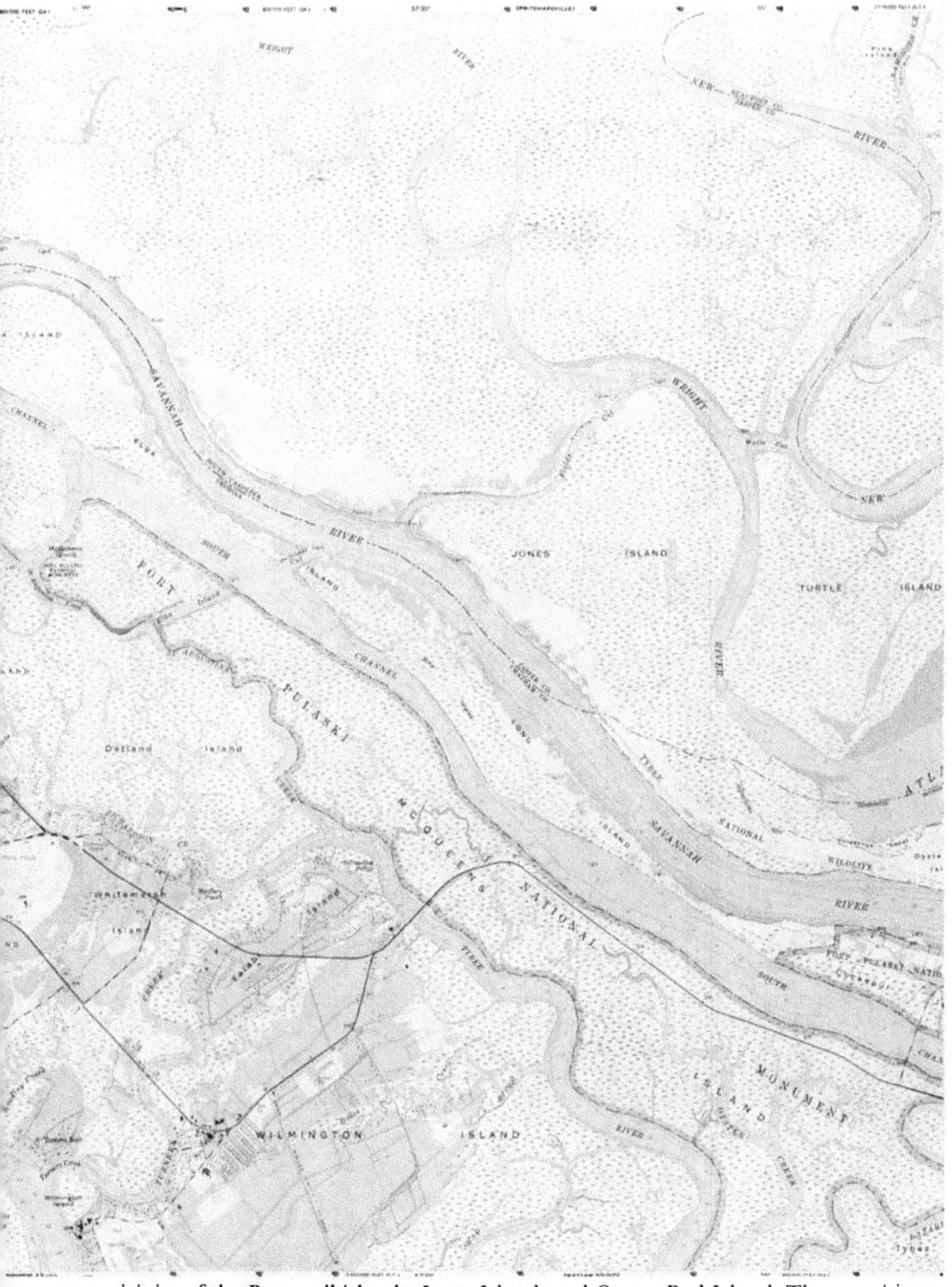

vicinity of the Barnwell islands, Jones Island, and Oyster Bed Island. These revisions did much to focus interest on the boundary issues during the 1970s. (Original map sc 1:24,000 has been reduced by 70%.)

SAVANNAH BEACH NORTH QUADRANGLE
SOUTH CAROLINA–GEORGIA

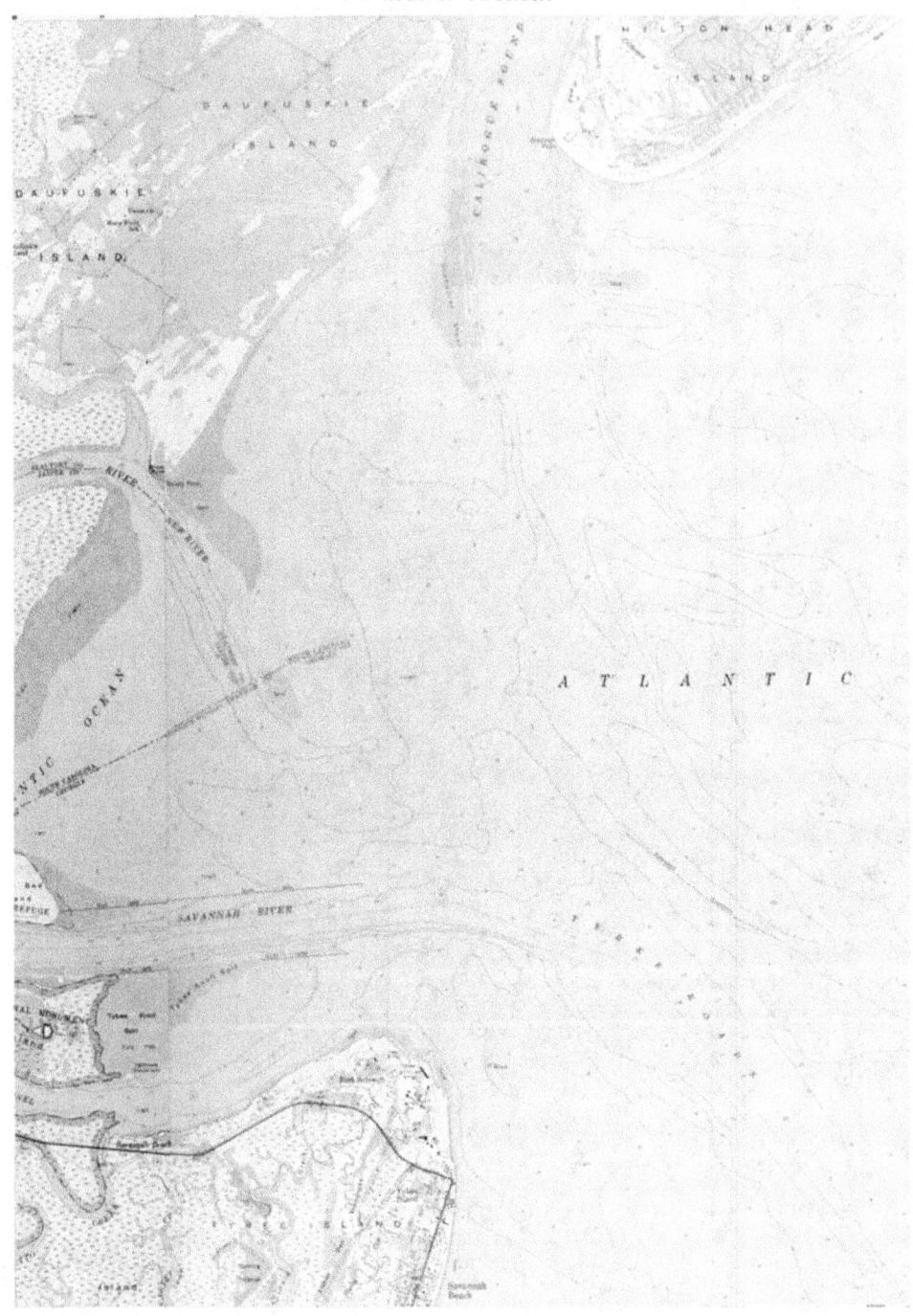

channel of the Savannah River, artificially created by the Corps of Engineers;

"4. That the peninsula of land known as 'Oyster Bed Island' lies within the boundaries of the State of Georgia; and

"5. That the Governor and the Attorney General are hereby requested and directed to take whatever measures are necessary, including negotiation, litigation, or both, to resolve the dispute concerning the boundary line between the State of Georgia and the State of South Carolina in the lower reaches and the mouth of the Savannah River."

17.

The boundary line dispute between Georgia and South Carolina involves over 10,000 acres of waters and waterbottoms and more than three thousand acres of high ground and marshland.

18.

Representatives from the State of Georgia and the State of South Carolina have met on several occasions since 1968 in an effort to resolve the dispute concerning the boundary line in the lower reaches and the mouth of the Savannah River and concerning the lateral seaward boundary between the two states. Such efforts at negotiation have not been successful, and it appears highly unlikely that any agreement as to the boundary dispute can be reached.

19.

The existence of the dispute between Georgia and South Carolina as to the boundary line in the area of Barnwell Island and other tracts now on the north bank of the Savannah River has created serious problems for the State of Georgia. Barnwell Island and other tracts now on the north bank of the Savannah River are prime sites for port and industrial development, and the uncertainty as to the jurisdiction over and title to these areas prevents their development.

20.

The existence of the dispute between Georgia and South Carolina as to the location of the boundary line in the mouth of the Savannah River and out to the three-mile limit has created serious problems for both states and for the citizens of both states in regard to the enforcement of laws, particularly laws relating to commercial fishing. The State of Georgia has made diligent efforts to reach a temporary agreement concerning enforcement of these laws in the disputed area, but all such efforts at agreement have failed.

21.

On June 29, 1977, a resident of South Carolina licensed as a commercial shrimp fisherman under South Carolina law was apprehended by law enforcement officers of the Georgia Department of Natural Resources while engaged in illegal commercial fishing in Georgia waters. The South Carolina shrimp fisherman resisted arrest, assaulted the Georgia Conservation Rangers, and fled to South Carolina. On July 15, 1977, the Governor of Georgia requested the Governor of South Carolina to extradite the South Carolina fisherman to Georgia to stand trial on charges of obstruction of officers, simple battery, and illegal commercial fishing. On July 22, 1977, the Governor of South Carolina refused the request for extradition, basing his refusal on the existence of the boundary dispute.

22.

Continued existence of the boundary dispute has caused and will continue to cause serious problems and inconvenience to the State of Georgia, the State of South Carolina, and citizens of both states with regard to the enforcement of laws in the disputed area and the determination of property rights as to land and waterbottoms within the disputed area.

23.

The original jurisdiction of this Court is invoked because there is a pressing need for prompt and final settlement of the controversy, and because the question in issue, the location of the boundary between the State of Georgia and the State of South Carolina, can be resolved by this Court alone.

WHEREFORE, the State of Georgia prays:

(1) That process be issued against the State of South Carolina and that the State of South Carolina be required to answer this Complaint;

(2) That a decree be entered declaring the true and correct boundary line between the State of Georgia and the State of South Carolina in the lower reaches and the mouth of the Savannah River and in the territorial sea to the three-mile limit;

(3) That the boundary be declared to be the middle of the northernmost stream or branch of the Savannah River, as such river existed in 1787, as changed by natural accretion and erosion but not as altered by avulsions, reserving all islands, including Barnwell Island, Jones Island, and Oyster Bed Island, to Georgia, thence running to a point midway between Tybee Island, Georgia and Hilton Head Island, South Carolina, and thence due east to the three-mile limit;

(4) That the Court issue a preliminary injunction prohibiting the State of South Carolina from enforcing its laws or asserting jurisdiction within the area in dispute; and

(5) For such other and further relief as this Court may deem to be proper.

Following its acceptance of the case in October 1977, the Supreme Court appointed Judge Walter E. Hoffman, senior judge of the U.S. District Court for the Eastern District of Virginia, as special master to hold hearings at which legal and factual arguments would be presented by counsel for each state. Important to these arguments was testimony of expert witnesses, as well as large numbers of documents and maps that were entered as evidence by both Georgia and South Carolina. After hearing all of the arguments and testimony and considering the masses of documentary and cartographic evidence, Judge Hoffman was to submit a detailed report of his findings and opinions on the questions raised in the litigation to the Supreme Court. In effect, his report would take the form of a recommendation as to what sort of decree the Supreme Court should ultimately award in the case. His report is, however, subject to challenge by both sides, and a final period of oral argument will be available before the assembled Supreme Court before any decree or decision is forthcoming.

In the remainder of this book, several of the issues basic to Georgia's claims in the litigation are explored from a historical-geographical point of view. This material is by no means the whole of Georgia's case, but it does provide a view of a significant number of the basic historical-geographical underpinnings of that case. Many of the accounts of events and interpretations which seem almost self-evident and obvious when read here were challenged and rigorously tested by South Carolina during the course of the hearings held by Judge Hoffman. Experts from a number of professional fields and academic disciplines were called and provided insights that pointed to conclusions contrary to the ones suggested here. Out of this testing and challenge, the special master and Supreme Court will ultimately find the "true and correct boundary line between the State of Georgia and the State of South Carolina in the lower reaches and mouth of the Savannah River and in the territorial sea to the three-mile limit" (State of Georgia, Motion of Leave To File Complaint and Complaint, U.S. Supreme Court, No. 74 Original). Based on that finding the lateral seaward boundary between Georgia and South Carolina from the limit of the territorial sea out to the limit of the outer continental shelf will then be established.

PART ONE

The Georgia–South Carolina Boundary as Determined by the Treaty of Beaufort, April 28, 1787

DISCUSSION OF THE GEORGIA–SOUTH CAROLINA BOUNDARY in the lower Savannah River and Sound region must begin with a consideration of Georgia's Charter of 1732. The general historical background of that charter is fully outlined in Albert B. Saye, ed., *Georgia's Charter of 1732* (pp. 1–16) and will not be repeated here. Rather, this section will focus on the bounds of the territorial grant which the charter included. In that charter, Georgia was described as being formed by

> all those lands Countries and Territories Situate lying and being in that part of South Carolina in America which lies from the most Northern Stream of a River there commonly called the Savannah all along the Sea Coast to the Southward unto the most Southern Stream of a certain other greater water or River called the Alatamaha and Westward from the heads of the said Rivers respectively in Direct Lines to the South Seas and all that space Circuit and Precinct of land lying within the said boundaries with the Islands in the Sea lying opposite to the Eastern Coast of the said lands within twenty leagues of the same which are not already inhabited or settled by any Authority derived from the Crown of Great Britain together with all the Soils Grounds Havens Ports Gulfs and Bays Mines as well Royal Mines of Gold and Silver as other Minerals Precious Stones Quarries Woods Rivers waters Fishings as well Royal Fishings of whale and Sturgeon as other Fishings Pearls Commodities Jurisdictions Royalties Franchises Privileges Prehemmences within the said Territories and the Precincts thereof. [Albert B. Saye, ed., *Georgia's Charter of 1732*, p. 39]

In addition to Saye's published version of the charter, researchers can consult an original manuscript version housed in the Georgia Archives and Records Building in Atlanta. Interestingly, this manuscript resided in South Carolina from 1735 until 1965, when it was presented to Georgia by the neighboring state.

It is significant that Georgia was described as extending "from the most Northern Stream" of the Savannah to "the most Southern Stream" of the Altamaha. Although no official map is known to be associated with the charter description, it is informative to read it with Henry Popple's "A Map of the British Empire in America with the French and Spanish Settlements Adjacent Thereto," drawn in 1733, in view (Map 3).

Although Popple's map was not an "official" map in the full sense of that term, it comes very close to being one. It was undertaken by Popple "with the Approbation of the Lords Commissioners of Trade and Plantations" and endorsed by Edmund Halley, Britain's most celebrated astronomer-scientist ("A Map of the British Empire in America"). Popple's grandfather and father both served in the office of secretary to the British Board of Trade and Plantations, as did his brother Alured. Henry Popple left a position as clerk with the Board of Trade in 1727, the same year he was appointed. He did, however, prepare a colored manuscript map of the American colonies in that year. Popple clearly enjoyed an unusual access to the extensive collection of American records, surveys, and maps held by the Board of Trade. As William P. Cumming and Helen Wallis have written:

> Popple's map is a product of those years when departments of state urgently required accurate maps, but had no official cartographic organization to supply the need. They depended therefore on the enterprising individual and the commercial map publishing trade. The maps themselves had to be compiled from a range of available materials, good, bad, and indifferent. . . . Popple's map could not be better than its sources. Even if it did not win the full support of the Lords Commissioners of Trade and Plantations, the fact that they ordered its distribution to each of the Governments in America remains an impressive testimonial. ["A Map of the British Empire in America with the French and Spanish Settlements Adjacent Thereto," p. 2]

Popple showed the seaward outlets of both the Savannah and Altamaha rivers as cluttered, island-studded areas. If one were attempting to formulate a verbal description of a colony to be located between South Carolina and hostile Spanish Florida, it is easy to see how the qualifiers "most Northern Stream" and "most Southern Stream" would be used. With this same image in mind, it is easy to see how the concept developed which awarded all Savannah River islands to Georgia. This concept is clearly predicated upon the assumption that the

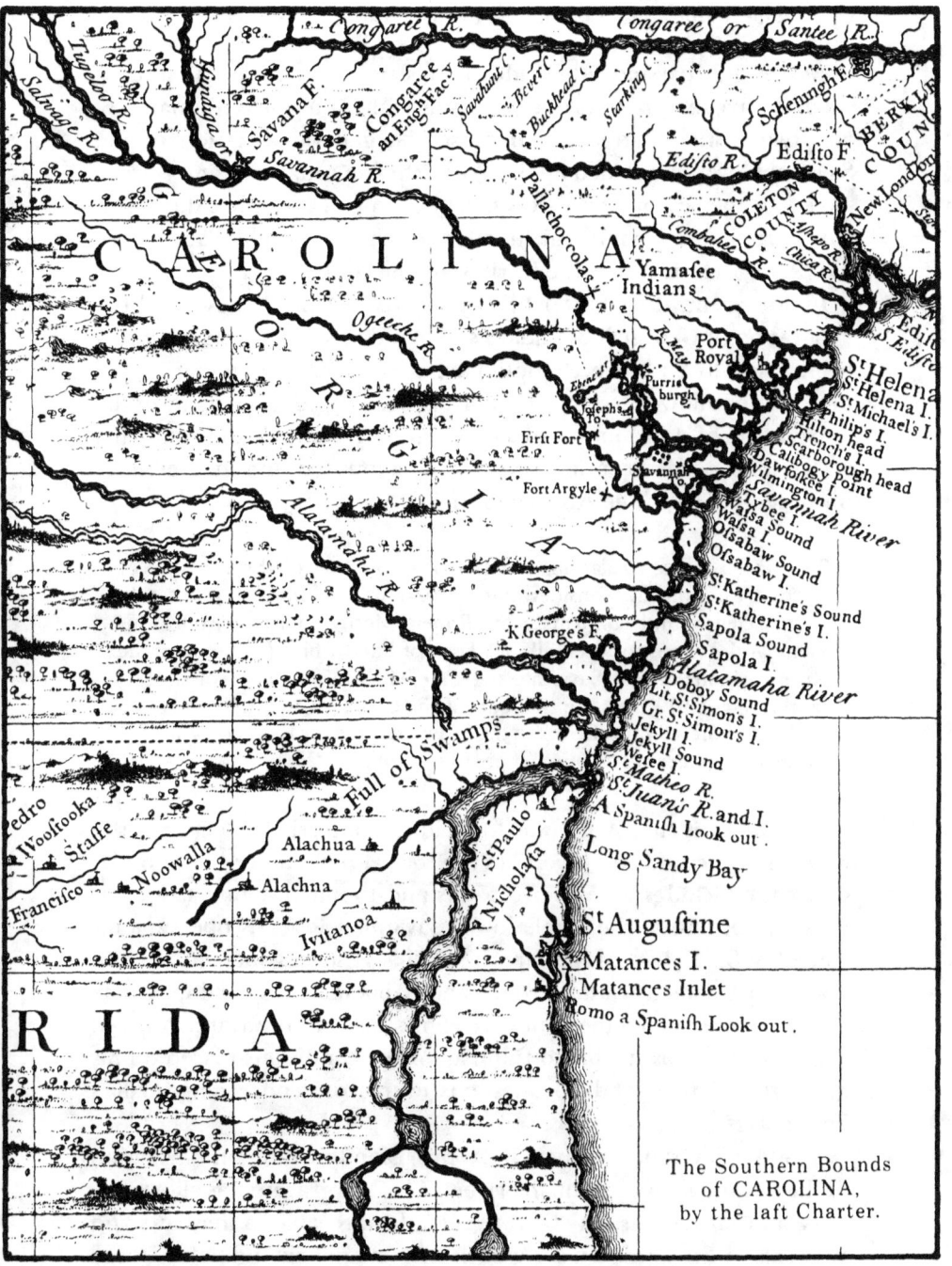

3. Section of "A Map of the British Empire in America with the French and Spanish Settlements adjacent thereto, by Henry Popple, 1733." Popple's map appeared following the period when the Georgia Charter was being written and can aid in understanding that crucial document as it bears on the Georgia–South Carolina boundary dispute.

flows of water passing either side of an island in a river are to be considered "streams" of that river. Thus any island in the Savannah creates two distinct "streams." Because the general direction of the Savannah was construed to be from the mountainous interior or "west" to the sea or "east," it was logical to conclude that the "most Northern Stream" bound, included in the charter, would place Savannah River islands within the territorial limits of Georgia.

In any event, the Charter of 1732 more specifically described the geography of Georgia's boundaries than did an earlier grant that had been made to Sir Robert Montgomerie in 1717. Montgomerie petitioned to be allowed to erect a distinct province under the name of the Margravate of Azilia in the area between the Savannah and Altamaha rivers. The Lords Proprietors of Carolina granted him that territory on June 19, 1717. The Abstract of the Grant stated:

> The under-written Palatine, and Lords Proprietors of the Province of Carolina, do, on the Considerations herein after mention'd, grant, sell, alien, release, and confirm to Sir Robert Montgomerie, Baronet, his Heirs and Assigns for ever, all that Tract of Land which lies between the Rivers Altamaha and Savanna, together with the Islands, Ports, Harbours, Bays and Rivers, on that Part of the Coast which lies between the Mouths of the said two Rivers to the Seaward. [Trevor R. Reese, *The Most Delightful Country of the Universe*, p. 36]

It is significant that Azilia was to include the territory "between the Mouths of the said two Rivers" in the coastal zone. Since the "mouth" of a river includes at least two banks and the intervening stream, it would appear that the whole lower Savannah River proper was included in Sir Robert Montgomerie's Azilia. If strictly interpreted, the boundary between South Carolina and Azilia was thus the line of normal high water along the South Carolina shore of the Savannah River. Montgomerie was unable to fulfill all of the conditions placed on his grant so it lapsed and no questions ever arose concerning Azilia's boundaries.

The Azilia Grant also included a provision touching on navigation in the Savannah and Altamaha rivers. The Margravate was allowed to pass laws "as near as may be conveniently agreeable to the Laws and Customs of England; but so, as such Laws do not extend to lay Duties or Custom, or other Obstruction, upon the navigation of either of the said Rivers, by any Inhabitant of South or North Carolina, or their free Commerce and Trade with the Indian Nations either within, or to the Southward of the Margravate" (Reese, *The Most Delightful Country of the Universe*, p. 37). Thus the Azilia Grant can be seen to have guaranteed the Carolinians free navigation over the whole of the Savannah River. On this point the Georgia Charter of 1732 was mute.

The abortive attempt to establish Azilia and the eventual founding of Georgia in the area between the Savannah and Altamaha were easily construed as an encroachment on South Carolina. The territorial limits of the colony were described in the Charter of 1663 as embracing "All that Territory or Tract of ground . . . extending from the North end of the Island called Luck Island, which lies in the Southern Virginia Seas and within six and Thirty Degrees of the Northern Latitude, and to the West so far as the South Seas; and so Southerly as far as the River Saint Mathias which borders upon the Coast of Florida, and within one and Thirty Degrees of Northern Latitude; and West in a direct Line as far as the South Seas aforesaid" (Mattie E. Parker, ed. *North Carolina Charters and Constitutions, 1578–1698*, pp. 76–77). These limits were enlarged in 1665 to give South Carolina a claim on the belt of territory between 29° and 36° 30' north latitude (Richard Lonsdale, ed., *Atlas of North Carolina*, pp. 41–42). The southernmost limit of South Carolina was extended deep into Spanish-held Florida to a line approximately one hundred miles south of the present Georgia-Florida boundary. The Popple map showed the "Southern Bounds of Carolina" well south of the Spanish city of St. Augustine in Florida.

In the years that followed the creation of Georgia, two major areas of dispute concerning territorial limits and claims developed with South Carolina. The first of these involved the boundary along the Savannah River, particularly in the stream's upper reaches. The Tugaloo and Keowee (now Seneca) rivers are the two tributary streams that were later found to join and form the major stream known as the Savannah from their confluence to the sea. Georgians preferred to think of the more northerly tributary, the Keowee, as forming the "most northern stream of a River . . . commonly called Savannah." This construction would have had the effect of enlarging Georgia to include the territory found between it and the Tugaloo (roughly the area of present Oconee County, South Carolina). A study of the Popple map reveals that the Keowee is identified as the "Isundiga or Savanna R." South Carolina took a more precise view of the charter language and argued that neither the Tugaloo nor Keowee was intended and that the Savannah River ended at their confluence. From this point, the South Carolina argument ran, a line should be drawn due west as stated in the charter. The effect of this construction would have been to add to the colony of South Carolina a thirty-five-mile wide strip of territory as far west as Britain's authority extended.

The second major area of contention involved South Carolina claims to land south of the Altamaha River. At the time of the writing of the Georgia Charter this area was in dispute between Britain and Spain and international diplomacy made it expedient to omit reference to it in that document. During the War of Jenkins's Ear (1739–43), Georgia's leader, James Edward Oglethorpe, established posts and settlements as far south as the St. Marys River. Oglethorpe, however, was then acting for the royal authority of Britain in an international conflict and not strictly as a Georgian.

The most serious overt dispute between South Carolina and Georgia concerning the territory south of the Altamaha appears to have developed in 1752 when the governor of South Carolina issued land grants in the area. Georgia's chief executive sent a member of his council to remonstrate against the action in Charleston and forwarded an official complaint to London. During the ensuing discussions it became clear that the British government had not intended such a development but was faced with a very embarrassing fait accompli on the part of South Carolina. The South Carolina grants were ordered to be copied for recording in Georgia, and such lands were considered to be a part of that colony. In 1763, following the conclusion of the Seven Years' War, Georgia's southern limit was extended from the Altamaha to the St. Marys River, and the new British colony of East Florida was created out of the former Spanish possession to the south.

Questions concerning navigation rights on the Savannah River caused debate with South Carolina during Georgia's first half-century of existence. Controversy between Georgia and South Carolina grew out of one of the only three laws the Trustees for Establishing the Colony of Georgia enacted for their colony. Two of those laws, reflecting General Oglethorpe's and other trustees' ideals for the colony of Georgia, forbade Negro slavery and closely regulated the Indian trade. The third law, which was to lead to the controversy and subsequent debate concerning navigation rights on the Savannah River, forbade the importation of "Rum or Brandys nor any other kind of Spirits or Strong Waters by whatsoever Name they are or may be distinguished" into the colony of Georgia (Allen D. Candler, comp., *The Colonial Records of the State of Georgia*, 1:45).

Oglethorpe promulgated these laws in 1736. Shortly thereafter the magistrates and Savannah's chief bailiff, Thomas Causton, apprehended two South Carolina vessels in Savannah harbor that were on their way to the Indian trading center at Savannah Old Town (also known as New Windsor) high up the Savannah River on the Carolina side. Causton reported that the vessels were loaded with "Indian Trading Goods, and amongst other Things, had each of them sundry Casks of Rum on board." He read the rum law to the hapless traders, staved "ten small Caggs . . . and three Hogsheads" of rum, and then released them to continue their voyage (*Report of the Committee Appointed to Examine into the Proceedings of the People of Georgia with Respect to the Province of South-Carolina, and the Dispute Subsisting between the Two Colonies*, p. 115). In the *Journal of the Commons House of Assembly, November 10, 1736–June 7, 1739*, eighty-five pages are devoted to the report of "The Committee Appointed to Examine into the Proceedings of the People of Georgia with Respect to this Province and the Disputes Subsisting between the Two Colonies." In addition to the committee's opinions on the two crucial concerns—Indian trade and navigation rights—the report includes an Appendix composed of many reports, letters, and depositions (see J. H. Easterby, ed., *The Colonial Records of South Carolina*, 1:72–157). The report was also printed contemporaneously as *Report of the Committee Appointed to examine into the Proceedings of the People of Georgia with respect to the Province of South Carolina, and the Disputes Subsisting between the Two Colonies* (Charles-Town: Printed by Lewis Timothy, 1736). In addition to these sources, the disputes are also treated in the *Calendar of State Papers, Colonial Series, America and West Indies*, Vol. 42, 1735–36 (London: Her Majesty's Stationery Office, 1953), 261–69, 367–75.

In their report, the South Carolinians examined the Georgia charter in some detail and observed in respect to that colony's boundaries that "it was His Majesty's most gracious Intention that the most Northern Stream of Savannah River and the most Southern Stream of Altamaha River should be the boundaries of Georgia: And that since his Majesty has been pleased to confine his Grant . . . to the Lands within those Boundaries, the Boundaries themselves cannot pass by the said

Charter or Grant" (*Report of the Committee*, p. 5). Thus the Carolinians argued that the Savannah and Altamaha were not really in Georgia but merely bounded it. They failed, however, to state to whom the rivers did belong. In a later section of the report dealing with the Savannah rum incident, they elaborated as follows:

> Your Committee have always understood, that the Right of Passage on Navigable Rivers and Highways throughout all his Majesty's Dominions was free to all his Subjects. . . .
>
> If it were admitted that the River was included within the Grant in the Charter of Georgia, yet your Committee have heard, that there is a known distinction in the Laws of England between the Property, and the Right of Passage in publick Rivers and Highways—that they are the King's High-ways and Free for all the King's People; though the Property of the Soil, Water, or Fishing may be in private or particular persons. [Ibid., p. 44]

This statement could be interpreted as a tacit admission that at least a portion of the Savannah River was within Georgia's boundary. The committee emphasized South Carolina's long-standing employment of the Savannah River as her only highway to the garrison at Fort Moore "on the North-side . . . near Three Hundred Miles from the Mouth of the said River" (ibid.), as well as to the settlements of New Windsor and Purrysburgh also along the stream.

The South Carolinians made their views known to Oglethorpe and the trustees as well as to crown officials. In a communication sent to Oglethorpe, the South Carolinians proposed "That the Use and navigation of the Savannah River be left open and free to all his Majesty's Subjects of Carolina, to all Parts and Places within the Province of Carolina without any Interruption, Molestation or Hindrance whatsoever" (ibid., p. 105). South Carolina was seeking only a limited freedom to navigation of the Savannah to allow access to her own remote territories along the northern bank.

Oglethorpe, however, refused to agree to even this limited demand. In his response to the committee, he observed:

> It would be Presumption in me to determine finally anything concerning [navigation rights] but the Officers of this Province must continue to act according to the Laws of this Province till his Majesty's Pleasure be known. However, till that be known theron, I shall suffer all Boats and Pettiaguas from Carolina to pass up the same, they delivering a manifest

of their Cargo and of the Place or Places to which they are bound in Carolina upon Oath to the Proper Officer or Officers of Savannah, and I at the Expense of the Trustees putting an officer on board such Boats to see the same delivered at the Place or Places expressed in the Manifest. [Ibid., p. 107]

Significantly, Oglethorpe's proposed arrangement in no way surrendered Georgia's sovereignty over the river with regard to enforcement of the trustees' laws.

Oglethorpe's posture was consistent with the attitude adopted by his fellow trustees in London. In his diary Georgia's most influential trustee, Lord Egmont, wrote the following on August 26, 1736:

> We find the Carolinians understand our charter not to restrain the whole navigation of Savannah to Georgia, but that all his Majesty's subjects may pass it, and they interpret our understanding it to a restraint, as a thing contrary to their liberties and privileges and to the law of Carolina, which gives Carolina liberty to trade up that river. But upon consultation together, and reviewing our charter, we judged that the whole navigation of that river is reserved to Georgia, and that His Majesty having erected Georgia into a distinct Province, the Carolina law for trading up that river ceases, only if the traders of that Province will take out a license from the magistrates of Georgia they may trade as our own people do, provided they do it in such goods as our law allows of, and carry not rum, which is forbidden with us. [Historical Manuscripts Commission, *Manuscripts of the Earl of Egmont*, 2 : 296]

In a letter to the Speaker of the Georgia House of Assembly on October 19, 1786, one of Georgia's first U.S. senators, William Few, included a lengthy historical review of Georgia–South Carolina boundary problems including the earlier Savannah navigation issue. On this issue he wrote:

> Here it may be necessary to add an observation respecting the exclusive right of Navigating the River Savannah, which I find was claimed at a very early period by the Province of Georgia and contested by So. Carolina, as appears by an extract of a report of the Lords Commissioners of trade and plantations, to the Lords of the Privy Councel, as follows. "Pursuant to their Lordships order of the 8th of Decemr. 1736 and the 4th of Feby 1737 on the consideration of the Humble Petition and Representation of the Councel and Assembly of South Carolina dated July 17, 1736 complaining of several obstructions given to the trade of that Province by the persons employed in the Government of the New Col-

ony of Georgia. As to the Navigation of the River Savannah we think that the northern branch of it ought to be free, and no vessel should be stopped going up either side of Hutchinson's Island (a little Island in the said Northern branch opposite to new Savannah) on account of having rum on board unless offering to trade at any of the Settlements in Georgia." The Carolinians consider this, as a determination clearly in their favor; but to me I confess it does not appear explicit, except only so far, as respects the River beyond Hutchinsons Island; but the implication seems to be in favor of the exclusive right in Georgia to the River above the Island and on the South Side, Rum only excepted, I do not from hence infer, that the sole and exclusive right is in Georgia; believing that if it was absolutely in Georgia she would not exercise it, unless So. Carolina should by some offensive measures urge her to it on a principle of revenge or self defence: for it must be acknowledged that the air and water was made free for the common use and benefit of man. The laws of Nature vests the equal right. An attempt to obstruct, or monopolize either, to the injury of man, would be a manifest deviation from that rule which ought to be the basis of all Laws. [William Few to Speaker of the Assembly of Georgia, October 19, 1786, Georgia–South Carolina Boundary File, Georgia Archives, Atlanta]

William Few's comments in 1786 clearly show that a controversy that had taken place half a century before had not been forgotten.

His review of the incident yields important insights regarding opinions on navigation rights of the Savannah River during the colonial period. For navigation purposes, many Georgians clearly had chosen to construe their charter limits as including the whole of the Savannah. Few himself seems to deny that Georgia possessed the sole control of the river but implies that her right was somehow superior to that of South Carolina. The Board of Trade, on the other hand, felt that navigation on the northern or bounding branch or stream of the Savannah ought to be free to the commerce of both colonies generally. In the immediate vicinity of the city and port of Savannah, however, they seem to have specified a greater degree of freedom for the Carolinians. Here, in the environs of Georgia's main commercial center, they appear to have decided that access to Savannah wharfs should be guaranteed. Thus vessels should not be stopped "going up either side of Hutchinson's Island (a little Island in the said Northern branch opposite to new Savannah) on account of having rum on board unless offering to trade at any of the Settlements in Georgia." This wording is relevant because both rum and slavery had been excluded from Georgia during the early period of the trusteeship. Although the words Few quotes from the Board of Trade suffer from a lack of clarity, they apparently were indicating that even rum-laden vessels should be free to navigate in these specified Savannah waters and that only in the case of illicit rum-running into Georgia settlements might Georgia authorities interfere with South Carolina vessels.

In July 1782 the British withdrew from Savannah and, finally, in December, from Charleston. In the spring of 1783 the states of South Carolina and Georgia, at last free from occupying troops, began to take formal steps to resolve their differences with respect to boundaries and territorial claims. On February 6, 1783, the South Carolina House of Representatives resolved that three commissioners be appointed to meet with commissioners from Georgia to treat "on the proper mode of fixing the Boundaries between the two States in an Amicable manner and determine the principles on which the Line of Jurisdiction shall be finally Established" (Copy of S.C. House Resolution in Georgia–South Carolina Boundary File, Georgia Archives). Only two days before, the Georgia House had passed a similar resolution indicating that the leadership of both states shared a perception of urgency and importance in the matter of boundaries. (Most of the correspondence with accompanying documents touching on these matters is found in the Georgia–South Carolina Boundary File collection in the Georgia Archives, Atlanta. See the *Calendar* of those papers prepared by Pat Bryant, deputy surveyor-general of Georgia.)

The sole concern of both states, as revealed by official correspondence and legislative statements, was the disputed territory high up the Savannah between the Keowee and Tugaloo rivers. Settlers were pushing into this attractive area, and western lands were of tremendous concern in South Carolina and Georgia during this period. Although both states professed a desire to settle the boundary question amicably, tensions were intensifying and little or no progress was made. It was not long before the potentially volatile problem came to the attention of the Continental Congress. William Houston, one of Georgia's representatives to that body, wrote to Georgia Governor Samuel Elbert:

> I have been able to collect from the agents of South Carolina that they are in momentary expectation (from their Governor's letter) of receiving instructions for an appeal to Congress in respect to the disputed territory between the two states . . . I am aware your Honour will pay that due consideration of this very important point which it deserves. I shall

only mention the rooted prejudices in Congress against our State may subject us to disadvantage. [Edmund C. Burnett, ed., *Letters of the Members of the Continental Congress*, 8:83]

Houston's prediction was verified when the government of South Carolina petitioned Congress to the effect "that a dispute and difference hath arisen and subsists between the State of Georgia and this State, concerning boundaries, the said States claiming respectively, the same territories" (*Journals of the American Congress*, 4:529–30).

Congress was requested to settle the dispute under article nine of the Articles of Confederation. An appointed committee considered the matter and recommended that agents be named by the two states and meet on May 8, 1786, to work out a settlement of the problem. The meeting date was twice postponed through the inability of one or another group of commissioners to attend on assigned dates. The two delegations finally met on September 4, 1786. William Few, George Walton, and John Houston represented Georgia, and John Kean, Charles Pinckney, and John Bull, South Carolina. This group did not feel that it possessed sufficient authority and requested that Congress allow them to establish a court empowered to settle the dispute. Congress responded by directing them "to appoint, by joint consent, commissioners or judges to constitute a court for hearing and determining the matter in question" (*Journals of the American Congress*, 11:154). After a further week of fruitless meetings, the South Carolinians, without informing their Georgia counterparts, petitioned Congress to appoint a court and set a time and place for its convening. Predictably, the Georgians were upset by this maneuver and contended that the Carolinians had no right to make such a petition unilaterally. They did, however, accede to the action in an effort to speed a settlement. Congress was requested to appoint a court as prescribed in the Articles of Confederation for such cases.

Congress named three members from each of the thirteen states. From this slate, Georgia and South Carolina were permitted to strike names until the number was reduced to thirteen. Of this group, nine were drawn by lot to make up the thus assured nonpartisan court. In order to permit time for argument preparation, the third Monday in June of 1787 was picked for the court's opening.

Despite the careful selection of an unbiased court, the Georgians showed no desire to have the dispute settled by the Continental Congress, but clearly preferred direct negotiation with South Carolina. On February 3, 1787, both branches of Georgia's legislature agreed to the appointment of John Houston, James Habersham, and Lachlan McIntosh as commissioners to ascertain and settle the boundaries with South Carolina. On February 15 Governor George Mathews of Georgia wrote to the state's three commissioners to wish them well in their important task. He also informed them that they were to strive to have "the Trial at the federal court set to a more distant period than it now stands" in the event that direct negotiations broke down (Governor Mathews to Commissioners, February 15, 1787, Georgia–South Carolina Boundary File, Georgia Archives).

In writing to their South Carolina counterparts, the Georgians proposed that a meeting be held at Beaufort on a convenient date. The meeting at Beaufort extended from April 24 to April 28, 1787, with Charles Pinckney, Andrew Pickens, and Pierce Butler representing South Carolina.

A signed and sealed copy of the "Convention, between The State of Georgia and The State of So. Carolina. Beaufort, April 28th 1787," as originally recorded in book A.3, folio 107.125, of the Georgia Secretary's Office, is located in the Georgia Archives Building in Atlanta. Page 1 of the convention document is headed "The Full Power of the State of Georgia," and page 2 is similarly headed "The Full Power of the State of South Carolina." A reading of these statements leaves no doubt that a majority of the commissioners who gathered at Beaufort were fully authorized to enter into a binding agreement regarding the location of the boundary. Further, it was stated that they were "to establish and permanently fix a Boundary between the two states." As events transpired, one Georgia commissioner, John Houston, dissented from the majority view and did not sign the convention document. He did, however, issue a statement that amounts to a minority opinion. Although Houston's statement is not included with the original copy of the Beaufort Treaty, it is included with the first printed version (Horatio Marbury and William H. Crawford, *Digest of the Laws of the State of Georgia*, pp. 666–67).

The treaty preamble, which forms an official summary of the problems existing between the two states, includes no mention of navigation on the Savannah or any other rivers. The treaty states:

That South Carolina claims that lands lying between the North Carolina line, and a line to run due west from the mouth of Tugoloo river, to the Mississippi, because as the said state contends, the river Savannah loses that name at the confluence, of Tugoloo and Keowee rivers, consequently that spot is the head of Savannah river—The State of Georgia, on the other hand, contends, that the source of Keowee river is to be considered as the head of Savannah river.—That the State of South Carolina also claims all the lands lying between a line to be drawn from the head of the river St. Mary, the head of Altamaha, the Mississippi, and Florida, being, as the said State contends, within the limits of its charter, and not annexed to Georgia by the said proclamation of one thousand seven hundred and sixty three. The State of Georgia, on the other hand, contends, that the tract of country last mentioned is a part of that state. [Convention between The State of Georgia and The State of South Carolina, Beaufort, April 26, 1787, Georgia Archives]

Thus it is clear that the stated dispute dealt with two tracts of interior territory as shown on Map 4. The map is, perforce, only an approximation of the territories suggested by the convention language quoted above. No official map was ever prepared to illuminate or illustrate the features, lines, and areas discussed at Beaufort, nor is it certain that the delegates at Beaufort had or consulted any maps during their deliberations.

One of the best general maps that would have been available to the commissioners at Beaufort in 1787 was titled "An Accurate Map of North and South Carolina with Their Indian Frontiers, Shewing in a distinct manner all the Mountains, Rivers, Swamps, Marshes, Bays, Creeks, Harbours, Sandbanks and Soundings on the Coasts; with the Roads and Indian Paths; as well as The Boundary or Provincial Lines, The Several Townships and other divisions of the Land In Both The Provinces; the whole from Actual Surveys By Henry Mouzon and Others, 1775" (Map 5). Like its title, Mouzon's map is large and, for its time, very detailed. It was first published in London, May 30, 1775, by the firm of R. Sayer and J. Bennet. Four sheets, each measuring 23¼ × 19⅞ inches, join to form the map, which is approximately 4 feet 8½ inches × 3 feet 3¾ inches. William P. Cumming, an expert on southeastern maps, calls it "*the* Revolutionary War map of North Carolina and South Carolina" and points out that it was not significantly improved upon until the nineteenth century (William P. Cumming, *The Southeast in Early Maps*, p. 59). It was also published in a number of

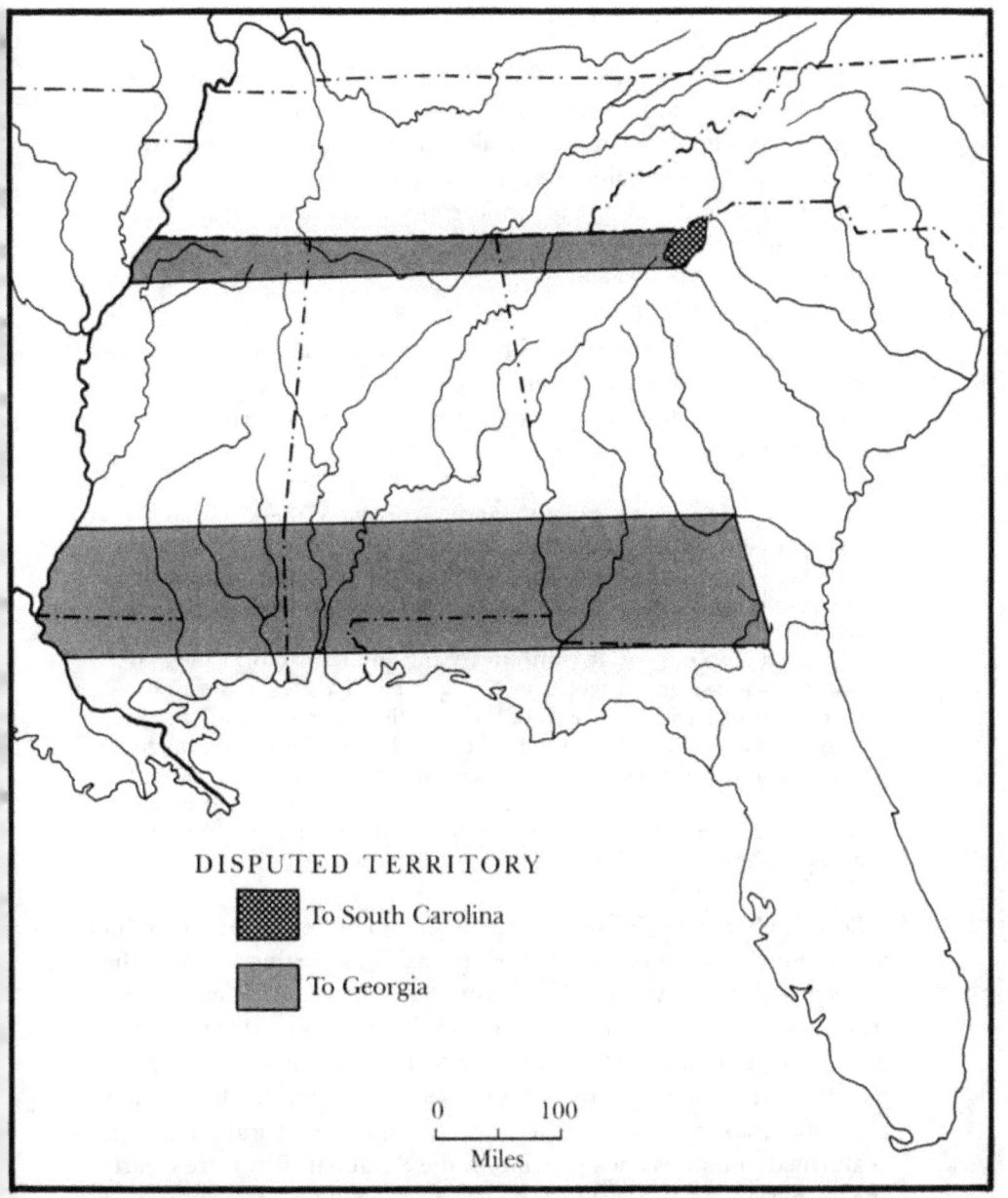

4. Disputed territory described in the Beaufort Convention Preamble. This map shows the major territorial settlement achieved by the Beaufort Treaty. South Carolina surrendered its claim to the extensive tracts of western lands in return for a clear title to the area between the Tugaloo and Keowee Rivers.

French editions and atlases. As late as 1794, the Mouzon map was reissued by the firm of Laurie and Whittle, who apparently had acquired the plates from the original publishers. Several eighteenth-century leaders, including George Washington, General Rochambeau, and General Henry Clinton, are known to have owned copies. Mouzon advertised the availability of his map as well as its content and accuracy in the *South-Carolina and American General Advertiser* (Charleston) on May 6 and June 3, 1774. It is reasonable to assume that this map would have been known to some or all of the commissioners at Beaufort. In any event, it forms a useful reference map to follow the verbal descriptions comprising the various articles of the treaty entered into at Beaufort:

> Article first, The most northern branch or stream of the River Savannah, from the Sea or mouth of such stream, to the fork or confluence of the Rivers now called Tugoloo and Keowee, and from thence the most northern branch or stream of the said River Tugoloo 'till it intersects the Northern boundary line of South Carolina, if the said branch or stream of Tugoloo extends so far North, reserving all the islands in the said Rivers Savannah and Tugoloo to Georgia; but if the head spring or source of any branch or stream of the said River Tugoloo does not extend to the north boundary line of South Carolina, then a west line to the Mississippi, to be drawn from the head spring or source of the said branch or stream of Tugoloo river, which extends to the highest northern latitude, Shall forever hereafter form the separation, limit, and boundary between the States of South Carolina and Georgia.

Several elements of this treaty article should be kept clearly in mind as one addresses the present boundary problem existing between the two states in the Savannah River from Savannah downstream. First, "the most northern branch or stream" of the river "from the Sea or mouth" is specified as forming the boundary. The word "stream" clearly covers areas where the river bifurcates or divides to flow around islands in its channel (see note 1). Thus the Georgia charter is reaffirmed and all islands existing in the Savannah River are clearly the property of Georgia. The term "branch" would be descriptive of a tributary or distributary of the main river. In view of the problems outlined in the treaty's preamble, it is probable that the commissioners chose to include the term to eliminate the possibility that any of the Savannah's other large tributary streams, such as the Broad or Rocky rivers, might be identified in place of the Tugaloo. Also, it would

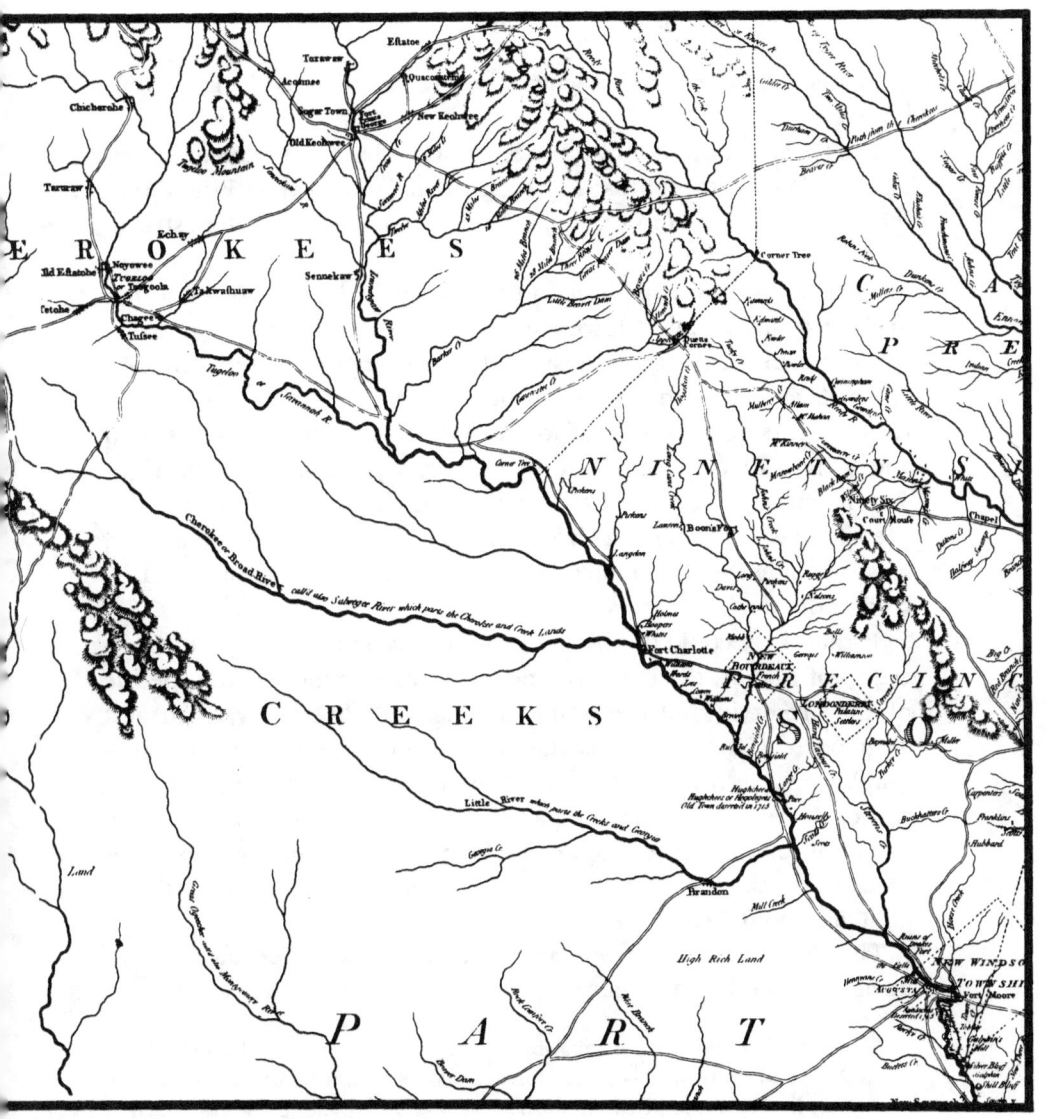

5. Section of "An Accurate Map of North and South Carolina with Their Indian Frontiers, Shewing in a distinct manner all the Mountains, Rivers, Swamps, Marshes, Bays, Creeks, Harbours, Sandbanks and Soundings on the Coasts; with the Roads and Indian Paths; as well as The Boundary or Provincial Lines, The Several Townships and other divisions of the Land In Both The Provinces; the whole from Actual Surveys By Henry Mouzon and Others, 1775." This map by Mouzon was very widely circulated in the late eighteenth century and shows the upper Savannah River valley as it was construed by South Carolinians. Notice that the Tugaloo fork of the Savannah River is named "Tugeloo or Savannah R."

serve to clarify the situation where the river was divided by numerous islands.

The specification of "from the Sea or mouth of such stream" is significant. Why is the phrase "of such stream" employed? Why didn't the commissioners simply write, "The most northern branch or stream of the River Savannah from the sea"? The sense of this important language is understandable in light of the confused geography existing in the Savannah valley downstream from Savannah. This language, "or mouth of such stream," ensures that all of the possible distributary channels as well as the main Savannah channel are included.[1] Thus, the flow passing northeast of Jones Island sometimes known as Mud and Wright River is embraced by this description. During the eighteenth century, the Savannah's mouth was consistently placed at Tybee Island with the phrase "from the bar and mouth." The other land mass forming the Savannah's "mouth" was the tip of Hilton Head Island to the north.

So that there could be absolutely no confusion concerning the ownership of islands, the commissioners took care to include the specific phrase "reserving all the islands in the said Rivers Savannah and Tugoloo to Georgia." Thus the island-studded and confused geographic area in the lower Savannah is further clarified with "*all*" the islands declared to be in Georgia. The final caveat in this treaty article makes all of the preceding arrangements and boundary calls time-specific in that they "Shall forever hereafter form the separation, limit, and boundary."

The second article of the Beaufort Treaty deals specifically with navigation on the Savannah:

> Article the second. The navigation of the River Savannah, at and from the bar, and mouth, along the Northeast side, of Cockspur Island, and up the direct course of the main northern channel, along the northern side of Hutchinson's Island opposite the town of Savannah, to the upper end of the said Island, and from thence up the bed or principal stream of the said River to the confluence of the Rivers Tugoloo and Keowee and from the confluence up the Channel of the most northern stream of Tugoloo River to its source; And back again, by the same channel to the Atlantick Ocean, Is hereby declared to be henceforth, equally free to the citizens of both States, and exempt from all duties, tolls, hindrance, interruption, or molestation whatsoever, attempted to be enforced by one State on the Citizens of the other; And all the rest of the river Savannah,

to be southward of the foregoing description, is acknowledged to be the exclusive right of the State of Georgia.

There can be no doubt that navigation was considered as a major issue by the commissioners at Beaufort in spite of the fact that the treaty preamble did not mention it. The South Carolina commissioners at Beaufort probably were aware of an act passed by the Georgia legislation on February 10, 1787, and titled "An Act for regulating the trade, . . . and also an impost on the tonnage of Shipping" (Robert and George Watkins, *Digest of the Laws of the State of Georgia*, pp. 351–53). This act was intended to raise a fund to finance the clearing of revolutionary war wrecks and obstructions in the Savannah River. This second article of the treaty assured South Carolina citizens that they were "exempt from all duties, tolls, hindrance, interruption, or molestation whatsoever." Inclusion of this exemption doubtless served as the motivation for the treaty's second article which, as mentioned above, dealt with a problem not hinted at in the formal preamble or statement of problem found in that document.

In attempting to interpret the intent of the article on navigation still another eighteenth-century map is helpful. This is titled "The Coast, Rivers and Inlets of the Province of Georgia, Surveyed by Joseph Avery and others. Published by Command of Government by J. F. W. Des Barres. 1st Feby. 1780" (Map 6). It was very detailed, showing water depths in the Savannah as well as islands and shoals. This map had been included in the collection of charts Des Barres had prepared for use by British forces in the American Revolution. These charts, distributed to Admiralty ships operating in North American waters, were known as "The Atlantic Neptune."

The cartographic technique employed to show topographic relief results in a somewhat exaggerated impression of terrain in this low-lying, marshy, coastal plain area. Once an allowance is made for this stylistic attribute, the map can be appreciated for its detailed planimetry. Its two-dimensional properties of shape, position, distance, and direction are impressive both for detail and apparent accuracy. These properties can be appreciated best by overlaying the Avery–Des Barres 1780 chart on a more modern chart of the area it depicts (Map 7).

The navigation article of the Beaufort Treaty specifies that "the navigation of the River Savannah, at and from the bar, and mouth" is

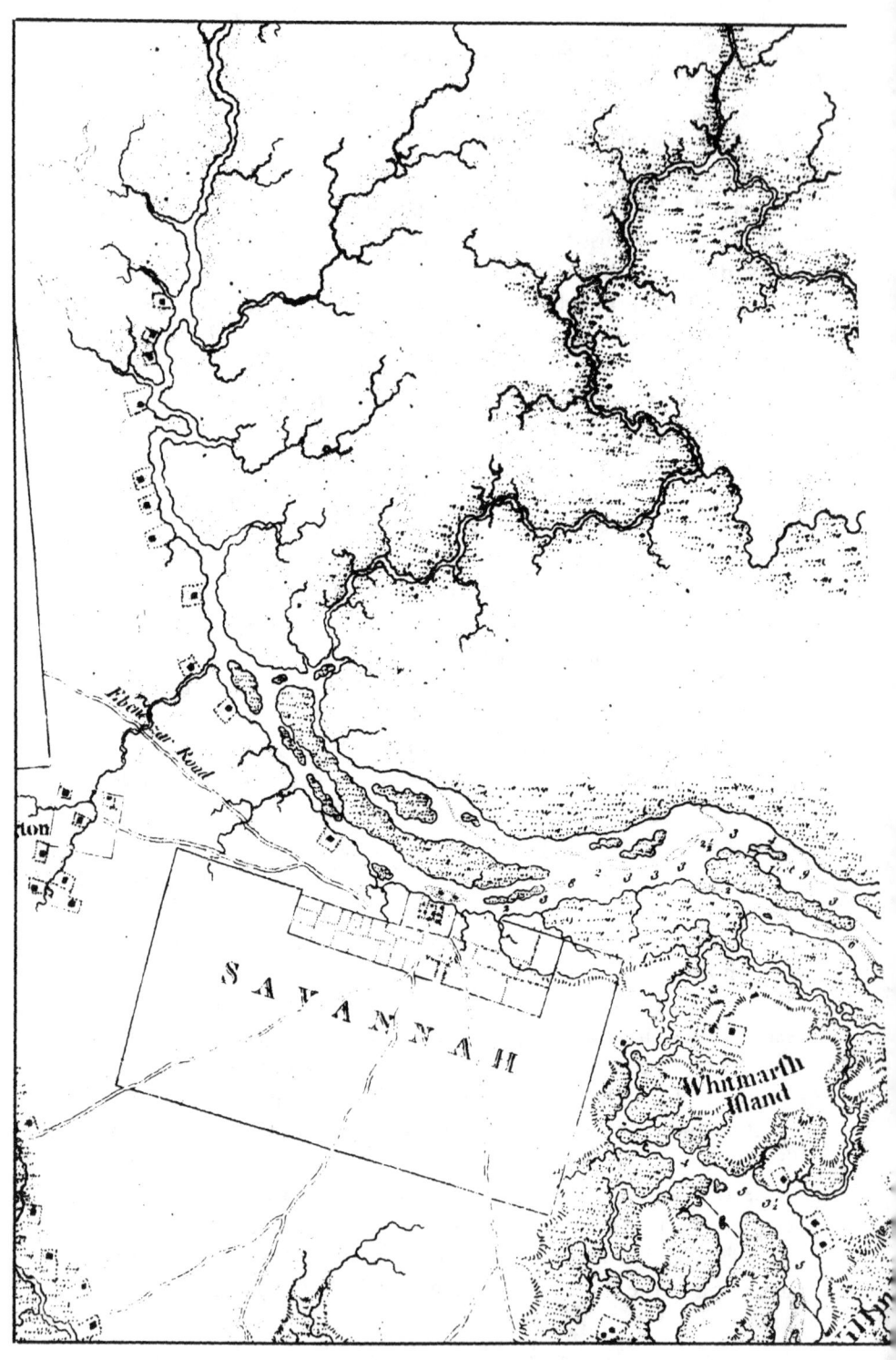

6. Section of "The Coast, Rivers and Inlets of the Province of Georgia, Surveyed by Joseph Avery and others. Published by Command of Government, by J. F. W. Des Barres. 1st Feby. 1780." This map was included as part of the

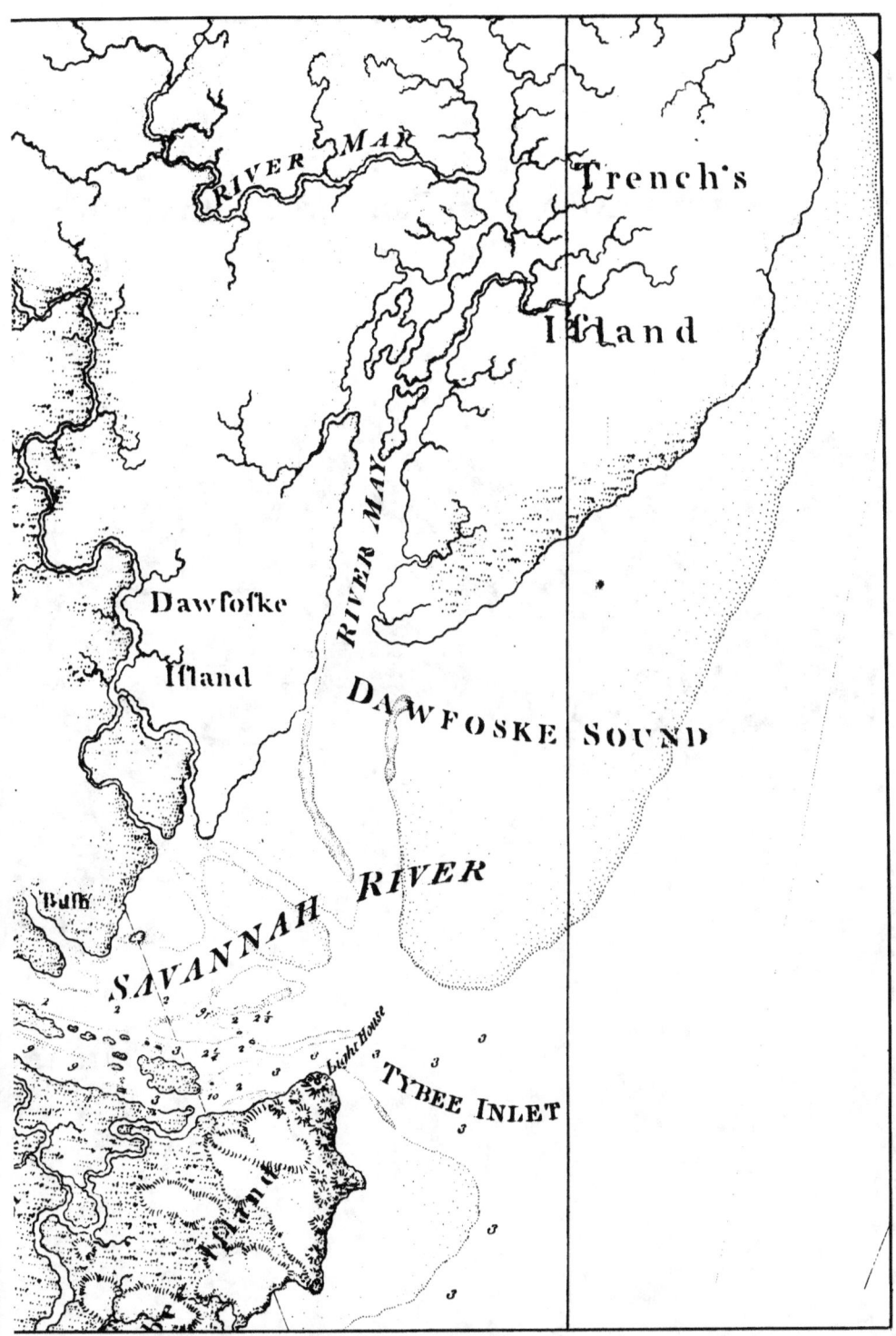

Atlantic Neptune, the collection of maps Des Barres produced for use by British forces during the Revolutionary War. It is important for its detailed depiction of channels and islands in the lower Savannah River.

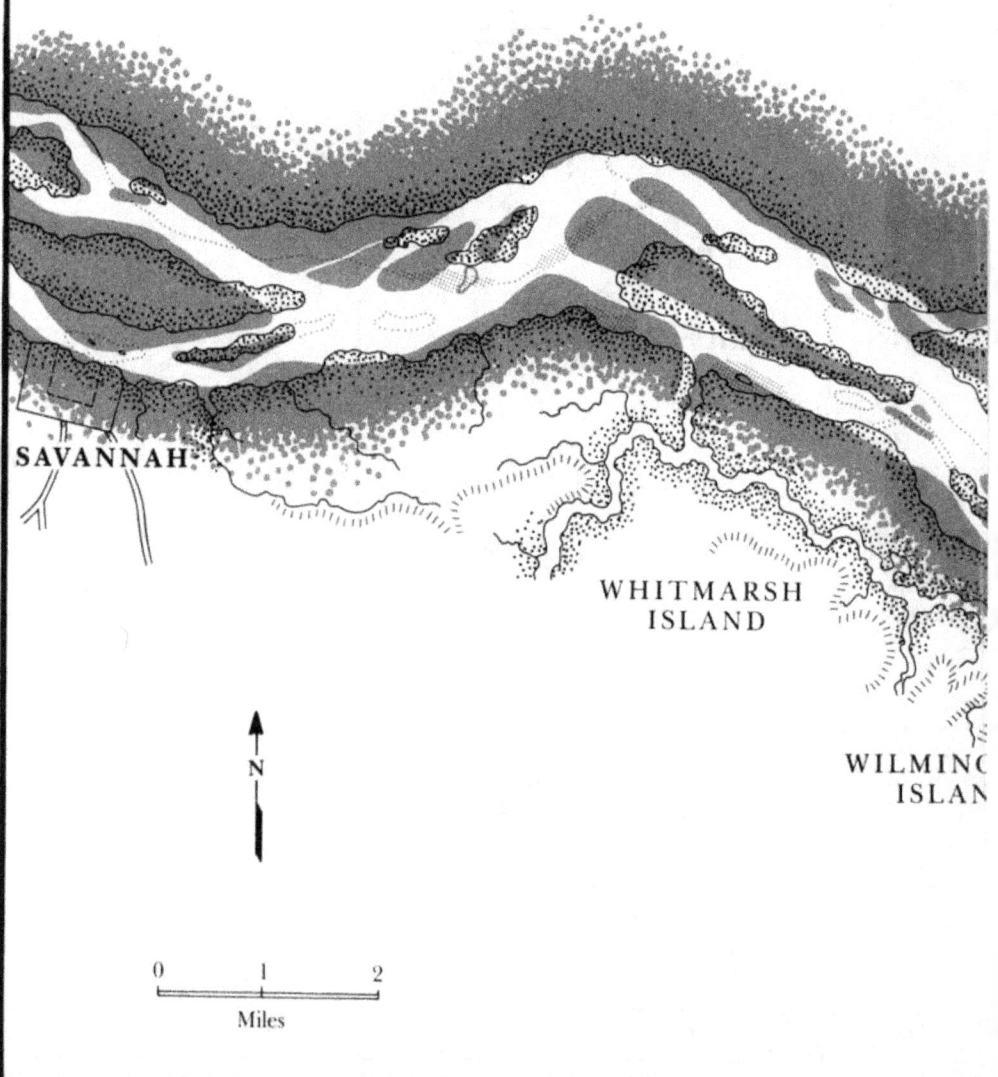

7. U.S. Coast Survey Preliminary Chart, 1855, overlaid on the Avery Map, 1780. To achieve this overlay the relevant portions of both maps were re-

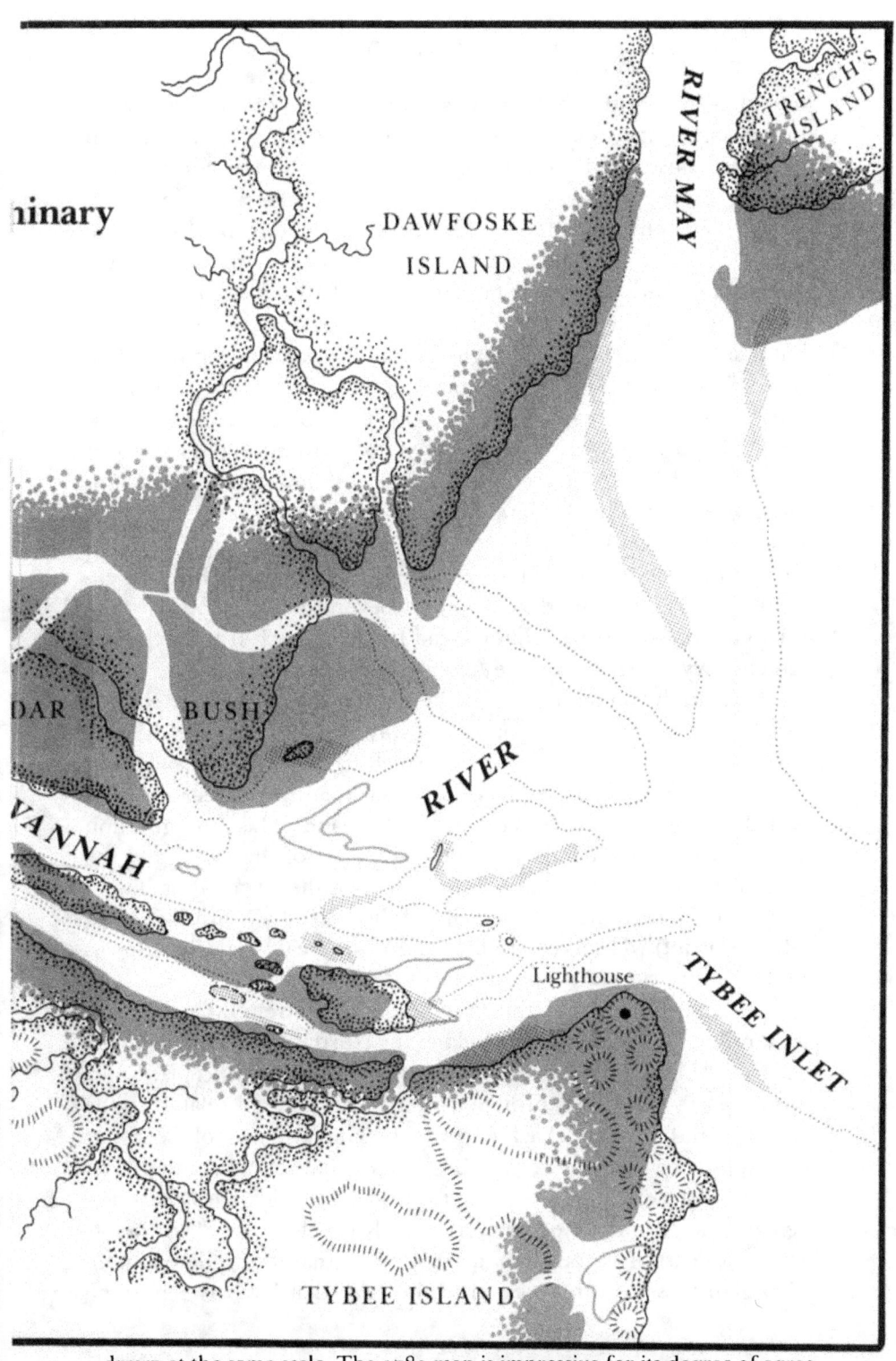

drawn at the same scale. The 1780 map is impressive for its degree of agreement with the first scientifically surveyed chart of the lower Savannah River.

intended along with other portions of the river. Since the river's "bar" is mentioned first, it is reasonable to conclude that commissioners at Beaufort construed it to come first as a mariner would normally encounter the river, that is, from the sea. The bar of a river is now and was in 1787 generally understood to be a deposited bank of silt, sand, gravel, or other earth material that forms a shoal or partial obstruction at the mouth of a river where the waters flow into the sea or some other body of water. A bar often builds up to or near to the surface but is submerged, at least at high tide. To the navigator, it was a feature of potential danger and consequently great concern. On the Avery–Des Barres map of 1780 the bar of the Savannah is indicated by small figures signifying the depth of water over it in the vicinity of Tybee Island. The preferred passage over the bar is named Tybee Inlet on the chart. The *American Coast Pilot* by Lawrence Furlong, published in 1798, states that Tybee Island lies at the mouth of Savannah River, to the southward of the bar. The name "Savannah River" is extended across the sound area to and beyond any closing line that might be drawn between Hilton Head Island (Trench's) and Tybee Island as they are shown on the Avery–Des Barres map.

There can be no reasonable doubt that the Savannah River was entered as one crossed the bar and came abreast of Tybee Island. Therefore the "mouth" of the river was formed by Tybee to the south and some other feature to the north. It is clear that the northern feature was the end of Trench's (Hilton Head) Island. This configuration would clearly accommodate both the language of the treaty and the placement of the name "Savannah River" on the Avery–Des Barres chart. No other configuration such as Tybee Island–Daufuskie Island (Bloody Point) will serve both the calls of the treaty and the patterns on the chart or other supportive historical materials.

This interpretation of the term "mouth" is strengthened by the next call in the treaty which is "along the Northeast side of Cockspur Island." Although unnamed on the Avery–Des Barres chart, Cockspur is easily identified through its shape and location relative to the Tybee Lighthouse and Lazaretto Creek. The long axis of Cockspur Island as shown on the Avery–Des Barres chart runs from approximately west-northwest to east-southeast. Therefore, the call that designates the free right of navigation as lying along the "Northeast" side of Cockspur is consistent and logical in that it would keep non-Georgian vessels in the portion of the river that lay between South

Carolina territory and occupied Georgia territory as represented by Cockspur Island. It would also assure that ships were following one of the main navigation channels of the day.

The next call in the treaty is "and up the direct course of the main northern channel." Once again, the call, as written, agrees closely with the content of the 1780 Avery–Des Barres chart. On the chart, a clear and continuous chain of depth soundings indicates the "main northern channel" up to the area just downstream of Hutchinson and Fig islands below the town of Savannah. Savannah was the main port and obvious destination for the most seagoing vessels navigating in the lower river, hence this information was vital to any useful chart of the area. Other charts, both predating and postdating the Avery–Des Barres make it clear that the main navigation channel with the greatest water depths was located generally along the northern sides of most of the larger islands located between Savannah and Tybee in the late eighteenth century (see the Henry Yonge chart of 1751 and John Le Conte chart of 1821, Maps 11 and 13).

The next call in the treaty article is very difficult to interpret at first reading because it denied South Carolina vessels free access to Savannah's wharves and landing stages. It reads, "along the northern side of Hutchinson's Island opposite the town of Savannah." Hutchinson Island was clearly located to the north of the city of Savannah. Why was free navigation guaranteed along the northern side of the island and not in the river between the island and city? The charts invariably show the main navigation channel focusing on Savannah, so this call seems to break the chain of logic well established in the treaty language up to this juncture. Further, it would appear to have failed to guarantee the South Carolinians freedom to navigate and trade in Savannah Harbor without let or hindrance. Was this its purpose? The answer to this question is to be found in the purpose of the Georgia "Act for regulating the trade . . . and also an impost on the tonnage of Shipping" mentioned above. Because a primary intent of that act was to raise funds for use in clearing revolutionary war channel obstructions and wrecks from Savannah Harbor, there was obvious utility for Georgia in writing the treaty in a way that would not exempt South Carolina vessels from paying the impost.

As written, the Beaufort Treaty did not impinge on Georgia's right to collect these needed charges on all vessels using the anchorages and facilities of Savannah Harbor. Thus, South Carolina vessels merely transiting the Savannah River, from a place like New Windsor Township, South Carolina, to Charleston, for example, would be exempted from the Georgia imposts. On the other hand, a South Carolina vessel engaged in the trade between Charleston and Savannah would be required to pay—not an unreasonable arrangement. The above discussion and argument gain strength when one reads further in the treaty's second article: "Is hereby declared to be henceforth, equally free to the citizens of both States, and exempt from all duties, tolls, hindrance, interruption, or molestation whatsoever, attempted to be enforced by one State on the citizens of the other; And all the rest of the river Savannah, to the southward of the foregoing description, is acknowledged to be the exclusive right of the State of Georgia."

The call in the treaty after "the northern side of Hutchinson's Island" follows logically once the conditions outlined above are understood. It states: "to the upper end of the said Island." This call has the effect of strengthening and making absolutely clear the intent of the one preceding it. There can be no doubt that the freedom of navigation declared in the treaty does not include Savannah Harbor, which would be along the southern side and at the lower end of Hutchinson Island.

From the upper end of Hutchinson Island, the next call describes the right of free navigation or passage as running "from thence up the bed or principal stream of the said River to the confluence of the Rivers Tugoloo and Keowee." This wording is very important because it guarantees South Carolina's right of navigation in the "principal stream" or channel of the Savannah, whereas the boundary would follow the "most northern branch or stream" of the river. In cases where the "principal stream" was totally within Georgia's territorial limits, South Carolinians would enjoy a guaranteed right of transit. It also represents an important compromise because South Carolina had maintained that the Savannah ended as a discrete entity at the point of confluence of its two major tributaries, the Tugaloo and Keowee.

The next call also represents considerable compromise and concession on the part of Georgia. The designation of the Tugaloo River as the boundary river was one of South Carolina's firm positions as outlined in the Beaufort Treaty's preamble. The call specifies that free navigation rights also extend "from the confluence up the Channel of the most northern stream of Tugoloo River to its source." Thus the debatable land lying between the Tugaloo and Keowee, roughly the area of present Oconee County, South Carolina, and the navigation on the Tugaloo are guaranteed to South Carolina.

The final call serves to emphasize and reaffirm what had been just defined. It reads: "And back again, by the same channel to the Atlantick Ocean." Thus, in a logical and geographically coherent manner, South Carolina's free right of navigation on the streams forming her common boundary with Georgia was ensured while in no way diminishing Georgia's territorial integrity as specified in her Charter of 1732. The above point is further emphasized in the final treaty caveats, which state: "Is hereby declared to be henceforth, equally free to the citizens of both States, and exempt from all duties, tolls, hindrance, interruption, or molestation whatsoever, attempted to be enforced by one State on the Citizens of the other; And all the rest of the river Savannah, to the southward of the foregoing description, is acknowledged to be the exclusive right of the State of Georgia."

The meaning and intent of the Treaty of Beaufort were brought to the attention of the general public soon after its signing. On May 3, 1787, for example, the *Gazette of the State of Georgia* (p. 3, col. 1), provided the following account:

Savannah, May 3

We hear that the Commissioners appointed by the Honourable the Legislature to settle the Boundaries between this State and the State of South Carolina have adjusted every point relative thereto, by a Convention, which was concluded the 28th ult. at Beaufort in South Carolina.—The Outlines of this important Business, it is said, are, That the most Northern Branch or Stream of the River Savannah, from the Sea to the Fork or Confluence of the Rivers Tugoloo and Keowee, and from thence the most Northern Stream of the main Branch of Savannah River, now called Tugoloo, 'till it intersects the Northern Boundary Line of South Carolina, is declared to be hereafter the Boundary Line between Georgia and South Carolina, leaving all that is South and West of it, as far as East and West Florida and the Mississippi, to the State of Georgia: And that the uninterrupted Navigation of the main Stream of that River, from its Source to the West End of Hutchinson's Island, and from thence along the North Side of said Island, and Cockspur Island, to the Sea, is to be the common Right of the Citizens of both States, leaving the Streams South of that Description to be the exclusive Right of Georgia.

The Treaty of Beaufort clearly confirmed Georgia's territorial limits along her riverine frontier with South Carolina, as these were articulated in the Charter of 1732. The charter had described Georgia as occupying the territory "from the most Northern Stream of a River there commonly called the Savannah," and the treaty confirmed the boundary as being "the most northern branch or stream of the River Savannah." With regard to South Carolina's right of passage or navigation on the river, however, a significant change occurred in the half-century from 1736–37 to 1787. During the 1730s, when a dispute concerning navigation rights arose between the colonies, the British crown was of the view that "the Northern branch of it ought to be free, and no vessel should be stopped going up either side of Hutchinson's Island . . . on account of having rum on board unless offering to trade [it] at any of the Settlements in Georgia." With the enactment of Georgia's "Act for regulating the trade . . . and also an impost on the tonnage of Shipping," in early 1787, a new dimension was introduced into discussions of Savannah navigation rights. The treaty authors were careful to exclude the stretch of river south of Hutchinson Island from the article guaranteeing South Carolina's right to use the river for navigation because this was Savannah Harbor. Savannah Harbor, in turn, was where most of the duties and imposts were to be collected for the purpose of clearing the wrecks and obstructions that had been left in the wake of the revolutionary war.

NOTES

1. In the printed *Communication to His Excellency Governor Cobb, on the Boundary between South-Carolina and Georgia; by the Attorney-General of South-Carolina*, which was published in Charleston in 1853, p. 10, the following statement appears: "Your Excellency is, I think mistaken in supposing that the expression, 'the most northern stream,' was ever applied exclusively above the confluence of the Tugaloo and Keowee. Such an idea is contradicted, as well by the character of the river, as the uncontroverted language elsewhere used in defining the boundary of Georgia. The river, as I have said, in point of fact, is divided at and below Savannah, into several streams, and in the 2d Article of the Convention of Beaufort, 'mouths' are spoken of in the plural, the 'main northern channel' is specified, implying of course other channels, as likewise the 'principal stream' implying necessarily other streams. And again the Charter begins to define the boundary by taking as a corner the point at which 'the most northern stream' enters the ocean, and runs thence not up the river, but southwardly. The reference here obviously cannot be to the streams above the confluence."

PART TWO

The Lower Savannah River and Mouth Area in the Eighteenth Century

IN TERMS OF GEOMORPHIC CHANGE, the lower Savannah River valley and mouth area is a dynamic region. The tremendous forces provided by a large river and the tidal surges of the Atlantic Ocean, influenced by wind and storm, are continuously sculpting and resculpting unstable shorelines formed by recent and erodible delta sediments. In this section, a summary is provided of verbal and cartographic descriptions of this dynamic region as it existed in the eighteenth century before large-scale engineering projects were undertaken in efforts to maintain the navigability of the river and the stability of its shores. These descriptions will enable the modern reader more clearly to understand and interpret the words and intentions of the authors of the article in the Beaufort Treaty describing the boundary between the states of Georgia and South Carolina. It should be kept in mind that no map or survey accompanied the treaty agreed to in 1787. All that the authors of that document provided for succeeding generations was the descriptive language discussed and analyzed in Part I of this book. It is not even certain that the commissioners consulted a map or chart during their deliberations at Beaufort, although that they did so seems highly likely.

The following review will provide a base of information from which the geographic realities existing in 1787 can be reconstructed. Second, and perhaps more important, it should provide insight into the general perceptions and attitudes held by eighteenth-century inhabitants of Georgia and South Carolina. Their perceptions of geographic and other conditions, like our own, were influenced by their value systems, political allegiances, and personal ambitions. The state of technology, particularly in respect to shipping and the productive use of the low-lying marsh and island-studded landscape found in the region downstream from Savannah, also had a direct influence on how these areas were assessed and evaluated.

The history of the founding of Georgia is inextricably bound to the perceptions and ambitions of the colony's resident trustee and principal designer, General James Edward Oglethorpe. In his letter to the Board of Trustees written in 1733, soon after his arrival in the new colony, Oglethorpe provided an excellent description of the site of his intended capital Savannah as well as the character of the river from which it was named:

> I went myself to view the Savannah River. I fixed upon a healthy situation about ten miles from the sea. The river there forms a half moon, along the south side of which the banks are about 40 foot high and upon the top a flat which they call a bluff. The plain ground extends into the country five or six miles and along the riverside about a mile. Ships that draw twelve foot water can ride within ten yards of the bank. Upon the riverside in the center of this plain, I have laid out the town. Over against it is an island of very rich land fit for pasturage, which I think should be kept for the Trustee's Cattle. The river is pretty wide, the water fresh. And from the quay of the town you see its whole course to the sea, with the Island of Tybee, which forms the mouth of the river; and the other way you may see the river for about six miles up into the country. The landscape is very agreeable, the stream being wide and bordered with high woods on both sides. [Mills Lane, ed., *General Oglethorpe's Georgia: Colonial Letters, 1733–1743*, pp. 4–5. This letter was published in *Gentleman's Magazine* 3 (April 1733): 168.]

This description of the area on the eve of its permanent occupation by Europeans is valuable with reference to the present boundary dispute because the mouth of the Savannah River is clearly defined as being formed in part by Tybee Island.

A few days earlier, in a letter to a friend in Port Royal, William Kilbury indicated the deep interest in the Savannah River by members of Oglethorpe's first party:

> As to giving you a particular account of the water, it is out of my power, as yet not having a man on board that knows the river nor how the channel is. The bluff where the town is designed to be built has a fine fresh. Water runs by it within 10 foot, where the sloop can float too at an hour's flood.... In about a week more I shall go down the river to sound it and

likewise the bar. I have made the best as I can a-coming up, which will be some help to my second proceeding. [Lane, ed., *General Oglethorpe's Georgia*, 1:6]

A Charleston merchant who developed an interest in promoting the commerce and exports of Georgia reported his first visit to Savannah on April 6, 1733. Samuel Eveleigh wrote to the trustees:

We arrived on Friday morning, an hour before day, at Yamacraw, a place so called by the Indians, but now Savannah, in the colony of Georgia.... This is a very high bluff, forty feet perpendicular from the high water mark. It lies, according to Captain Gascoigne's observations, in the Latitude of 31-58, which he took off Tybee, an island that lies at the mouth of the Savannah River.... There's about a 11 foot at high water on the bar, which I look upon to be of advantage to a young settlement, for in case of war no vessel of force can enter to disturb them. [Ibid., pp. 12–13]

The fact that a well-informed Charleston merchant identified Tybee Island as "at the mouth of the Savannah River" is especially important because that portion of Eveleigh's letter was printed in the *South Carolina Gazette*, March 24, 1733.

In a letter to the trustees written from Charleston on June 9, 1733, Oglethorpe reported his purchase of "a sloop with all her rigging good and Cable, anchors, sails, boat, etc. for 50 Sterling" (Lane, ed., *General Oglethorpe's Georgia*, p. 17). Among other uses for the vessel he included the "piloting in of shipping." This early reference can be seen as the commencement of Georgia's primary concern with and responsibility for the safety of navigation in the lowermost reaches of the Savannah River.

In this same June 9, 1733, letter, Oglethorpe discussed the potential value of land in Georgia: "You may judge the value of your lands here by the price of those of Trench's Island, which lies *at the mouth of the Savannah River on the Carolina side*" (ibid., p. 19; emphasis mine). The italicized words show clearly that in Oglethorpe's mind the mouth of the Savannah was formed by present-day Hilton Head (Trench's) Island to the north and Tybee Island to the south. That this was a widely held and consistent view becomes clear as succeeding documents and statements are reviewed.

Oglethorpe again expressed concern for the safety of navigation in the approach to his growing capital town on Yamacraw Bluff in a letter to the trustees in September of 1733: "A beacon upon Tybee for to direct ships on their making land is very necessary. I have therefore thought that you would not be displeased at an expense which will be but small, if compared to the great usefulness of it" (ibid., p. 24). Thus from the very outset of the colony, Georgia authorities felt responsible for navigation safety from the Savannah's mouth and bar upstream. The Tybee lighthouse was to become one of the man-made wonders of the colonial seacoast of eastern North America.

In December Oglethorpe again mentioned the beacon or lighthouse he was having built on Tybee. In this letter he described the structure then under construction: "The timber is already cut and squared and the upper and lower door framed. They reckon it will be finished in March. It is an octagon of 90 feet high, 25 feet wide at bottom and 12½ feet wide at top, weatherboarded 26 feet high and the rest open. It is all framed here of the best light wood and to be carried down and set upon the point of Tybee. The foundation will be secured with cedar piles" (ibid., p. 29).

Hector Beaufain, the collector of customs in Charleston, provided news of the progress of Oglethorpe's lighthouse in a letter he wrote on January 23, 1734: "Before I leave Savannah Town I must not forget to tell you who are concerned in the navigation of the river that there is a fine lighthouse making by Mr. Oglethorpe's order to be erected upon a point in Tybee Island." In the same letter Beaufain confirmed Oglethorpe's perception regarding the location of the Savannah's mouth: "We entered the river at Tybee Island without a pilot. Mr. Oglethorpe had been so kind as to send one to meet us, but the weather being foggy he missed us at sea" (ibid., pp. 35–36).

In a lengthy letter written to the trustees from Frederica on May 18, 1736, Oglethorpe revealed an important and apparently widely held view concerning jurisdiction and control of the river: "The Magistrates of Savannah have seized and staved large quantities of rum upon the river under the hill at Savannah. The channel being between Hutchinson's Island and Savannah, they deem that the water between the island and the town is Georgia since the islands are so (ibid., p. 267).

Such a logical interpretation of Georgia's charter apparently did not find favor among groups in South Carolina. Oglethorpe noted, "The People of Charles Town have taken this extremely ill and sent me a representative upon it." Thus, Georgians considered that the Savannah River south of any islands was wholly within their colony's territorial limit whereas many South Carolinians disagreed.

The *Journal of the Commons House of Assembly* of South Carolina for the years 1736–37 contains a lengthy report with appendixes concerning the rum controversy, discussed in Part I. Several of the appended documents contain statements indicating the geographic perceptions of contemporary South Carolinians concerning the lower Savannah River region. The deposition of Alexander Crombie made before the governor of South Carolina, for example, reveals an important statement as to where an active trader of that colony felt he entered the Savannah River on his way from Charleston to Savannah Town or New Windsor high up that river. In his deposition, Crombie recounted his knowledge of the rum-staving episode in Savannah Harbor, Georgia, and makes it clear that the South Carolinians considered Bloody Point to be "near the Mouth of Savannah River" (Easterly, ed., *Journal of the Commons House of Assembly*, p. 150). The waters south of Bloody Point also appear to have been considered as forming a portion of the river. Another deposition by Bacon Myers repeats this interpretation (ibid., p. 15).

Peter Shepherd, Patroon, revealed an intriguing view of a Savannah island that may be the same as the one now known as Jones Island. On April 8, 1736, Shepherd deposed that:

> Capt. Vanderplank told him that Mr. Oglethorpe designed to write Home to the Trustees to address the Parliament to enlarge the Bounds of his Government so far Northerly as Bloody Point up a straight Line in order to take in Purrysburgh and so up Back River, that he might command all that Part of the Country.
>
> That the said Shepherd was informed that there is a Law passed at Georgia which inflicts a Penalty of 50 Sterling upon any one that shall presume to pass up the River which is called the Back River, having its Entrance at the mouth of Savannah River at the Sea Coast and runs up behind an Island claimed by Mr. Oglethorpe, and comes out 5 miles about Georgia into Savannah River again, so that any one having a Plantation or Settlement on the said Back River must not go to it by Water, under forfeiture of Fifty Pounds Sterling.
>
> And the said Peter Shepherd further says that Capt. Vanderplank at

the same Time told him . . . that he had heard Mr. Oglethorpe say he would build a House on Bloody Point to hinder Pettaguas carrying Rum up Savannah River. [Ibid., pp. 151–52]

It must be kept in mind that Shepherd was repeating hearsay and may have scrambled his geography.

Although the town of Savannah was growing in size during the first years of Georgia's existence, little appears to have been done to improve the natural harbor found at the foot of Yamacraw Bluff. In a letter to the trustees written on February 10, 1737, John Brownfield, Savannah's register and naval officer, mentioned that "the town of Savannah is subject to several disadvantages in its trade from the want of a wharf and landing place." He continued: "We have two or three vessels this summer from Jamaica and Saint Christopher's and I was sorry to hear the complaints which the masters of those vessels made for want of a good crane and wharf to unload upon. I heard men of judgement say that ships are above three times longer unloading here than at other ports" (ibid., p. 297).

Whether the trouble was caused by the lack of berthing facilities alone or by the additional difficulty of conning deep-draft vessels through the channel to Savannah is difficult to determine, but it is apparent that many ships anchored at Tybee Island with passengers and freight being carried in small boats to and from the town. The importance of the presence of boatmen at Tybee is amusingly emphasized in the following passage from a letter Oglethorpe sent to the trustees on October 11, 1739:

I shall use my utmost endeavours to see your orders executed. Some things, I believe, you will think necessary to alter in them, particularly the allowing of an alehouse at Tybee, which would be the occasion of making boatmen drunk and might be the loss of many boats and men and would be attended with the same ill consequences as the alehouse on the Carolina side hath been, which, on the losing of several boats and drowning fourteen of my men, I have applied to have suppressed. [Ibid., p. 417]

Peter Gordon, the artist of the perspective view showing the town of Savannah in the forest clearing on Yamacraw Bluff (Map 8), also provided an excellent verbal description of the site. In his journal of his experiences in crossing the Atlantic aboard the *Anne* with Oglethorpe and the original contingent of Georgians, Gordon wrote:

> Next morning being the first of February Old style calendar—New style February 12, 1733., we sailed from Jones's Island,[1] with a fair wind and arrived the same day at Yamacraw Bluff in Georgia, the place which Mr. Oglethorpe had pitched upon for our intended settlement. . . . And as soon as we landed, we sett emediately about getting our tents fixed, and our goods brought ashore, and carryed up the Bluff, which is fourty foot perpendicular height above by water mark. This by reason of the loos sand, and great height, would have been extremely troublesome had not Captain Scott and his party built stairs for us before our arrival, which we found of very great use to us in bringing up our goods. . . . The 19th Mr. Oglethorpe went in the scout boat to the Island Tybe in the mouth of our river to pitch upon a proper place for a small settlement for some people from Carolina who desired to be admitted under his protection, and to serve as a look out for our settlement. . . . About seven in the evening Mr. Oglethorpe returned in the scout boat from Tybe. This day our new crane was putt up. [E. Merton Coulter, ed., *The Journal of Peter Gordon, 1732–1735*, pp. 35, 39, 40–41]

Peter Gordon's engaging remarks are best read with a copy of his engraved "a View of Savannah As It Stood the 29th of March, 1734" at hand (Map 8). The view is taken from Hutchinson Island, which appears in the foreground across the Savannah River to the steep bank of the bluff. A large cleared area on the bluff top is occupied by the distinctive rectangular plan of lots, streets, and squares that was the hallmark of Oglethorpe's planned settlements. The "stairs" and "crane" which Gordon mentioned as providing access between the river edge and bluff-top town appear in the foreground. Gordon's mention of Tybee Island as being "in the mouth of our river" is consistent with the concepts of others in his era.

Baron Georg Philipp Friedrich von Reck, who helped lead the first band of German-speaking Protestant exiles from Salzburg, arrived in Georgia in March 1733. Von Reck recorded the following observations concerning the lower Savannah region:

> At noon we cast anchor because of the Tide: at eight, during the Evening Prayers, we entered the River of Savannah; and were shelter'd by the Divine Goodness, from all dangers and Inconveniencies of the Sea. This River is in some Places broader than the Rhine, and from 16 to 25 Foot

8. "A View of Savannah as it Stood the 29th of March 1734," by Peter Gordon. Peter Gordon was an early visitor to Savannah. His "View" and

commentary assist in gaining an appreciation of early-eighteenth-century conditions in the area.

deep; and abounds with Oysters, Sturgeon, and other fish. Its banks were cloathed with fresh grass; and a little beyond were seen Woods, old as the Creation; resounding with the Musick of Birds, who sung the Praise of their Creator.

The Magistrates of the Town sent on Board our Ship an experienced Pilot; and we were carried up to the Town of Savannah by 11 in the Forenoon. [Trevor R. Reese, ed., *Our First Visit in America*, p. 46]

Francis Moore, author of *A Voyage to Georgia Begun in the Year 1735*, included valuable references to the lower Savannah region in his book published in 1744:

I took a View of the Town of Savannah; it is about a Mile and Quarter in Circumference; it stands upon the flat of a hill, the Bank of the River (which they in barbarous English call a Bluff) is steep and about 45 Foot perpendicular, so that all heavy Goods are brought up by a Crane, an Inconvenience designed to be remedied by a bridged Wharf, and an easy Ascent, which in laying out the Town, care was taken to allow room for, there being a very wide Strand between the first Row of Houses and the River. From this Strand there is a very pleasant Prospect; you see the River wash the Foot of the Hill, which is hard, clear, sandy Beach, a Mile in Length; the Water is fresh, and the River 1000 Foot wide. Eastward you see the River increased by the Northern Branch, which runs round Hutchinson's Island, and the Carolina Shore beyond it, and the Woody Islands at the Sea, which close the Prospect of 10 or 12 Miles Distance. Over against it is Hutchinson's Island, great part of which is open Ground, where they mow Hay for the Trust's Horses and Cattle. The rest is Woods, in which there are many Bay-trees 80 Foot high. Westward you see the River winding between the Woods, with little Islands in it for many Miles. [Ibid., pp. 96–97]

Moore's description of the Savannah River's bifurcated channel opposite the city of Savannah is noteworthy in that he refers to "the Northern Branch, which runs round Hutchinson's Island." The term "northern branch" appears in the first article of the Treaty of Beaufort in reference to the location of the boundary between Georgia and South Carolina.

Benjamin Ingham, an active member of the Oxford Methodist group, accompanied John and Charles Wesley to Georgia in 1736. His journal of the voyage includes an illuminating description of the Savannah mouth area which serves to reinforce the perception of others quoted: "On Tuesday we found Ground; on Wednesday we Saw

Land, & on Thursday afternoon Feb. 5, we got safe into the Tybe Road in the mouth of the River Savannah in the Province of Georgia in America" (ibid., p. 174).

As mentioned above, German-speaking Protestants formed an important and numerous component of Georgia's early population. After an unhappy sojourn at their original inland settlement site named Ebenezer, they were granted a new tract on the Savannah River upstream from the town of Savannah. Johann Martin Bolzius was pastor of the group and also its unquestioned temporal leader. Toward the end of the trusteeship period he was frequently solicited for detailed information about Georgia by interested persons in Europe. In responding to one of these, he wrote the following:

> We are well provided with general and special maps from Halle and Augsburg. Nothing accurate has as yet been published about our colony and Carolina. Our colony is separated from Carolina by the beautiful, wide, rapid, healthy, rich-in-fish, also navigable Savannah River, which like all main rivers in America flows into the sea from northwest to southeast. While passing Purrysburg it forms several small and large islands which are very adequate for rice planting, and all of which belong to Georgia by Royal Patent. [Klaus J. Leowald, ed. and trans., "Johann Martin Bolzius Answers a Questionnaire on Carolina and Georgia," p. 64]

Bolzius obviously had no doubts concerning Georgia's charter limits insofar as the islands in the Savannah River were concerned. His opinion was very important because of his position as spokesman for one of Georgia's most numerous and productive communities in the middle decades of the eighteenth century.

Although the foregoing descriptive statements were made by persons representing a diversity of backgrounds and interests and offer a generally consistent view, they are more impressionistic than scientific. The first truly scientific verbal description of the lower Savannah area appears to have been provided by William Gerard De Brahm.

De Brahm was a highly trained German military engineer who arrived in Georgia in 1751 in charge of a large group of immigrants bound for Ebenezer just upriver from Savannah (see Louis De Vorsey, Jr., "William Gerard De Brahm," pp. 204–9). His first map of the Savannah River was drawn during his first year in Georgia. Now a part of the Faden Collection in the Library of Congress, Geography and Map Division, it is titled "A Map of Savannah River beginning at

Stone Bluff or Nexttobethel, which continueth to the Sea; Also, the Four Sounds Savannah, Hossabaw and St. Katherines with their Islands Likewise Newport or Serpent River from its mouth to Benjehova Bluff."

As joint surveyor-general of lands for the royal colony of Georgia, an interim surveyor-general in neighboring South Carolina, and surveyor-general for the entire Southern District of British colonial North America, De Brahm had access to the fullest record of detailed geographic information available. This knowledge, along with his considerable talents as a geographer and surveyor-cartographer, qualified De Brahm as an expert on the geography of eighteenth-century Georgia. In addition, he was an accomplished navigator well acquainted with the watery margins of the colony, particularly the lower Savannah region.

In the comprehensive report that he prepared and personally presented to King George III is included a wealth of detailed scientific descriptive material on the lower Savannah region presented in both verbal and cartographic form. Although the report that includes the material quoted below was completed during 1772, the conditions described probably were applicable in the mid-1750s and early 1760s during De Brahm's residence in Savannah. He left Georgia in 1765 for St. Augustine, East Florida, which remained his base of operations through his productive tenure as surveyor-general of the Southern District.

In describing the Savannah River below the town, De Brahm drew attention to the shoaling that was already becoming a problem in the middle decades of the eighteenth century:

> The Savannah Stream forms a Sound at its own Outlet into the Ocean, which altho' it is not barred, yet there are many Banks in the Road between the Sound and City, on a distance of 17 miles, which these 40 years have rather increased in Extent and Shallowness, a Consequence owing to nothing else, but the great Currents yearly wheeling down a distance of 290 miles, especially at the time of great Freshes, by which great Trees with their Roots and many Shrubs are grubbed up, which and along with them great Quantity of Ground, Sand and Gravel is hurried down, and before the precipitating Stream breaks into the Sea, the Ocean's Flood checks its Velocity; thus suddenly stopt, the Stream drops its Gravel and Sand on Places where Currents give way to contre-Currents (Eddys). So that a Man-of-War Sloop with Difficulty goes up to the City at this time; when thirty-six years ago a forty-gun Ship found no difficulty to come up

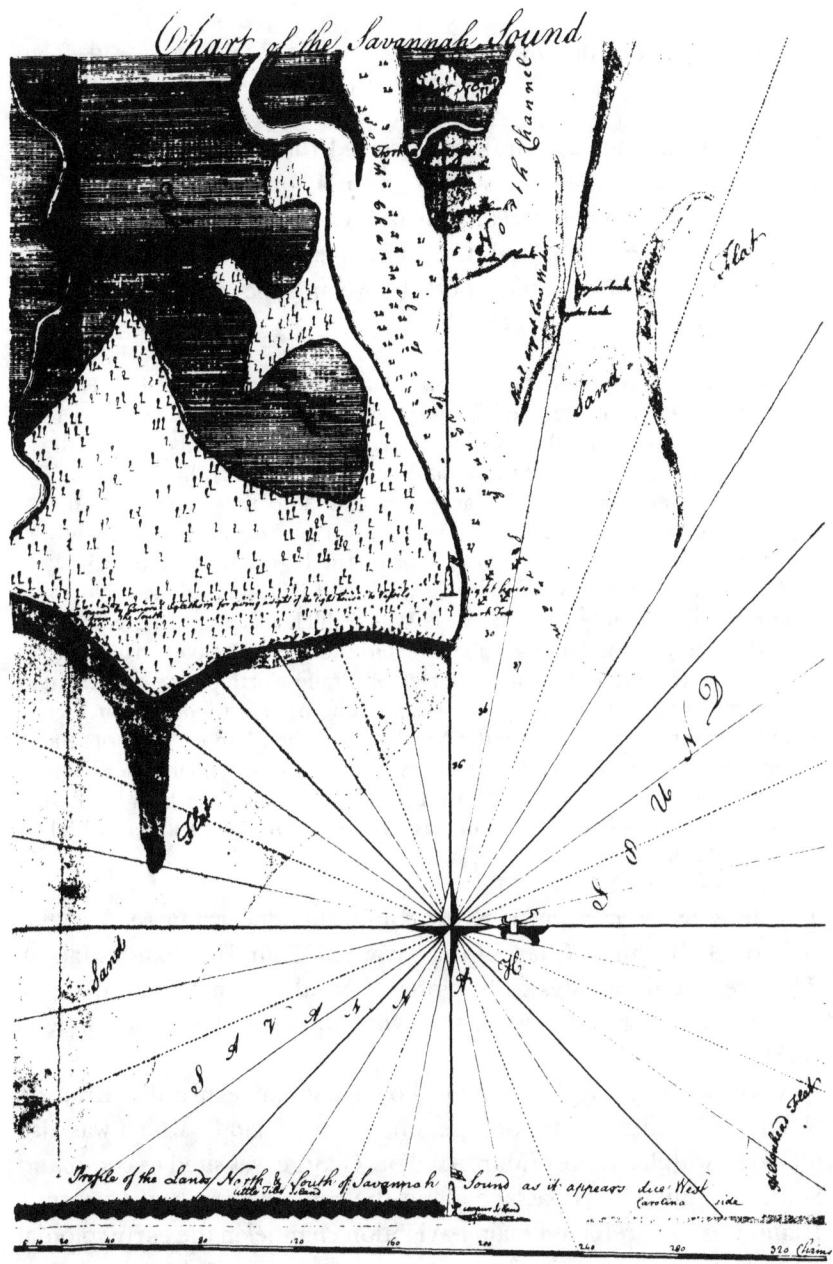

9. "Chart of the Savannah Sound," by William De Brahm. De Brahm served as Surveyor General of Lands in Georgia's first royal administration. His maps and verbal descriptions of the lower Savannah River region are extremely valuable. (Photograph of original in Kings Ms. 210 supplied through the courtesy of the Trustees of the British Library.)

and anchor before the Town. [Louis De Vorsey, Jr., ed., *De Brahm's Report of the General Survey in the Southern District of North America*, p. 159]

It is significant that De Brahm perceived the "Sound" of Savannah River as a part of the river system and not something apart from it, stating that "Savannah Stream forms" the Sound. In the paragraph that follows, he supported the eighteenth-century perception of the location of Savannah's mouth between Tybee and Hilton Head islands:

> The Sound is formed by a great Sand-flat, which runs from Hilton Head (the north Point of the Sound) three miles to the East, and six miles to the South; and by another Flat, which runs from Great Tibe Island (the south Point of the Sound) three miles on a S.E. course. The Breakers of both these Flats have a fine large Entrance into the Sound, which is made, by taking a small Pine Tree (grown on the East of the Light House) a little to the North, so as to bring the Light-House to bear W. ½ N., and keep this course until the East Point of Hilton Head bears North, and the west Point bears N. by W. ½ W., at which time the North Shoal is cleared, and a Vessel may at Liberty avoid the South Breakers, run up to the Light House, and come a quarter of a mile North of the said Light House to anchor in a very good Ground. The Breakers from Great Tibe and from an Oyster Bank on the North side of the Channel, opposite the Light House, are so visible, that a Vessel needs no written Direction. The least Water from the Light House up to Coxpur Island, which lay East and West a mile from each other, is 12 feet at low, and 19 feet at high water. [Ibid.]

This lengthy description is easily comprehended when read with a copy of De Brahm's "Chart of the Savannah Sound" at hand (Map 9). The area he designates as Savannah Sound is clearly seaward of a closing line that would run from Tybee to Hilton Head on modern charts.

A portion of Cockspur Island is shown in great detail on De Brahm's "Plan and Profile of Fort George, on Coxpur Island," which was also included with his report (Map 10). Fort George was sited to command South Channel. This passage along the southern flank of Cockspur Island was the preferred main navigation channel in the early colonial period.

De Brahm had been appointed as surveyor-general of the newly established royal government of Georgia jointly with Henry Yonge in 1752. Yonge, though much less well known than De Brahm, was his equal as a surveyor-cartographer. In 1751, Yonge prepared a large

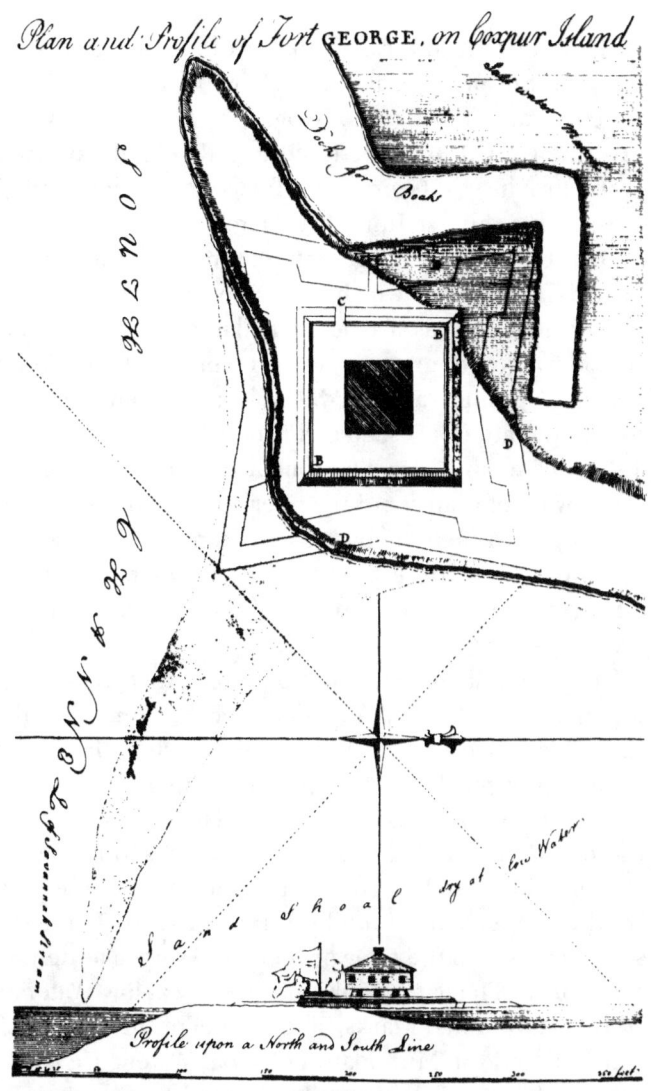

10. "Plan and Profile of Fort George, on Coxpur Island," by William De Brahm. De Brahm included this detailed depiction of a portion of Cockspur Island in his "Report" delivered to King George III in 1772. (Photograph of original in Kings Ms. 210 supplied through the courtesy of the Trustees of the British Library.)

and detailed chart of the lower Savannah from the town to Savannah Sound. The manuscript original of this chart is also in the Faden Collection of the Library of Congress, Geography and Map Division (see Map 11). Its title is "A Plan of the Inlets and Rivers of Savannah and Warsaw in the Province of Georgia. Performed by order of the President and Assistants this 1st June Ano Dom 1751 per Henry Yonge Surv." This chart grew out of a presentment made by the first General Assembly held in Georgia, which was convened in January 1751. Rather than functioning as a true lawmaking body, this group resembled a modern grand jury, bringing problems and questions to the trustees' resident administrators in the last year of their tenure. Three of the first four matters presented dealt with navigation and commerce on the Savannah River. The fourth presentment dealt specifically with the "want of a survey of the river" (Hugh M'Call, *The History of Georgia*, 1:234). In their reply, the president and assistants stated that a survey would be undertaken "as soon as persons qualified could be procured" (Lilla Hawes, ed. "Proceedings of the President and Assistants . . . 1749–1751").

Henry Yonge's excellent chart is ample proof that the Georgia administrators had indeed found a qualified person for this important task. A cartouche labled "Explanation" makes it clear that Yonge was as astute an observer of the natural processes operating in the lower Savannah as was his colleague De Brahm. He and De Brahm both showed the broad, sandy shallows that extended south from Hilton Head and Daufuskie islands to constrict the entrance to the Savannah River from the deeper water found off Tybee Island. These shallows as well as similar areas in the river proper were shown as described in his "Explanation": "The Sand Banks that are dry at low Water are distinguished by Yellow doted Marks, The Chanel of the River is shaded with Indian Ink, and the Mud Flats and shoal Waters are left White" (Henry Yonge, "A Plan of the Inlets & Rivers of Savannah & Warsaw in the Province of Georgia"). In addition to the ink shading, the channels are indicated by lines of figures representing water depths in either feet or fathoms. Several small oyster banks are identified, as are prominent trees along the riverbanks that served as landmarks. Yonge also provided a basic scheme for improving the navigability of the Savannah through methods that were to become standard hydraulic engineering practices a century later. Thus Yonge created both the first detailed chart of the lower Savannah and the first large-scale river improvement scheme.

The river improvement scheme is implicitly stated on his chart through the placement of several small arrow-shaped symbols at strategic points along the Savannah's course to the sea. In the "Explanation" on the chart Yonge noted that these symbols "are shoals and narrow Places in the River Savannah which if stoped up would probably open the main Chanel." For example, Yonge suggested a dike to connect Fig Island and Hutchinson Island to increase the flow and scouring capacity of the river along the Georgia shore just below the town limits of Savannah. A short distance below this, he recommended the same action in two narrow channels between two islands that became known as Barnwell and were later joined to the fast land of the South Carolina shoreline through the efforts of the U.S. Army Corps of Engineers. Below this he recommended a similar blockage that would have joined a small island to the upper end of Elba Island. He also advised the closing off of the Mud River branch of the Savannah, which flowed around Jones Island, to be joined by the tidal creek known as Wright River.

In two places on his chart, Yonge termed the main northern navigation channel the "North Branch" of the Savannah River. At a point about midway betwen Tybee and Cockspur islands he placed a symbol that was explained as a "Proper Place for a Buoy in Savannah River." Taken together the work and observations of Yonge and De Brahm provide a detailed description of the lower Savannah River region as it existed a generation prior to the signing of the Treaty of Beaufort.

A lengthy letter written by James Habersham, partner in the Savannah trading company of Harris and Habersham, to Benjamin Martyn, the secretary of the Trust, in the same period included a detailed discussion of the difficulties being encountered by ships using the port of Savannah. These problems must have inspired the request for a survey of the river that led to Yonge's outstanding chart and scheme. Habersham wrote:

> I cannot omit mentioning, what must give the Trustees, as well as all, who wish well, to this Colony a great Concern, that the river between this Town and Tybye is thought to be extreemly bad, and I am afraid, unless it can be made better, will prevent this Place from ever becoming a Market for this Colony—I have for Two Years past been apprehensive of it, and when Complaints was made against David Cunningham, who was Pilot before the present one, I urged, upon several Occasions, that the River might be surveyed, when it wou'd appear, whether He was faulty; But People were so prejudiced in Favour of the River, that it was almost

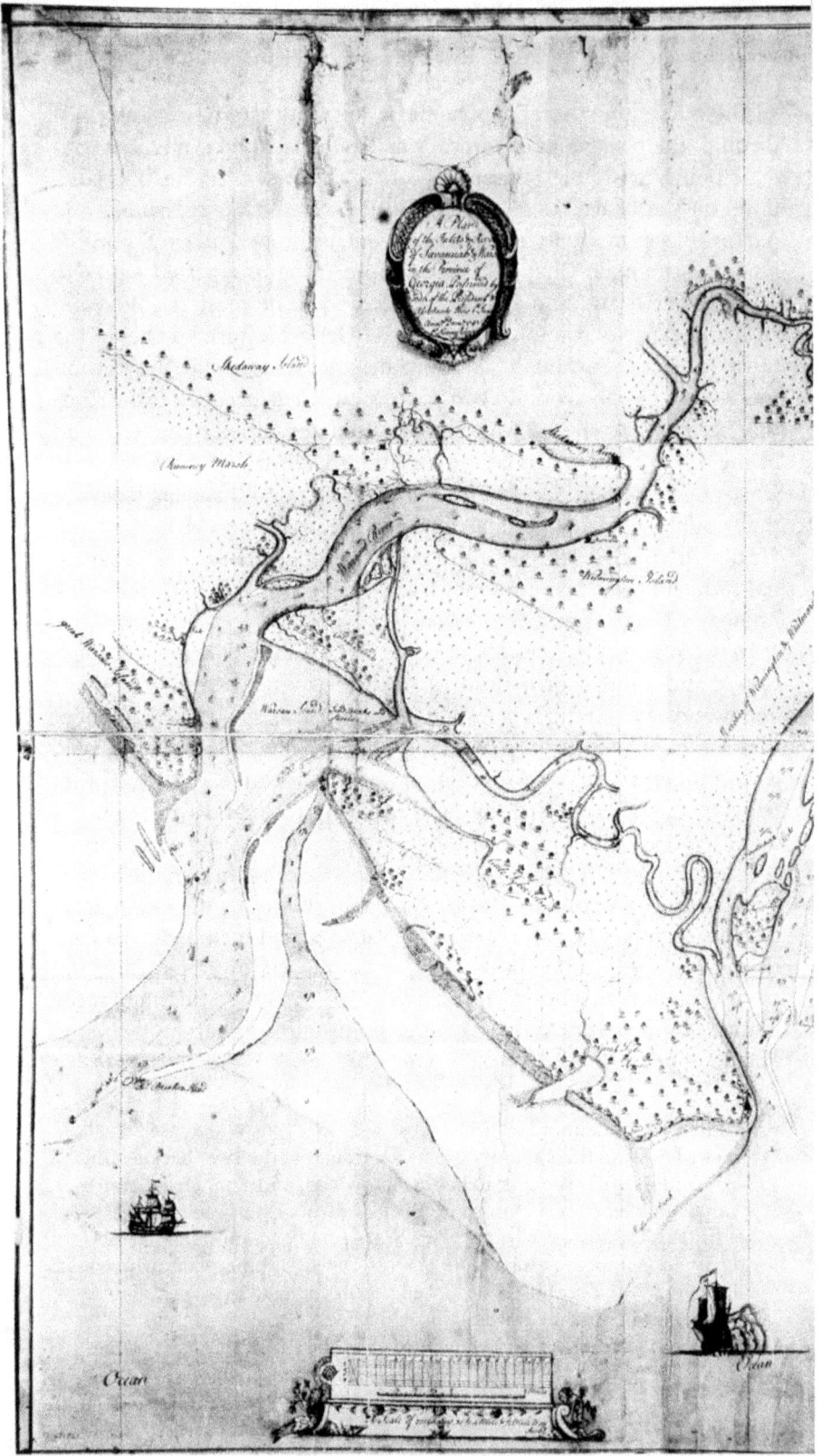

11. "A Plan of the Inlets and Rivers of Savannah and Warsaw in the Province of Georgia. Performed by order of the President and Assistants this 1st June Ano Dom 1751 per Henry Yonge Surv." In addition to charting the lower Savannah River's channels and islands Yonge provided suggestions to improve the river's navigability on this detailed map.

deemed Treason to contradict the received Opinion—Mr. Cunningham was displaced, and Mr. John Penrose was put in his Room—Since which, almost every Vessell has been run on Ground in going down, and He now refuses to carry any Down, that draws above Ten Feet—I cannot determine, whether either of these Pilots have wanted Judgement, as the River has not been surveyed (for want indeed of a judicious Seaman to accompany our land Surveyers therein) but if they are not culpable, it cannot be expected, unless (as I before observed) the River can be mended, that any Exportation of Consequence can be carried on here.— It is not to be doubted, but that Ships of Two Hundred Tons or upwards have come up to this Town, but I dont understand, that every any, of near that Burden, has been carried down loaded without running on Ground, which is too dangerous to be suffered, if it can be avoided—It has not, I suppose, been considered ('till Experience has taught us) that a Ship, which draws Twelve Feet Water or upwards, can better come up with a flowing Tide, than of Ten Feet go down with the Ebb; Likewise, the Vessels come in much lighter into these Parts, either from Europe or elsewhere, supposing them loaded with our usual Imports, than they go out, especially with Rice Cargoes. I mention these Observations to shew, how easily Persons unacquainted with shipping may be mistaken in their Judgment of the Navigation of Rivers, which appears to have been the Case with our Inhabitants.—The Snow Mary Capt Pearson, which my Partner and I loaded here last July wou'd not carry One Hundred Ton of Rice and drew, when loaded, about Elleven Feet; and notwithstanding, she took in about Thirty barils of rice, and some of her Water at Cock Spur, yet she met with such Difficulty in going down, and was so often run on Ground, that it almost drove the Master mad; and indeed I did not wonder at his being uneasy, as his Vessel might be suffered, beyond repair, besides the Danger of damaging, if not loseing her Cargoe.—I wish she did not suffer, and I am in some Pain about her, as I don't hear of her Arrivall. Six Days agoe, A large Sloop freighted by us, fell down the River about two thirds loaded, and the Master of her is just now come up, and informs me, that she has been ground Four Times, since she left our Wharfe, and was in great Danger on the last Bank, she was upon, they having slipt one Cable, and parted another by her thumping, occasioned by a violent Wind, which came on, while she was on the Bank; And that He does not expect to get to Cock Spur, 'till the Tides lift, which may be in two or three Days—She now draws something less, than Ten feet and a half, and that she might go down without Danger, we loaded our Schooner with Corn, Pease and Rice to be put on Board at Cock Spur, which from the Time the Sloop went down, she will deliver them—These are insufferable Inconveniences, and our Commodities will be hereby loaded with such an Expence (unknown to our Neighbours) that I cannot see, how we can do Business upon a Footing with them, or to any Purpose—This has been the Case with (I believe) every Vessel of upwards of Ten Feet draught, which has loaded at this Town for Two years past, in which Time, we may date our Exports. The

Board have consulted on Means to remedy this Grievance, and proposed to get the Land Surveyors to examine the River, who say, they can return a Draught of it, but won't be at a Loss to propose a Remedy, as they don't understand the setting of the Tides, and the Method of turning the Force of the Current into the proper Channel to deepen it, and that this must be reported by experienced Seamen, which we are at present in Want of—Capt David Cutler Braddock, who I mentioned in my Journal of the 21st November last to be sailed for New England, is proposed to accompany the Surveyors in this Enquiry, when He arrives here—He is allowed to be an excellent Seaman, and to be well acquainted with this river; But it is a Doubt with me, whether it can be remedied with any tolerable Expence, for as it is bounded below this Town with Marshes, which are sometimes overflown by spring Tides, it branches out into several wide openings, and divides about four Mile below into, what is called, the North and South River, one of which, and perhaps some of the other smaller Branches must be stoped up, to force the Current to deepen the other, unless raking the Banks, and thereby losening the Sand or Mud, for the Tides to carry it off, may answer the same Purpose.—As I am no ways acquainted with the Method of making Rivers navigable, my Thoughts thereon must be very imperfect; but in the mean Time, the Navigation of this is become so much out of repute, that I question, whether we could get a Vessel of any Burden (of any that know it) to come to this Town to load, and the Expence and Trouble of loading at Cock Spur must be intollerable, and, I suppose, impractable in Lumber Cargoes, as rafts are liable to be lost in carrying down, and when there, if the Wind is at East, it causes such a Swell, that the Lumber Ports cannot be opened—This we have experienced in a Ship, we lately loaded with Lumber, which took in a small Part at Cock Spur—I am persuaded, this Account of our River will give the Trustees great Concern, especially as they have always thought Savannah happily situated in this Respect; And it must be an uneasy Reflection in my Partner and me, as we have laid out more Money in Improvements in this Town, than any private Persons, since its first Settlement—Our Wharfe, which is now finished will cost us upwards of Two Hundred Pounds, Mr Harris has near finished a very handsome House which will cost him more, the Buildings I have put on my Lott has stood me in as much, which with the Repairs and Additions, we made to our Stores in this Town will probably amount to Eight Hundred Pounds Sterling, and all the Improvements are new, and in very good Condition—I dont mention this, as tho' we were the only Sufferers, in Case the River shou'd be found incurable, but the Fear of it's being so will make all the present Improvements invaluable, and will probably strike a Damp on People making more, which seemed (of late) to be the Desire of all that could—The Ship Caesar, which was suffered to sink before this Town, is supposed to hurt the River (as it certainly has done) by gathering a Bank, and forcing the Current against our sandy Bluff, which has doubtless carried away great Quantitys of Sand into the River, but however it may have encreased the shoal Places a little below the Town, I cannot think, it has made any great Alterations six, seven or Eight Miles below, where some of the worst Banks are—It will afford me the highest Satisfaction, if this Difficulty, which (while it remains) must obstruct the Welfare of the Colony, and this Town in particular, can be removed; And tho' I wou'd hope it may, yet I should think myself inexcusable, if I should delay to acquaint the Trustees therewith. [Lucian Lamar Knight, ed., and Allen D. Chandler, comp., *The Colonial Records of the State of Georgia*, 26:137–42]

Habersham's description of the lower Savannah River at midcentury was largely verified by Georgia's extremely able colonial governor Sir James Wright in a descriptive report he prepared on the colony in 1773. The report is in the form of answers to a list of questions that had been posed in an earlier communication from Lord Dartmouth, the secretary of state in the British government (James Wright, "Report of Sir James Wright on the Condition of the Province of Georgia, on 20th Sept., 1773," pp. 158–79).

The Georgia governor named Tybee Inlet as the entrance to the Savannah River and placed it at latitude 31°55' north and longitude 80° west from London. He specified that Georgia's northern boundary was "on the most Northern stream of Savannah River as far as the Head of the said River." He also stated that he knew of no dispute concerning the colony's boundaries "either with the adjoining Provinces or with the Indians."

In an answer to a query concerning rivers, he described the Savannah as follows:

The Principal Rivers are Savannah River, which extends back into the Country a North west by Northerly course to Augusta about three hundred miles, altho by Land not above 140. And above Augusta it extends above 200 miles into the Cherokee Country and is said to interlock with the Tanassee River, a branch from the Ohio, but does not join it. Pretty large trading boats go to Augusta, but no large Boats can go above that on account of a ridge of rocks and untill they are removed, it is only navigable for canoes. [Ibid., p. 161]

On the colony's harbors, he wrote:

The Principal Harbours are Savannah on the Bar of which call'd Tybee there is three fathoms and a half water at low water or better. And up the River to the Town, there is in general about thirteen feet water at high Water common Tydes, but there being three sand banks in different places therefore at present and untill they are removed Vessels at the Town do not load deeper than from twelve to thirteen feet and then are obliged to fall down to Cockspur to take in the rest of their loading. But for more circumstantial account of this Inlet etc. I beg leave to refer to the Inclos'd sketch mark'd A No. 1. [Ibid., pp. 163–64]

The sketch that Governor Wright enclosed with his report is in the map and chart collection of the British Public Record Office, London (M.P.G. 357). It is a detailed depiction of the main approach to the Savannah River bar off Tybee Island and the river mouth off Tybee to Cockspur Island. William Lyford, "Branch Pilot for the Barr & River Savannah in Georgia," drew the chart and dated it 13 December 1773, a week before Governor Wright dated his report to Lord Dartmouth. In addition to the chart showing soundings, shoals, channels, the lighthouse, and fort on Cockspur, Lyford included a short verbal description:

> In Lat. 31–55 Longitude 80 is the entrance of Savannah River. At Low water, you have 3 Fathoms & ½ upon the Barr. From which to sail into Cockspur, your Course is W ½ N about 5 Miles, carrying 3, 2½, 3¾, 3, 3½ Fathoms till you are abreast of the Lighthouse, in 4 Fathoms, then Steer WSW about 3 miles carrying in 3½, 3, 2 Fathoms to the point of Cockspur Island where you may anchor in 4 Fathoms at Low Water with room sufficient for a Twenty Gun Ship or Frigate. The flow of the Tides upon a Nieptide is Seven feet, and upon a Spring Tide Nine Feet. ESE makes high water upon the Barr, full & change. N.B.
> In Tybee Creek there is a proper place and water suffict. to heave down & careen, any ship of the abovementioned Size—W.L. [British Public Record Office Map, M.P.G. 357]

Unfortunately, Governor Wright did not have Georgia's branch pilot prepare an even more comprehensive chart to show the river channels between Cockspur and the town of Savannah. Certainly those channels were increasing in significance as the colony grew.

Wright indicated that the colony's maritime commerce had increased from 45 vessels accounting for only 1,604 tons which entered the "whole province" in 1761 to 217 totaling 12,124 tons in 1772. In this latter year, 161 vessels were cleared at the Savannah Customs House.

In describing Georgia's prerevolutionary fortifications, Wright provided detailed information on Fort George and Cockspur Island:

> Fort George on the Island of Cockspur opposite to Tybee Island being at the entrance of the River Savannah and a very necessary post as it is the Key to our Port and may command all Vessels that come in or go out; Enforce due obedience to the Laws of Trade and our Provincial Laws. And in case of War prevent Enemies Privateers from cuting out and carrying off our shipping or from coming up the River to plunder etc. This Fort was built in the Year 1762 being mud walls faced with Palmettoe Trees, but is now almost in ruins for as it stands on a point of Land exposed to the Easterly winds from the Sea, it is very lyable to suffer by the sea beating and washing against it when there is strong Easterly Winds. On the inside is a Capaniere which serves for Officers Apartments and in lieu of Barracks, it used to be garrisoned by an Officer and Ten men but now as its almost in ruins there is only an Officer and three Men just to make signals etc. I look upon this Fort or having a proper Fort at this Place to be of the utmost consequence and shall propose building a new Fort of Tabby, but as our property is yet small and our taxes pretty high, I doubt much whether the Province can afford to go to the expence of building a Proper Fort. [Wright, "Report," p. 168]

Governor Wright's description of Fort George's vulnerability to wind and wave is excellent testimony to the dynamic nature of the lower Savannah region. Writing some seventy-two years later, engineer Lieutenant Barton S. Alexander confirmed Wright's worst fears for the future of Fort George. In a letter from Fort Pulaski on February 25, 1845, Alexander wrote of old Fort George as follows:

> Capt. Mansfield tells me that the site of Fort George is now almost entirely washed away. It stood on the South-east side of the island and the spot where the round beacon now stands; this is a small shell bank some 300 yards from the present shore. If this was the only fort that the British had on this island it would seem to indicate that the South Channel was then the main channel for it was much too far from the North Channel to defend it unless it too has greatly changed. [Keith Read Manuscript Collection, University of Georgia Libraries]

If Alexander's information was correct, it indicates that the erosion of the eastern extremity of Cockspur Island had totaled some nine hundred linear feet in just seventy-two years, or an average rate of almost twelve feet yearly! Also, South Channel ceased to be the main channel sometime between 1773, when Wright proposed building a new tabby fort to defend it, and 1845 when Alexander was at Fort Pulaski.

The rate of erosion reported at the eastern extremity of Cockspur Island is verified through a comparison of the 1780 chart by Avery with the U.S. Coast Survey's 1855 "Preliminary Chart of Savannah River" (Map 7). Measuring the retreat of Cockspur shown on these charts reveals roughly one thousand feet of westward erosion, very close to the nine hundred feet reported by Alexander. The similarity between Alexander's figure and Avery's chart further confirms the accuracy of the latter.

Although the date when the northern channel up to the city of Savannah became the main navigation channel is not known, it may have begun to assume this role by the early 1790s or only twenty years after Wright proposed the construction of a new Fort George. Emplacements on Tybee rather than Cockspur served as Savannah's outer defenses during most of the revolutionary period.

In her monograph *Savannah Harbor: Its Origin and Development, 1733–1890*, published in 1968, Mary L. Granger used several eighteenth-century descriptions. She was particularly impressed by the work of De Brahm. Granger wrote:

> The "Eddys" and currents which de Brahm considered so largely responsible for the shoaling problems as already briefly mentioned found a fertile spot at the lower end of Fig Island where Back and Front Rivers united to form a single channel to the head of Elba Island. This eddying of currents off the Fig Island shore produced natural shoaling which made it the logical site for easy blocking of the channel when the Revolutionary War made the town a prize for both the Royal government and the Patriots. The addition of artificial hazards to the Fig Island channel, already of critical depth, produced an effective barrier for the town. After the war, however these obstructions greatly increased future problems of navigation by providing a nucleus for more rapid shoaling. Since this time, "The Wrecks" has been the name by which this channel has been known. [P. 8]

Both the British and the Patriots deliberately blocked the Savannah's channel on several occasions during the Revolution. The master's log of H.M. Armed Vessel *Cherokee*, for example, describes the progress of the ship up the river in February 1776. On Monday, February 26, the master noted: "At 10 AM unmoored Weighed and come to sail and Dropt further up at 11 Anchd wth the Bt Br in 2 ffm at Low Water Veered to ⅓ of a Cable and moored wth the Stream Anchor to the so wd the Battery on Savannah Bluff WBS 3 Miles and the Rebels Guard House on Brewtons Plantation SW 1 mile found the Channell block'd up by a Hulk being sunk in the Middle of the Chan-

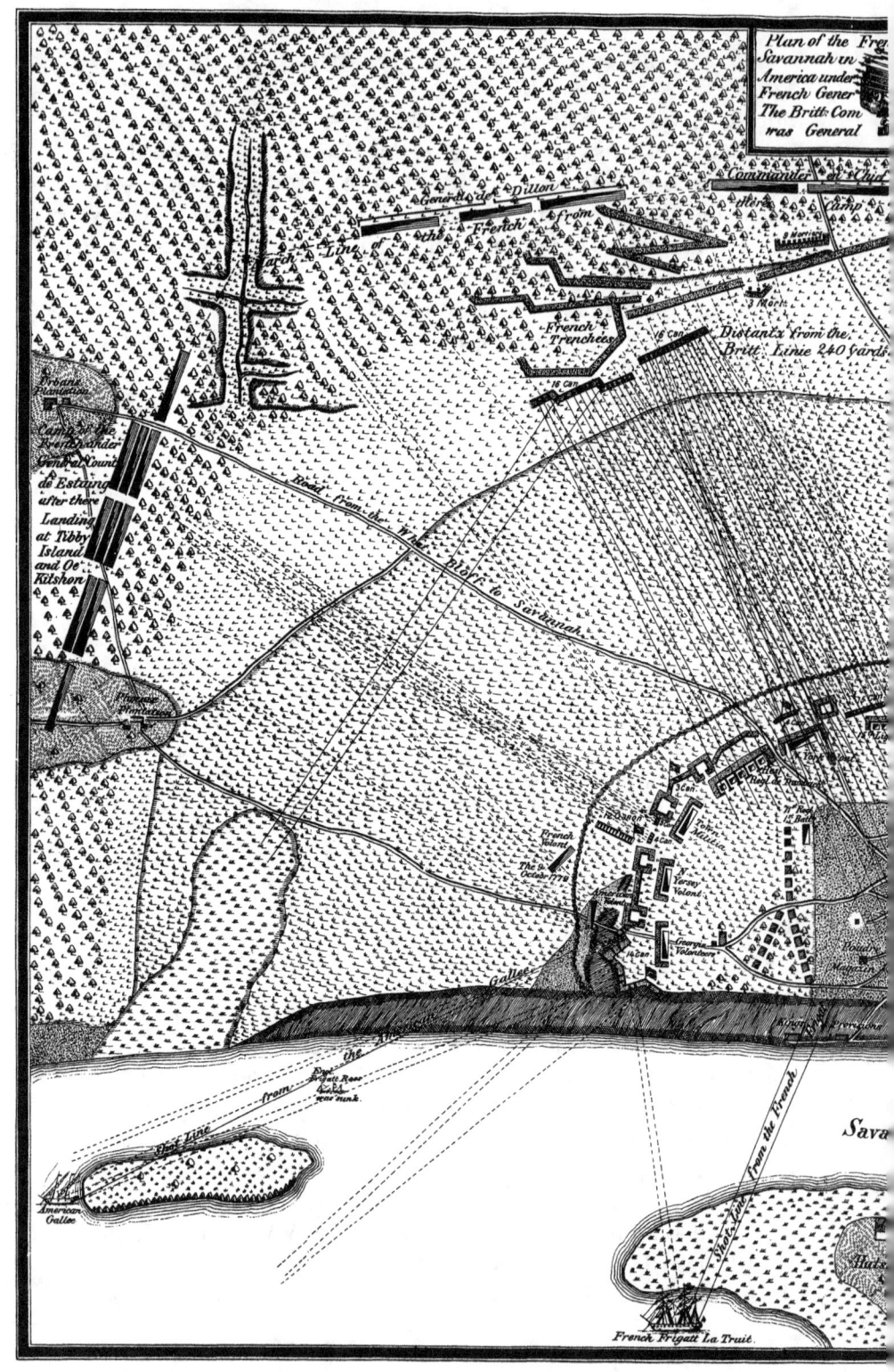

12. "Plan of the French and American Sieg of Savannah in Georgia in South America under Command of the French Gener. Count d'Estaing The Britt: Commander in the Town was General August Prevost, 1779." This battle

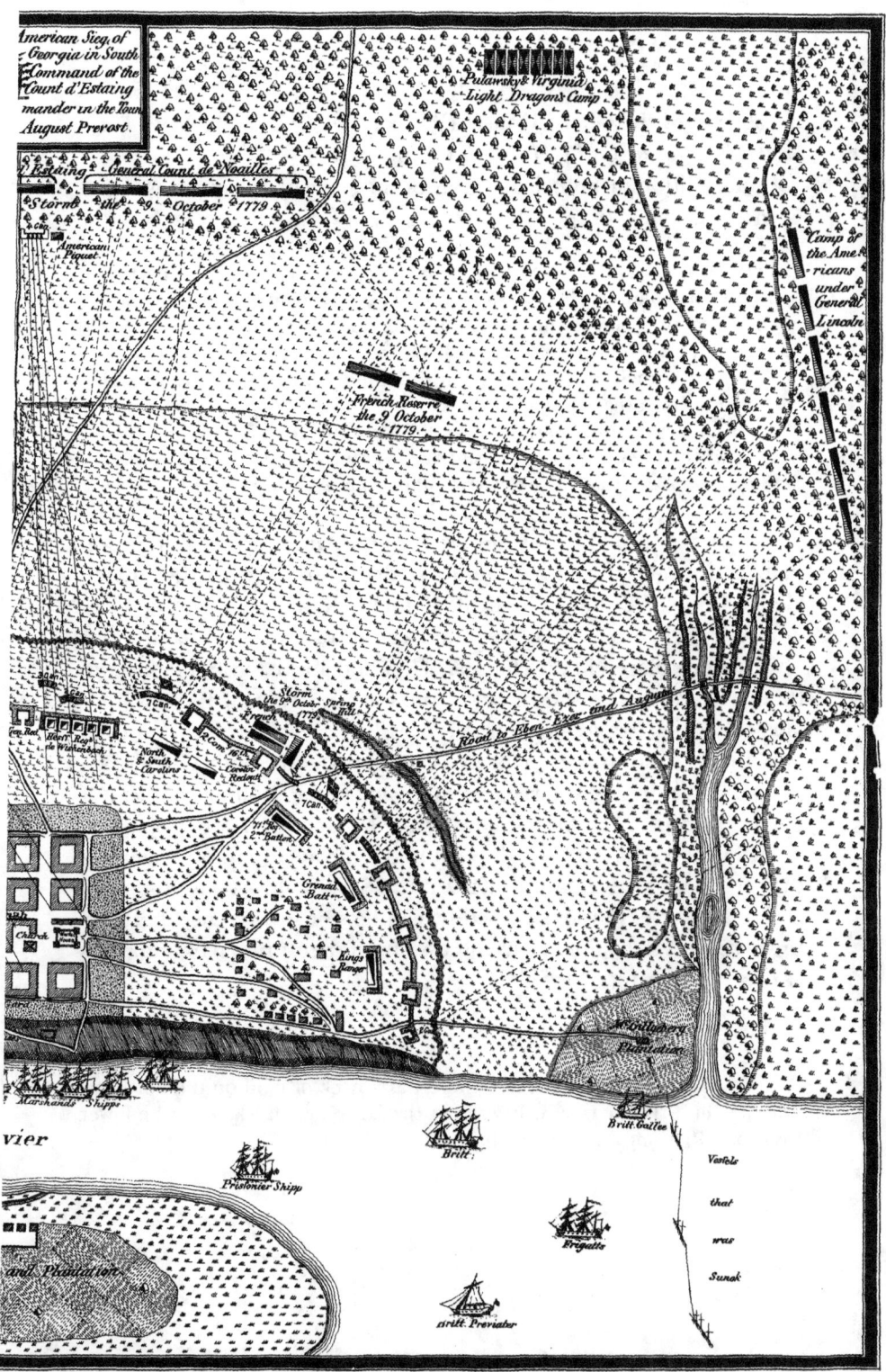

map shows some of the vessels that were sunk to block the channel to Savannah. These wrecks caused serious navigation hazards for several decades after the Revolutionary War.

nel abreast of the Guard House" (William Bell Clark, ed., *Naval Documents of the American Revolution*, 4:107).

In his edition of French accounts of the siege of Savannah in 1779, Charles C. Jones, Jr., noted:

> The ships *Rose* and *Savannah* and four transports were sunk in a narrow part of the channel of the Savannah river, below the city. Several vessels were also sunk above the town, and a boom was stretched across the channel to prevent the French and American galleys, which passed up the north branch of the river from rounding Hutchinson's Island and attacking from that direction.
>
> The *Rose* was sunk on the *Garden Bank*, on the 20'th of September to obstruct the river against the ascent of the French. [*The Siege of Savannah in 1779, as Described in Two Contemporaneous Journals*, p. 52]

The engraving, "Plan of the French and American Sieg of Savannah in Georgia in South America under Command of the French Gener. Count d'Estaing The Britt: Commander in the Town was General August Prevost," indicates the location of the wrecks and other obstructions placed in the channel below and above Savannah in 1779 (Map 12). Buildings shown below the bluff in front of the town are labeled "Kings Provisions Store Houses."

With the resumption of peace, Georgians and South Carolinians alike began to mend the ravages of prolonged and bitter conflict. Of particular concern to both states was the expanding frontier of settlement in the upcountry which was rapidly advancing into former Indian territories at the headwaters of the Savannah. As was discussed in Part I, above, tensions caused by conflicts of sovereignty there led the two states to begin serious discussions of their mutual boundary as early as the spring of 1783.

NOTE

1. The Jones Island referred to here was a neck of land on the northeast side of Hilton Head Island. It was not the large marsh island in the lower Savannah River now known by that name.

PART THREE

Changes
in the
Morphology
of the Lower
Savannah
River Area,
1787–1900

VERBAL AND CARTOGRAPHIC STATEMENTS by eighteenth-century figures such as the merchant James Habersham and the professional surveyors Henry Yonge and William De Brahm suggest that the dynamics of the morphological alterations in the lower Savannah area were reasonably well understood and appreciated during the middle decades of that century. In the first part of this section the changes that took place in island and riverbank morphology from Savannah downstream to Tybee Island will be traced from 1787 until 1855, when the first comprehensive scientifically prepared chart of the area was published by the U.S. Coast Survey under the supervision of Alexander Dallas Bache. The remainder of this section will deal with the period from 1855 until 1900, with major stress on the efforts and accomplishments of the U.S. Army Corps of Engineers as that organization attempted to tame and stabilize the river while ensuring safe navigation for deep-draft vessels.

In the preface to his monograph *The Hydraulics of a Tidal River as Illustrated by Savannah Harbor, Georgia*, Ralph F. Rhodes provided an insightful view of the river and its problems as conceptualized by hydraulic engineers who worked in the area for a century or more:

> Savannah Harbor, Georgia, is part of the tidal section of Savannah River and originally was probably part of a deep gorge which increased in dimensions toward the sea. This gorge filled slowly through the ages with material brought down by the river from the upper watershed. The amount and character of the material varied according to changing conditions on the watershed, and the travel of this material toward the sea stopped when the carrying capacity of the currents was sufficiently reduced by tide water. The upper part of the gorge filled first and the

lower part last, and it is the removal of the filling of this lower part that today constitutes the maintenance problem of Savannah Harbor.

To solve this and similar problems, it is necessary to have a thorough knowledge of the forces of nature involved, how best to control such forces toward the desired end, and the means in money and plant to carry out the plans.

The only force of nature over which the engineer has any material control are the currents moving through the channels and which are produced by the fresh water flowing toward the sea and the tides which move under the influence of the moon in and out of the tidal section.

The amount of the energy in these currents that can be utilized depends on the volumes of water in motion and the velocities at which they move. These can be regulated to a certain extent by alterations in the alinement and size of the channels. After as much reduction in the amount of material being brought into the harbor is effected as is practicable and economical, the remaining part of the problem is how best to utilize the available energy of the currents so that they will carry a large portion of their burden to the sea instead of allowing it to drop in the improved channels where it must be removed by dredging. [Pp. i–ii]

In 1787 the Georgia legislature first focused attention on problems of navigation in the Savannah River, passing "An Act for regulating the trade, laying duties on all goods, wares, liquors, merchandize and negroes imported into this State, and also an impost on the tonnage of Shipping, and for other purposes therein mentioned" (Watkins, *Digest of the Laws of the State of Georgia*, pp. 351–53). Among other provisions, the act directed that a fund be established for improving the navigability of the Savannah River downstream from the city of Savannah:

> And whereas it becomes absolutely necessary for the better navigation of the river Savannah below the town, that the wrecks and other obstructions be as speedily as possibly removed, and that a fund be established for that purpose; Be it therefore enacted by the authority aforesaid, That a further sum of three pence per ton shall also be levied on all shipping entering the port of Savannah, and shall be, and hereby is, appropriated and set apart as a fund for clearing the said river of the wrecks etc. And the commissioners of the pilotage for the port of Savannah herein after named, shall be and hereby are empowered to carry the same into effect. The said commissioners shall also be, and hereby are authorized to draw on the collector of said port from time to time, for whatever sums may accrue, and be received by him for that purpose. [Ibid., p. 351]

The commissioners of pilotage became the public body chiefly concerned with the physical condition of the lower Savannah until the United States federal government assumed that task. A harbor master was appointed to carry out the day-to-day legal responsibilities of the commissioners of pilotage. One of his important duties was providing the data needed for establishing the tonnage levy each ship should pay to the state. Harbor masters were appointed for Georgia's other ports, Sunbury, Brunswick, and Saint Marys. Ships entering those ports were also required to contribute to the fund for clearing the Savannah's obstructions.

Some of the minutes kept by the commissioners of pilotage in Savannah survive in the manuscript collections of the Georgia Historical Society in Savannah. A review of those recorded from 1791 through 1800 reveals that this little-known state agency engaged in a surprising range of activities. Their minutes give insight into conditions in the lower Savannah area during the last decade of the eighteenth century.

In March 1791, for example, it was noted that a river pilot named James Campbell operating under William Scranton's "branch" or license was fined for allowing the sloop *Polly* to go aground on one of the "wrecks." Clearly, the residue of revolutionary channel blockage was still causing serious navigation problems in the river. In an effort to cope with the problems confronting them, the commissioners resolved in 1793 to "make a further application for powers . . . for the purpose of altering the water courses of the River Savannah with a view of deepening the main channel" (Port of Savannah Commissioners of Pilotage, Minutes, 1:19).

During the early 1790s, several references to "The Machine" appear in the minutes. Apparently, a dredge, probably a bucket dredge, was being operated under the authority of the commissioners of pilotage in the Savannah area. This dredging operation was under the supervision of a Mr. Rice, who received fairly substantial sums for his efforts. In 1792 the commissioners wrote to a Colonel Stevens of New York to inquire about a "machine proper for removing the impediments in the River Savannah" (ibid., p. 11).

In December of the following year, 1793, mention was made of a letter from Ebenezer Stevens informing the commissioners that he had engaged two men to operate the dredge he was providing for use in the Savannah clearance projects. Several subsequent allusions to the operation of a dredging apparatus and the need for "flatts" or barges to carry the dredged sand to dumping places are clear evidence that channel depths in the vicinity of Savannah were undergoing improvement efforts. In 1795 an unspecified mishap caused the "Dredge Machine" to sink. Two weeks later a Mr. Shaw was paid $52.72 for raising it.

It seems doubtful that these early dredging efforts resulted in any significant alterations in the bank and island morphology of the Savannah area downstream from the city or on the South Carolina banks of the boundary stream, as indicated in the minutes for February 11, 1796: "The plan adopted of the Dredge Machine imported from New York at a considerable expense, has been found not to answer the great character given of it, or our expectation. Where the bed of the river consists of mud it is found to answer well, the scoop of the dredge doing great execution, but when the bed consists of sand it falls far short of our expectations and the sand fills up again nearly as fast as it is taken away" (ibid., p. 69).

At about this time more ambitious harbor improvement schemes began to occupy the commissioners, who had secured the services of a trained engineer-cartographer named Isadore Stouf. In January of that year, for example, they had "considered the propriety of placing obstructions between Hutchinson and Fig Island." Hutchinson Island, located opposite to the city of Savannah, has the effect of breaking the Savannah into two main streams, Back River between the island and the South Carolina shore and Front River between the island and the bluff site of Savannah. Fig Island was a smaller, low, marshy island that was later merged with the southeastern portion of Hutchinson. It shows as a distinct entity on such early maps as the 1855 Coast Survey Preliminary Chart of Savannah River. A facsimile copy of Stouf's "Plan of the River Savannah from Five Fathoms hole to the Town of Savannah with a Project of a Dike to Shut the Channel by Hutchinson Island for raising the water of the South Channel 1797," located in the Savannah office of the U.S. Army Corps of Engineers, shows two proposed closures which, if built, would have linked Hutchinson and Fig islands. The desired effect of such a closure was obviously to maintain a greater flow close to the Georgia shore, from Savannah's wharves downstream to the wrecks obstruction located below the eastern end of Fig Island.

Plans were afoot for the area upstream from the city as well, aimed at closing the channel between the upper end of Hutchinson and lower end of Argyle Island. This channel, known as Cross Tides, was frequently the object of closure schemes. The result sought was to block the main Savannah or Front River ebb flow from passing into the Back River behind Hutchinson Island, thus increasing the ebb flow scour effect in front of Savannah's wharves. On November 11, 1795, two of the commissioners went up the river with engineer Stouf to "view the situation of the wreck that was sunk by order of the Commissioners at Argyle Point and conduct a survey of the banks at the entrance between the points of Argyle & Hutchinsons Islands" (ibid., p. 58).

A little more than a week later, Stouf presented a "survey and plan for stopping the entrance between Argyle and Hutchinson Island, which appeared to be executed in a Masterly manner" (ibid., p. 59). According to their minutes, the commissioners were of the "decided opinion . . . that by sinking obstructions from the lower end of Argyle to the upper end of Hutchinson's islands, and thereby preventing the water from going down the Back River, that it would occasion a greater depth of water on the Garden Bank" (ibid.). They also stated that they had purchased "a few old hulks of vessels and had them sunk in a line from Argyle Point, and although they were not sufficient to reach above one-third of the way to Hutchinson Island . . . yet the increase of water it has occasioned on the Garden Bank sufficiently points out to us the utility of our proceeding . . . either by sinking more hulks or Piling across the channel" (ibid., p. 69).

In 1797, copies of a "plan of the River" drawn by Stouf were sent to Philadelphia, New York, Boston, and Newport with advertisements requesting proposals from "any person to undertake removal of certain wrecks . . . as laid down on said plan" (ibid., p. 117). By this time, conditions were alarming enough that the commissioners wrote the Georgia congressional delegation for aid in securing federal assistance in their efforts to clear the channel. They wrote, "We do not hesitate in pronouncing that if these wrecks are suffered to remain but two years longer in their present situation, the entire destruction of this Harbour must inevitably follow!" (ibid., p. 166).

Finally, in December 1798, Stephen Colver contracted to remove the wrecks for $9,000. During August of 1799, it was reported that Colver was dumping sand and mud into the river, contrary to the assurance he had given to prevent any injury to the channel. According to Colver, he was only allowing the current to sweep mud away and was carrying heavier materials such as brick and stone to "a proper place" for dumping.[1] The commissioners of pilotage seem to have approved of Colver's procedures but ordered the harbor master to check the situation and sound the channel depth once every fortnight.

On November 16, 1799, the commissioners drafted a more optimistic letter to the Georgia congressional delegation than the one of the year before. On this occasion, they wrote, "We have the pleasure to inform you that the wrecks lying below the Town . . . are wholly removed, or will be in a few days" (ibid., p. 260). They stressed their need for funds to meet the terms of the almost completed contract. On January 6, 1800, the chairman reported that he and another commissioner had gone down the river to view the wrecks raised by Colver and had found that they had been acceptably removed. It would appear, however, that their report was premature because a few weeks later a notice concerning the removal of the wrecks was ordered placed in the *Columbian Museum* with the offer of $100 for the best plan to deepen the river from the city to the sea.

Other activities carried out by the commissioners of pilotage during this period leave little doubt that the Georgians viewed the Savannah as their river all the way to the Atlantic. They licensed and regulated the pilots "of the Barr and River Savannah." They disciplined pilots for such faulty conduct as grounding ships in their charge and reluctance to board ships to the seaward of the bar. To correct the latter problem, the commissioners moved to increase the rates for bar pilotage while reducing those for river pilotage.

The commissioners of pilotage also had beacons and channel markers erected on Tybee and Bird islands. They were frequently concerned with problems arising from the indiscriminate dumping of ballast. The harbor master was often called upon to recommend proper dumping places. In 1797 four buoys for "this Bar and River" were shipped to Savannah on board the ship *Alexander Hamilton*. Great effort was expended in placing these buoys. Captain Throop, the harbor master, was joined by John McKinnon, the county surveyor, in supervising the exacting task. Two of the buoys appear to have been copper clad; the other two were of unprotected wood and were vulnerable to worms. In 1798 a buoy that had gone adrift was recovered on the southern side of St. Simons Island.

The beacons and buoys placed by the commissioners of pilotage during the 1790s are probably the ones described in the *American Coast Pilot* published by Lawrence Furlong in 1798. The section headed "Directions for Sailing into Savannah, in Georgia," includes the following:

> Mariners sailing into this port will observe the following marks and buoys, viz. a large buoy lies on the outer edge of the Bar, in the deepest water, having all the leading marks on, the Beacon and Light-House in one, bearing W. ½ N distant 4 miles, another buoy lies in the same direction, one mile within the Bar. A third buoy lies one mile farther, W. by N. from the second. A fourth buoy lies N. W. b. W. from the third; after passing which there is safe anchorage for a large fleet in 4 or 5 fathoms at low water, the Light-House bearing S.S.W.
>
> The buoys lie and lead in the deepest water, having a channel half a mile to the Northward, and one quarter of a mile to the Southward of them, (in the narrowest place) nearly the same depth of water, and there are 20 feet on the Bar at lowest tides.
>
> Tybee-Island lies at the mouth of Savannah River to the Southward of the Bar. It is very pleasant, with a beautiful creek to the West of it, where a ship of any burden may lie safe at anchor. A Light-House stands on the Island 80 feet high, is 7 miles E.S.E. ½ E. from Savannah, and 6 miles S.W. ½ W. from Port-Royal. Wassaw Sound is formed by the Southern end of this Island. [P. 129]

In the dozen years following the signing of the Beaufort Convention, it appears that the state of Georgia, through the commissioners of pilotage, was actively engaged in river improvement and navigation safety programs extending from the Savannah's bar off Tybee to the channel between Hutchinson and Argyle islands. Their attempt to close or restrict the flow of the river into the Back River channel is most noteworthy because this action might have been construed as an infringement of South Carolina's navigation rights under the treaty. A blockage of the Cross Tides channel, if successful, would have impeded vessels navigating from Back River into Front River on the way upstream and beyond Hutchinson Island. The treaty had guaranteed the South Carolinians "the navigation of the River Savannah, . . . along the northern side of Hutchinson's Island opposite the town of Savannah, to the upper end of the said Island, and from thence up the bed or principal stream of the said River." Since Front River was the "principal stream" of the Savannah, the blockage at the upper end of Hutchinson Island would have effectively blocked Carolina boats coming up or down the river. No evidence has been found to indicate either that the commissioners of pilotage took this fact into account or that any South Carolina complaint was lodged to protest the action. It was not until the 1830s, when a federal agency renewed the effort, that South Carolina lodged protests.

Extracts from the commissioners of pilotage minutes show that their attempts at channel improvement continued into the nineteenth century. In 1812, for example, they noted:

> Friday, December 18, 1812—The Committee appointed to point out the place in the Back River to be stopped by piling reports that they proceeded yesterday in execution of the duty, and on examining the several places that the stoppage would be most effectual and secure by commencing at Argyle Island just below the sunken vessels, and running in a direct line to the upper end of Hutchinson's Island so that the lower row of piles should be against the upper end of Hutchinson's Island and the upper row at eighteen or twenty feet to the westward of said Island, both rows projecting over or beyond the point—the distance is about fifteen hundred feet, and the present contractors will do the work for a price increased in proportion to the increase of distance, say eight thousand and one hundred and twenty five dollars. [Port of Savannah Commissioners of Pilotage, Minutes, 2:320]

By early July 1813, the long rows of piles were in place and the commissioners noted: "Proposals will be received until the first of August next for filling up with brush the vacancy between the double row of piles reaching from Argyle to the upper end of Hutchinson's Island, the length of the piling is two thousand feet and the distance between the rows is eighteen feet" (ibid., p. 345). The principal interests of the commissioners continued to focus on the damming of Cross Tides channel and eliminating the shoaling at the lower end of Fig Island and in the area of the wrecks into the 1820s. These projects, in one form or another, remained at the center of river improvement schemes until the Civil War.

In his *A History of the City Government of Savannah, Georgia, from 1790 to 1901*, Thomas Gamble stressed the vital need to improve the harbor and navigation conditions of the Savannah during this period and indicated that additional funds to finance such improvements were actively being sought from the federal government. In October 1825, for example, a committee of aldermen was appointed to look into the feasibility of deepening the river below the city in connection with the possible establishment of a naval depot by the federal government. At the end of December 1825 this committee recommended that a memorial be sent to Congress requesting financial aid. They estimated that at least $50,000 would be needed to clear the river, but the city was unable to provide that sum. Congress was to be urged to establish a naval depot "which would keep the government's eyes on the river" (p. 157). The committee opined that "this preference of the government would serve to disclose new sources of wealth, open a demand for many of our productions, and with spirited exertions in internal improvements by the State, show . . . that Savannah is destined to become the New York of the South" (p. 158). Gamble noted, "Savannahians of this time had abundant faith in the future of the port" (ibid.).

Congress reacted favorably to the City Council's memorial and appropriated $50,000 on May 18, 1826, "to be applied under the direction of the President of the United States, to remove obstructions in the river Savannah, below the City of Savannah" (Granger, *Savannah Harbor*, p. 11). Interestingly, this act was passed two days before the Omnibus Act of May 20, 1826, which is usually cited as the first rivers and harbors appropriation act.

The $50,000 appropriation was administered by a United States commissioner, Dr. William C. Daniell, who was appointed by the Treasury Department as its agent to superintend the removal work in the Savannah. Because Dr. Daniell was also a member of the Commissioners of Pilotage, good communications seemed assured. The commissioners were charged with the responsibility of having a survey of the river made preparatory to a plan of work for channel clearance. John Martineau, "an able engineer," in the words of the commissioners, was secured to make the survey. The estimated cost of the needed work was set at $30,389.50 for constructing dams between Hutchinson and Fig islands and Hutchinson and Argyle islands. Another $10,000 would be needed for removing the obstructions at the wrecks. A dredge boat with a ten horsepower engine and all necessary machinery for two sets of scrapers and four tenders of thirty tons each would cost about this amount. It was estimated that some thirty tons of mud, sand, and wrecks would need to be removed by the dredge at a cost of $6,000. The project was expected to increase the draft of water available up to the town by four feet and to cost just over $46,000 in all.

Although the federally funded improvement project of 1826 began as an effort to deal with the wrecks obstruction and Front River channel flow, its director, Dr. Daniell, was soon forced to consider enlarging its scope. In September 1827, he reported a meeting held with Lieutenant Jonathan W. Sherburne, who was conducting a survey of the port of Savannah for the navy; Sherburne told him that obstructions near the mouth of the river would have to be reported and that their presence on charts would "prove injurious to the reputation and character of our port, and increase the rates of freight and insurance." The obstructions in question were described:

> Opposite Tybee Island and abreast the light-house, there is a hard rough bottom of some breadth, upon which there is at low water 12 feet, consequently somewhat upwards of 18 feet at high water. This bottom is considered to be a hard incrustation of sand upon a bed of mud. It destroys what would otherwise be a good anchorage, at a very important point.
>
> There is another hard incrustation near what is called the Oyster Beds, of similar character and depth.[2] This latter again interferes with what would otherwise be an excellent and secure anchorage. [William C. Daniell, "Correspondence and Reports Concerning Savannah River Improvements, 1827–1830," pp. 10–11]

Lieutenant Sherburne suggested that the dredge boat intended for work on the wrecks could also be used to remove these offending banks.

On January 12, 1828, Daniell reported on an examination of the obstructions near the Savannah's mouth:

> I beg leave to submit to you the result of the examinations which have been made of the "Tail of the Knowl" a bank in the Savannah River, opposite the light-house on Tybee Island, and of the "Oyster Banks," about two miles higher up the river. . . . The first is composed of sand in a compact mass, and can be removed with the dredge boat. It will be necessary to remove about twenty thousand tons. The Oyster Banks are composed of oyster shells and mud, with some sand. These, it is believed, can also be removed with the dredge boat. About twenty-two thousand tons will be required to be removed. The removal of these two obstructions will be highly important, as it will enable ships arriving at the bar to come to a

safe anchorage at any period of the tide, in a Northeast storm, which at present cannot be done. [Ibid., p. 13]

Daniell felt that the removal of the Tail of the Knoll and oyster banks was even more important than the damming of Cross Tides between Hutchinson and Argyle islands. There was some feeling that the Fig Island to Hutchinson dam would create a stronger current in the Front River and make the Cross Tides closing superfluous.

Ill fortune overtook the construction of the Fig Island works when the contractor lost four of the large wooden cribs he was sinking to block the channel. According to Daniell's report, "Unfortunately for Mr. Bargy, as soon as one crib was sunk, (and without completing the filling up at once, with a strong force) he would commence preparations for sinking another, and he found himself with four cribs sunk which were not sufficiently filled up, and the water undermined first one and then another, and nearly all have been cast up by the force of the tide" (ibid., p. 15). To make the situation even worse, the contractor Mr. Bargy "was taken into custody by his creditors."

Bargy's failure caused other contractors to grow apprehensive of the dangers inherent in the Fig Island dam project. The effect was, in Daniell's words, "to add a considerable sum to the real cost of the work, as an inducement to . . . run the risk of failure." Daniell sought "the advice and scientific services of Mr. Gill, the Chief Engineer of the Savannah, Ogeechee, and Altamaha Canal Company," in determining cheaper construction techniques that might overcome this risk inflation. Daniell reported: "It is proposed to construct the body of the dam with green oyster shells, which can be obtained about ten miles from the place where they will be wanted. The clay with which it is proposed to line the dam can be had immediately adjacent. The stone may be had from vessels arriving in ballast, which ballast will answer very well, and usually may be obtained in sufficient quantity. If there should be a scarcity of ballast, its place could readily be supplied with the oyster shells" (ibid., p. 19).

Daniell proceeded to construct a shell and stone dam and in June 1829 reported the following design modifications in the interest of economy: "It was contemplated to place on the slopes or sides of the dams a layer of clay. It is now evident that this may be dispensed with, and the shells be sufficiently compact, as the interstices between them are now being rapidly filled up from the deposite of the river" (ibid., p. 26). On July 3, 1829, a serious break in the Fig Island dam was reported by Daniell: "After having been raised upwards of one foot above low water mark, the dam between Fig and Hutchinson islands gave way for about 35 feet, in consequence of the continued pressure of the water from above, produced by a freshet in the river. From the influence of the same cause afterwards, and the prevalence of strong Easterly winds since, the other portions of the dam have been reduced, though they are still above low water mark" (ibid., pp. 27–28).

Although a bitter disappointment, the dam break provided vital information that would certainly be important in future channel diversion schemes. Daniell wrote: "It was originally believed that, as the channel between Fig and Hutchinson Islands communicated with the main channel at each end of the former island, there would be as great an elevation of water on one side of the proposed dam as on the other, and that, consequently, the material would not wash. It is now apparent that there was an error in this opinion" (ibid., p. 28).

With the completion of the Fig Island dam project in view, Daniell wrote the following long letter, which is quoted here in its entirety because it indicates clearly the nature and degree of morphological change that was occurring near the southern end of Hutchinson Island. Daniell also details many of the mechanical and human problems that were being encountered in this ambitious pioneering effort at Savannah River improvement.

Savannah, 2nd January, 1830.

Sir: I have received your letter of the 24th ult. and accordingly submit the following statement. The dredging machine went into operation, as reported to you in my letter of the 21st January, 1829. She was placed to work upon the bank called "the wrecks," and with the exception of delays incident upon rough weather, the breaking of parts of her machinery, and the repairs of the boat itself, has been constantly in operation there since. The set of buckets with which she commenced operating, was found to be too large and too weak to work efficiently in the sand, which was found to obtain in many parts of the bank. In consequence, a new set was ordered, of a construction which it was thought would better fulfil the object in view, and I am happy to say, they have fully answered every expectation.

About the same time these buckets were received, the boat was found to leak so freely, after an unsuccessful attempt to caulk her, that it became necessary to raise her upon ways, and subject her bottom to a minute examination and thorough repair. She was a double boat, or rather two boats united together by strong timbers, and a deck in common with a race way between. This plan had been recommended to me by Watchman & Bratt, men of experience in such matters, as decidedly superior to any other. I had found however, that when there was a rough sea in the roadstead, where the boat operated, that it pressed so powerfully, upon the anchors, and gave such motion to her, that she could not work with effect. I availed myself of the opportunity afforded by the boats being placed upon ways, of closing up the race way between the two boats. Since, I find that in bad weather she operates more efficiently than before, and with far less strain upon the cables. Since these improvements, she discharges daily, from six to eight flat loads of mud and sand, each load being equal to twenty cubic yards. I am fully satisfied, that if they had been originally introduced, by this time much more would have been achieved than has been.

The progress that had been made with the dam between Fig and Hutchinson island, at the time the dredge-boat went into operation, was such as to increase essentially the force of the current in the main or south channel. The effect of this has been to carry down with the ebb-tide, considerable quantities of sand, which had lodged on the shallow places and much of this on "the wrecks," and in that way, has essentially increased the quantity of material to be removed by the machine. It was found that from the time of once moving the dredge-boat to another, there would be an accumulation of sand under the boat, and in her track, where she worked between the stern and bow anchors. But for this deposite of sand, the work at the wrecks would have been completed before this, as it is, we have there now, full fifteen feet water, at the high water of ordinary tides, and two feet more at Spring tides, which is a gain of three feet water. The former draught having been twelve feet at ordinary high water, and fourteen at spring tides. An increase of one foot more will achieve what was originally contemplated. The dam between Fig and Hutchinson's Islands, is now nearly finished. Its elevation generally, is about three feet above low water mark. The difficulties suggested in my letter of the 3d July last, has rendered it inexpedient to raise it six feet above low water mark, as was originally contemplated. The only materials furnished by the neighboring country, were shell stone and shells; with these it was, through its whole distance, built and raised about one foot above low water mark, when, owing to unforeseen causes, stated in the letter above recited, the dam gave way in some parts, and in one place, a thorough breach was effected of about fifty feet. With difficulty, broken brick were obtained in quantities barely sufficient to rebuild the dam, excepting the main breach, to its former height, and it remained in that situation until stone ballast, with which it was originally designed to build the upper three feet of the dams, could be obtained. Within the last month, I have been enabled to collect a considerable quantity, brought in as ballast, at fair prices, say from 75 to 95 cents per ton, chiefly, however at 50 cents per ton, exclusive of the cost of transportation from the wharves and vessels. A layer of stone, varying from one and an half to three feet, has been made through the whole course of the dam, and little else now remains, but to stop the breach. In this I have made some progress, as it is now reduced to about forty feet in width, and twelve feet in depth at low water mark. It is my belief that this breach may be wholly stopped, but I shall work it up from one side and watch attentively the effect, and if any danger should appear to be threatened, I will allow the remainder of the breach to be a permanent waste gate, securing the margins of it with additional weight, by an increased elevation of the dam at them. It is but proper that I should state that this dam, if finished by stopping the sluice will, by excluding myself and several of my connexions who have plantations on the South Carolina shore, from the use of the channel between Fig and Hutchinson's islands, increase the distance to our respective places. If the sluice should be left open, it may be by some attributed to the influence of my private interests. I merely state this now, to apprize you of the facts. I know my duty and will perform it. The object designed to be effected by the erection of this dam, was to throw the water of this channel into the Southern or main channel, by which it was believed that the latter would be so much strengthened as to enable it to cast the deposite upon the mouth of the channel from the back river, that becoming the weaker one, instead of, as heretofore, receiving it on its own bed, at the wrecks, by which the navigation of that channel has been injured. It is already evident that we shall not be disappointed in our expectations, for there has been considerable accumulation at the end of Hutchinson island, below the dam, and an extensive bed is forming at the mouth of the channel of back river, just above where it unites with the main or Southern channel, which, if it continues to increase for a few months, will be dry in places at low water. It will, I think, readily occur to you that the completion of the dam is not necessary to effect this object: for, although a body of water will pass with great velocity and power through a sluice of 40 feet, yet that cannot give an important impulse to a body of water 640 feet wide, which is about the average width of the channel between Fig and Hutchinson islands. In this instance the sluice exhausts itself in an eddy below the dam, and at a short distance below the eddy there is a shoal that has formed since I have been engaged in building the dam, that extends nearly across the channel.

I am equally confident that there is no occasion to raise the dam more than three feet above low water mark, even could it be done with safety, which is perhaps doubtful. The evidences are palpable that the channels and currents which formerly existed on the shore of Hutchinson island above the dam are filling up and disappearing, the water having been turned into the main channel by the obstruction caused by the dam below.

If a sufficient quantity of ballast stone shall arrive, of which there is every prospect, the dam will be finished in all February. The remainder of the appropriation may be advantageously expended upon the dredging machine.

I believe it will be more than sufficient for the complete removal of the wrecks. How much can be done upon any of the other shoals with what may then remain unexpended, my experience, derived from our operations on the wrecks, teaches me, cannot be foretold.

After the month of February, unless some unforeseen source of expenditure should occur, the monthly estimates will not exceed, I think, one thousand dollars, which should exhaust the appropriation about September next.

The estimates for the current month are:

For the dam,	$800
For the dredge-boat,	900
	$1,700

With the hope that the foregoing statement, made amidst a press of duties, and whilst suffering from indisposition, will be satisfactory to the President and yourself,

I am, sir, very respectfully,
Your obedient servant,
W. C. DANIELL

To S. Pleasonton, Esq.
    Fifth Auditor, &c. [Ibid., pp. 31–33]

Daniell wrote this letter in response to a request arising from complaints the president had received concerning the Savannah River project. These complaints grew in intensity in the early months of 1830 and culminated in a letter from Georgia Congressman James M. Wayne recommending that disbursements to Daniell cease and in future the work be supervised by the commissioners of pilotage. On March 30, 1830, Daniell was informed that work in the Savannah under the appropriation of 1826 should be suspended.

On April 10, 1830, a committee of the commissioners of pilotage made a detailed examination of the federally financed project which Dr. Daniell had supervised. They reported as follows:

REPORT:

That, in pursuance of the duty assigned them by the Board, the committee have gone into a careful examination of the dam erected between Hutchinson's and Fig Islands, and found as follows, namely: That said dam, if completed so as to connect the two islands aforesaid, would have been six hundred and ten feet in length; that there is a chasm or gap near the South end of said dam, about fifty feet in length, through which the water runs with great rapidity; that there was in this gap at low water, slack tide, about ten feet water. At low water the top of the dam was about four feet above the level of the water around it; the average breadth of the top of the dam, four feet above the water level, was ten feet. The committee also proceeded to examine and sound on the shoal ground, called the wrecks, and found, on the deepest part thereof, at high water, (on the tenth of the present month) thirteen and a half feet water, which the committee are of opinion is nearly the same depth that has been found on the same for four years past at the same time of the moon, and the same time of tide. They are of opinion that no perceptible alteration in the depth of water has been caused by the dam aforesaid, or from the application of the mud or dredging machine. That, if the dam remains in its present unfinished state, no benefit to the river can arise from it; and even should it be completed so as to connect the two islands, and to bring the top of the dam above the water at high tide, it is doubtful in the minds of the committee if it would have the effect to deepen the channel of the river.

WILLIAM CRABTREE, JR.
F. H. WELMAN,
WILLIAM J. HUNTER.

Savannah, April 12, 1830 [Ibid., p. 59]

This report, along with Dr. Daniell's letter of January 2, 1830, provides a good summary of the project. Little had been accomplished in a tangible sense beyond a partial closing of the channel between Fig and Hutchinson islands, but much valuable experience and knowledge concerning the hydraulics of the Savannah River had been gained.

As mentioned above, the United States Navy was considering the construction of a southern naval depot during the late 1820s. Not surprisingly, the lower Savannah River received considerable attention as the navy gathered data on which to base this important locational decision. Some of these data are reviewed here in an effort to form a more complete idea of the river below the city of Savannah. The following summary is based on materials found with a report from the secretary of the navy to the Senate, dated December 26, 1828 (J. P. Henry, "Report to Secretary of Navy Respecting the Harbor of Savannah, November 12, 1828," pp. 8–15).

In November 1828, J. P. Henry, the Savannah agent for the navy, provided a detailed report describing the conditions existing in the lower Savannah River. He reported that the depth of water on the bar varied between 18 and 28 feet depending on tidal conditions. Another 1 or 2 feet of increase or decrease in depth could also be experienced under certain wind conditions. The channel over the bar was three-quarters of a mile wide, and the bar itself was reckoned to be from one-half to three-quarters of a mile wide. Vessels drawing 9½ feet at lowest tides or 16 feet at high water could find safe anchorage in Cockspur roads at a distance of 6 or 7 miles from the bar. In the channel north of the Oyster Bed good anchorage could be found in any part after crossing the bar and abreast of Tybee Island. Here 5 or 6 fathoms of water prevailed.

In the river above, vessels drawing up to 18 feet could "with safety, at high spring tides, reach Four Mile Point, at the upper end of Gibbett Island, and from 16 to 17 feet at common tides; and to Fort Jackson 16½ at spring tides, and from 13 to 14½ at common tides" (ibid., p. 9).[3]

Henry listed six sand banks and mud flats as impediments to navigation in the river. He placed the first at 5 miles from the bar, the second 6 miles, the third 7 miles, the fourth 12 miles, the fifth 12¾ miles, and the sixth at Four Mile Point. Henry opined that all of these could be "removed or greatly reduced by a good dredging machine." If this were done, ships of 30 feet draft could be brought safely from the sea to Fort Jackson. Between Fort Jackson and the city of Savannah, however, the wrecks created conditions with only 6½ feet at low water and 13½ feet at high water. At spring tides the greater depth was increased to 14 or 15 feet at the wrecks. The improvement scheme at the wrecks was in progress when Henry reported these depths.

In summarizing the advantages Savannah offered as the location for a naval depot, Henry drew attention to Daniell's efforts then under way at the wrecks. Concerning the sand and mud flats in the river, he wrote,

> The sand and soft mud which form these impediments, are susceptible of removal without much difficulty, it is believed, by means of the improved excavating machine, impelled by steam, which has been so successfully applied in many instances for clearing rivers. That about to be put in operation here by the Commissioner for removing the wrecks, might possibly be beneficially employed for this purpose.... Were these shoals removed ... from 25 to 26 feet might be carried to Four Mile Point, in fresh water 15 miles from the sea, and but five from the city, by removing the shoals in the north channel. [Ibid., p. 12]

To support his findings, Henry included a sworn statement concerning the Savannah's characteristics signed by three of the port's most highly qualified pilots. From this statement a more precise idea of the shoal areas in the river can be gained. It states:

> Q. What are the impediments in the river from the bar to Four Mile Point and to Fort Jackson, and can they be lessened or removed?
>
> A. The first is the tail of the knoll from 4 to 5 miles from the bar, sandy bottom, the next is the head of the knoll, one mile from the tail, soft mud and shells; water from 4 to 4¾ fathoms may always be found between these two points at high water. The third shoal is the head of the white oyster bed, one mile further, sandy bottom, and may easily be removed, its extent in crossing is not more than 30 feet. Five miles further up is the next shoal, extending from Venus Point to the Horse Shoe, about ⅜ of a mile in extent, composed of soft mud, and may easily be removed. The next shoal at ¾ of a mile distance, is the lower mud flat, then the upper mud flat at Four Mile Point, the two making about ¾ of a mile, and of soft mud. Deep water and safe anchorage may be had at all times of tide between these shoals; their removal would give a channel of 30 feet and upwards from the Bar to Fort Jackson. [Ibid., pp. 12–14]

As can be seen, the river pilots used the position of the Savannah's bar as an important reference datum. It is, however, a reference datum that is difficult to fix with any precision on many early maps of the area that are still extant. An excellent and very detailed chart published in 1838 does provide a key to this reference datum with an apparently fairly high degree of accuracy. This is the "Chart of Southern Coast from Tybee Bar to Hunting Id. May River Surveyed by Charles Wilkes Lieutenant Commandant . . . in U.S. Brig Porpoise. 1838." It shows a "Bar Buoy" positioned to mark the Savannah River bar. The buoy bears 100° true from Tybee Light at a distance of approximately 11,750 feet, or about two and one-quarter miles. The buoys marking the Savannah River bar were described in E. M. Blunt's *American Coast Pilot* (10th ed., 1826) as follows:

> Note—Sailing into Savannah you will observe the following marks and buoys, viz. a large buoy lies on the outer edge of the bar in the deepest water, having all the leading marks on the beacon and light house in one, bearing W. ½ N. distant 4 miles. Another buoy lies in the same direction, one mile within the bar; a third buoy lies one mile farther W. by N. from the second; a fourth buoy lies N. W. by W. from the third; after passing

which there is safe anchorage for a large fleet, in 4 or 5 fathoms, at low water, the light-house bearing S. S. W. [P. 240]

The "Bar Buoy" shown on the Wilkes chart is probably the third buoy in from the outer edge of the bar as described by Blunt above. This would place the outer limit of the bar at about four miles distant from Tybee Lighthouse on a heading of 100° true. Although not explicitly stated, the "mile" used by Blunt and other mariners is probably a nautical mile and so slightly longer than a statute mile.

One other group was systematically investigating the lower Savannah River area during the 1820s. This was the U.S. Army Corps of Engineers, which was at this time primarily interested in matters of defense rather than internal improvement. The Board of Engineers for Fortification had conducted a comprehensive review of the American coast from 1817 to 1822. Cockspur Island near the Savannah's mouth was chosen as the site for a major defensive emplacement, with work beginning there in 1829. Fort Pulaski, constructed in the years that followed, is best known for the role it played in the defense of Savannah during the Civil War.

As a part of the fortification surveys, Captain John Le Conte prepared large-scale maps of the Savannah River and its mouth, which are in Record Group 77 of the National Archives in Washington. One of Le Conte's maps drawn in 1821 was later engraved for printing at a reduced scale and published in the widely circulated Blunt's *American Coast Pilot* (1837). Although Le Conte's map is somewhat imperfect when judged by today's standards, it provides a useful cartographic statement of conditions in the lower Savannah area as they were perceived by a trained observer in 1821 (Map 13). As included here, it has been redrawn from Le Conte's original.

Le Conte's map shows the river from Tybee Island to the city of Savannah. The main channel is clearly to the north of Cockspur Island. The Tybee Lighthouse appears with the plan of the Martello Tower defensive installation just to the east of it. Fort Pulaski is not shown on Cockspur Island. Small arabic numerals arranged in lines indicate water depths in the river's two channels, which join near the tip of Gibbet Island. Fort Jackson and Fig Island are key reference points along the channel leading to the wharves of Savannah. Gibbet Island was also known as Hogh's Island and is identified as Elba Island today. Despite its technical flaws, Le Conte's map is helpful in understanding

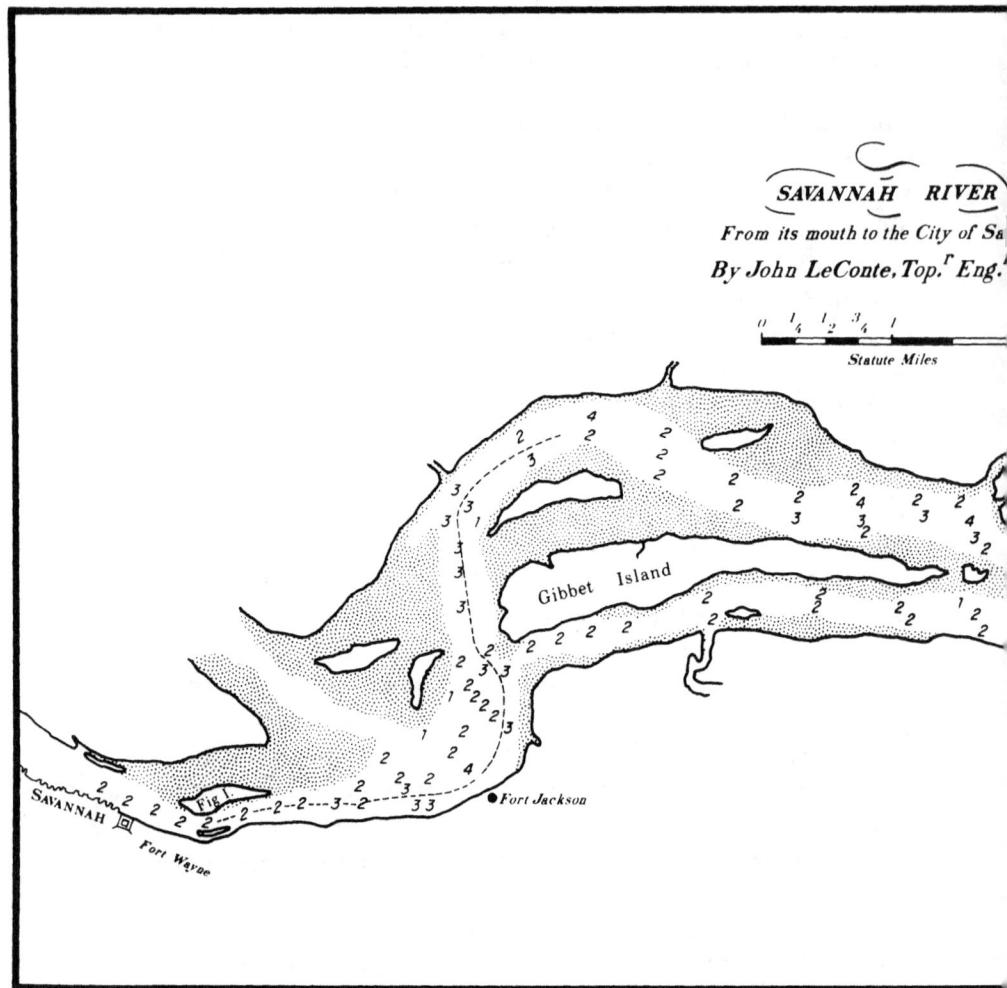

13. "Savannah River, From Its Mouth to the City of Savannah By John Le Conte, Topr. Engr., 1821." Redrawn from Le Conte's original for clarity, this map, while imperfect, aids in an appreciation of the complex geography of the lowermost Savannah River area.

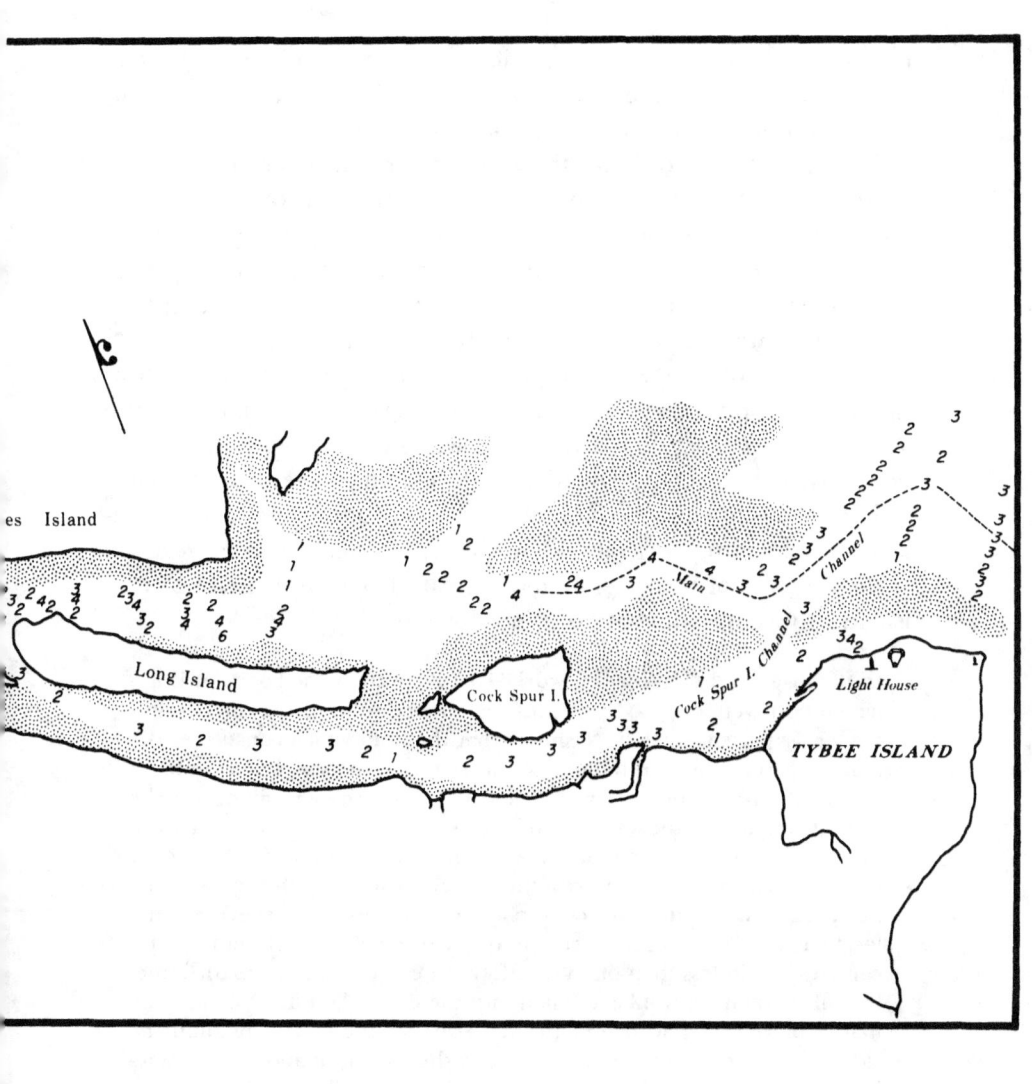

river conditions as they were described through the 1820s. It was certainly a vast improvement over the Savannah River chart found in earlier editions of the *American Coast Pilot.*

From about 1824 onward, the Corps of Engineers began to take a more active role in surveys and projects aimed at improving the country's transportation and commerce. Until the early 1830s, however, they appear to have played no direct part in Savannah River improvement schemes. Active participation began when Lieutenant Joseph K. F. Mansfield was ordered to take over the supervision of the Savannah improvement program after replacing Robert E. Lee at the fortification on Cockspur Island in the spring of 1831. In the same year, the War Department set up a division known as the Topographical Engineers as a separate body to handle the developing survey responsibility.

The following extract concerning an aspect of the engineers' experiences in building Fort Pulaski on Cockspur Island helps to confirm earlier reports of the erosion and retreat of the eastern end of that island. It was in a summary of work done in 1835.

> In the original design for this work [Fort Pulaski] by the board of Engineers, no revetment was contemplated for the sides of the ditches and feeder. Experience has since shown that the mud which constitutes the island when exposed to the influx and reflux of the sea, will assume, in combination with the water, a demi-fluid state, thereby filling up the ditches, impairing the strength of the fort and health of the garrison. Further, in cases of severe blows and high tides the water will flow over the dikes, and in case of no revetment-walls will sweep the earth of the slopes and dikes into the ditches in a few moments. It is believed by the local engineer that, if the revetment of the scarp of the demi-lune be not constructed, in less than one year after the completion of the fort, one-half of its rampart will have fallen into the ditch. An estimate has been made for revetting with masonry the scarp of the demi-lune, and the sides of the feeder, to the ditch between the advanced and remote tide-locks, amounting in the aggregate to $150,000; which is in part embraced in the estimate for the next year's operations, and will be so applied unless restricted by the act of appropriation. [Chief of Engineers, "Report from the Chief Engineer," p. 194]

In December of 1832, Lieutenant John Mackay of the Topographical Engineers was ordered to report for duty with Lieutenant Mansfield at Savannah. Reflecting his considerable talent and effort are several maps of the Savannah River, in the vicinity of the city of Savannah, now in the National Archives, Washington. Two printed sheets forming a detailed map from the eastern end of Argyle Island to the western tip of Elba Island are titled "Chart of Part of the Savannah River, 1833, Surveyed & Drawn by Lieut. John Mackay, 2d Regt. Arty." (Maps 14A and B). In their original state these sheets are at a scale of six inches to one mile and were prepared from a very large manuscript by Mackay which is in the same archive (Record Group 77b, Headquarters Map File, N14-1, N14-2, N15-3).

On Mackay's map three partial structures stretch between Fig and Hutchinson islands. Two of these are open lines of piling and the third is the "Stone Dam" on which Dr. Daniell expended so much effort and federal money. Another point of interest is a detailed sketch marked "Plan for an Obstruction" which was designed to block the Cross Tides channel between Argyle and Hutchinson islands. Pennyworth Island and two full and one vague Barnwell islands are close to the Carolina shore. A wealth of hydrographic data appears in the river areas, as well as soundings and notations on bottom composition and a line indicating the "Line Of Greatest Velocity" of the river current. In accuracy and completeness Mackay's survey of the Savannah near the city was a major improvement over all earlier maps.

The 1834 report of the Engineer Department included the following observation concerning the Savannah River project:

> The progress of the improvements on this river has not answered the expectations of the project for the year, or the anticipation contained in my last report. It was contemplated to complete the foundations of a permanent obstruction between Hutchinson and Argyle islands; and to remove by dredging the shoals at the Wrecks, Garden Bank, and upper Mud Flat. All the preliminary arrangements for the first mentioned object were made; materials were collected, and operations commenced, when the local engineer was made aware that, by the second article of the treaty of Beaufort, concluded in 1787, between the States of Georgia and South Carolina, no obstructions whatever should be made by the citizens of either State in the channel it was contemplated to close. A suspension of operations was therefore required by the department; the subject was referred to the United States attorneys in those States, and a consequent application will be made to the respective Governors at a suitable time. [Engineer Department, "Report from, 15 November, 1835," pp. 107–8]

For the first time, the Treaty of Beaufort navigation right provision had been invoked to stop a scheme designed to divert the Savannah's

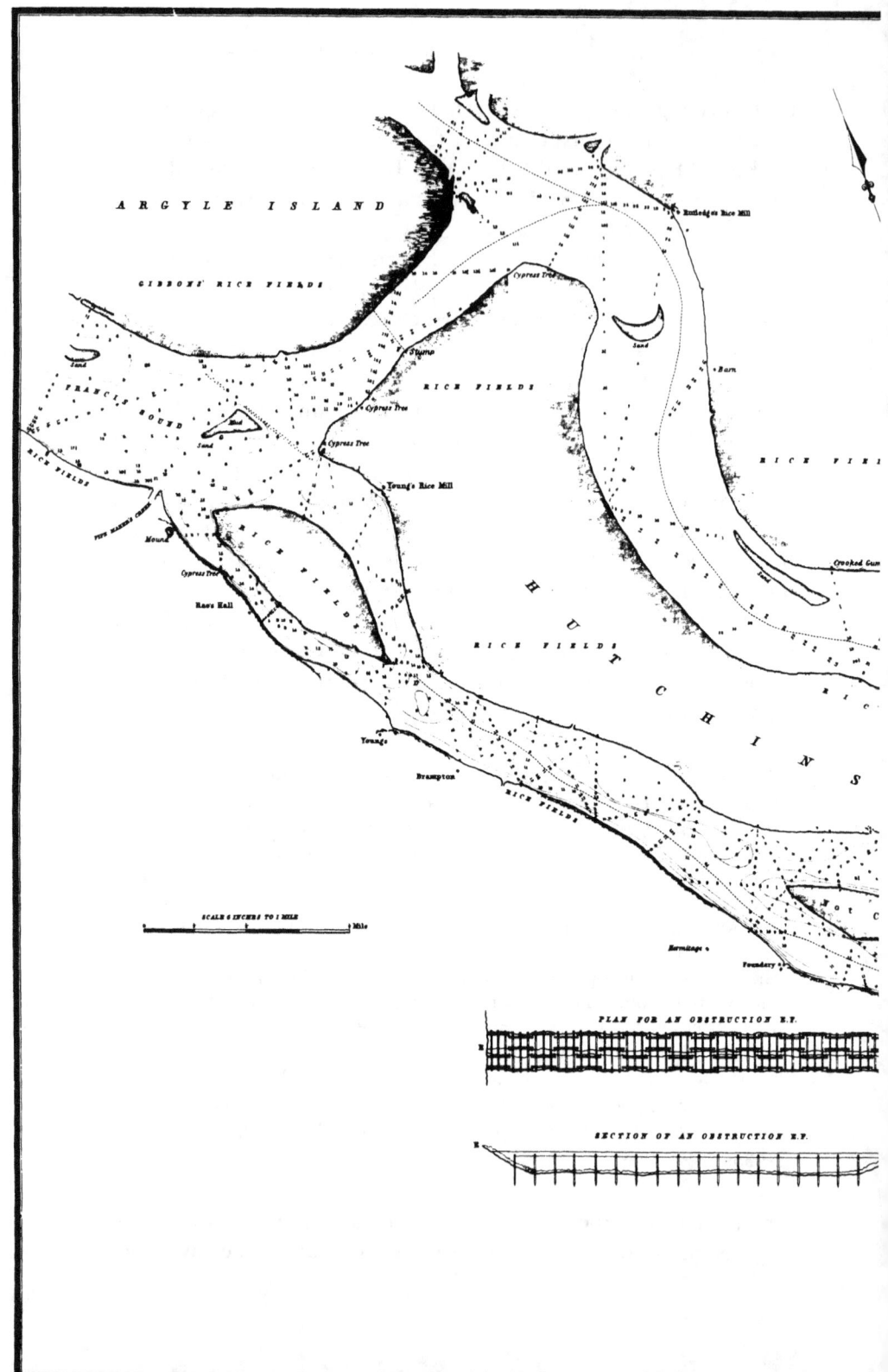

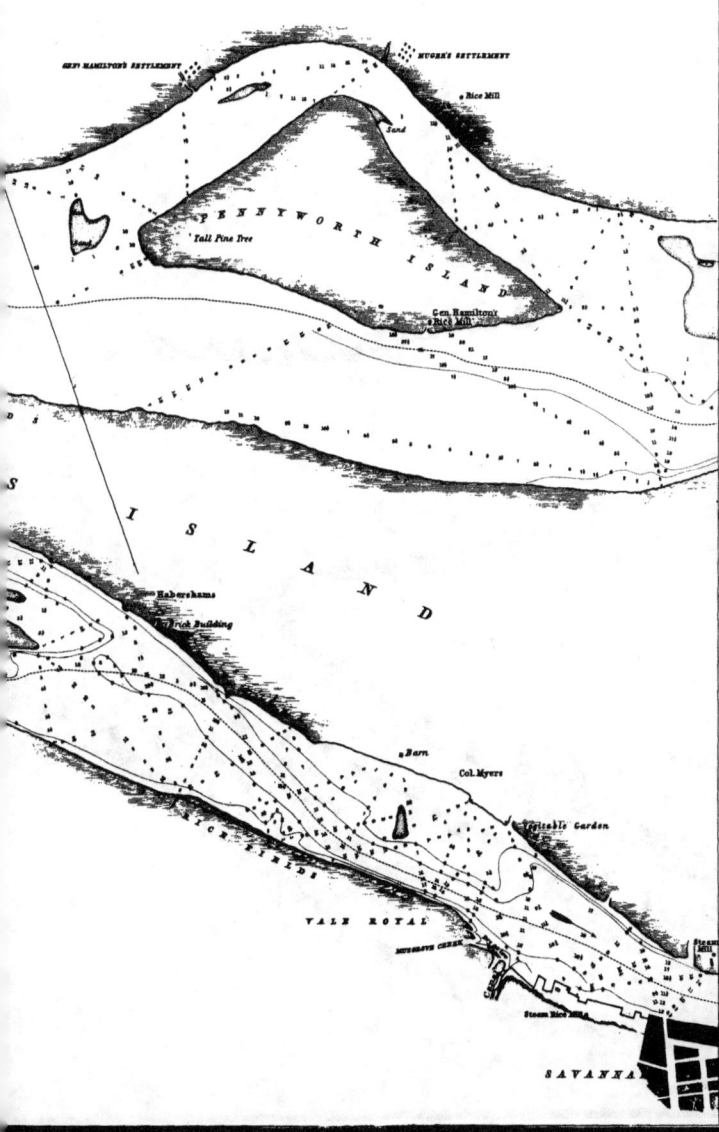

14A. "Chart of Part of the Savannah River, 1833, Surveyed & Drawn by Lieut. John Mackay, 2d Regt. Arty." Printed on two sheets, Lt. Mackay's map shows the Hutchinson and Barnwell islands area in considerable detail.

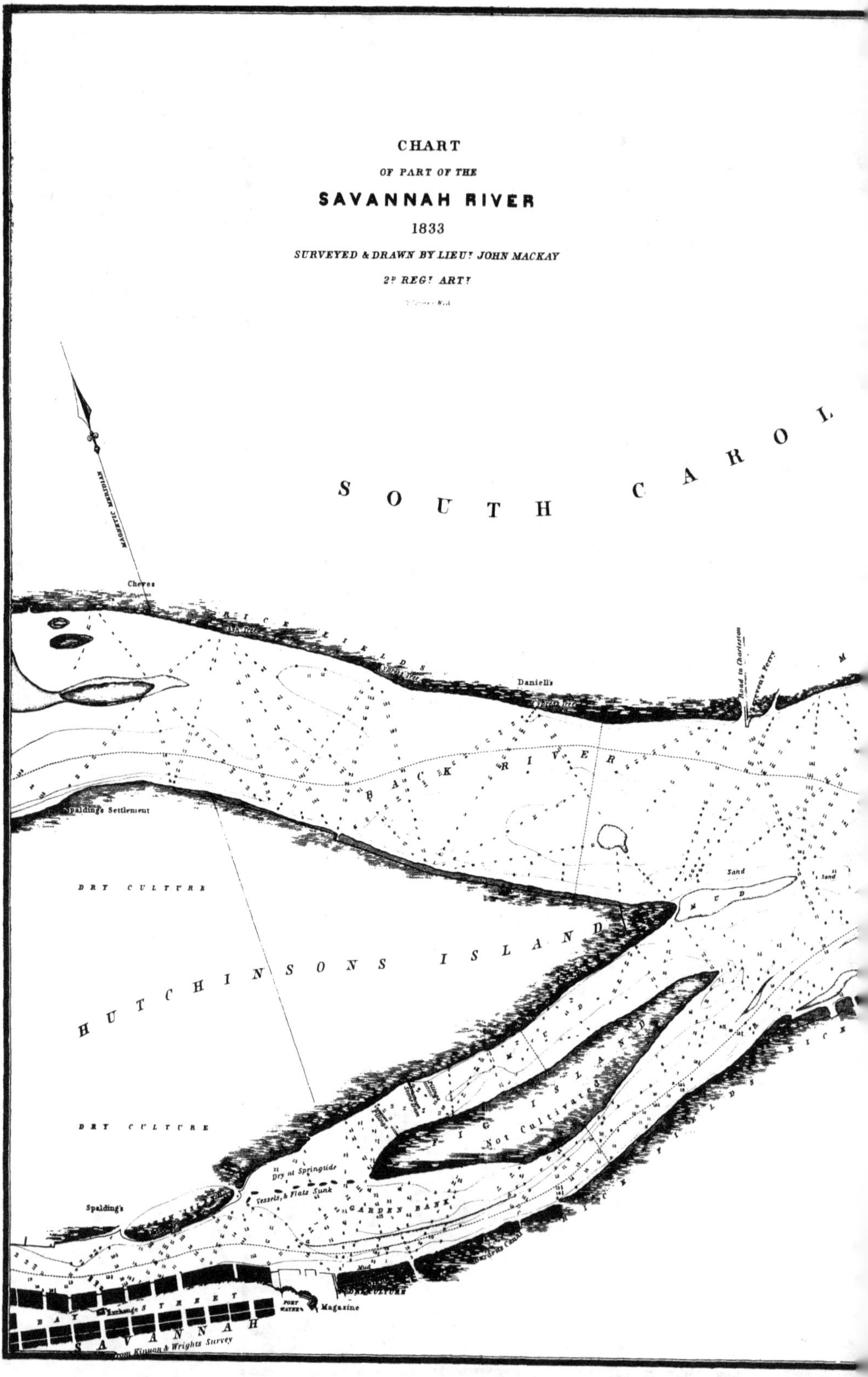

CHART
OF PART OF THE
SAVANNAH RIVER
1833
SURVEYED & DRAWN BY LIEUT. JOHN MACKAY
2D REGT. ARTY.
MAGNETIC MERIDIAN
SOUTH CAROL
Cheves
RICE FIELDS
Daniell's
Road to Charleston
BACK RIVER
Spalding's Settlement
DRY CULTURE
Sand
MUD
HUTCHINSONS ISLAND
DRY CULTURE
FIG ISLAND
Not Cultivated
Dry at Springtide
Vessels & Flats Sunk
GARDEN BANK
Spalding's
RICE FIELDS
Mud
BAY STREET
Exchange
FORT WAYNE
Magazine
SAVANNAH
from Kinnon & Wrights Survey

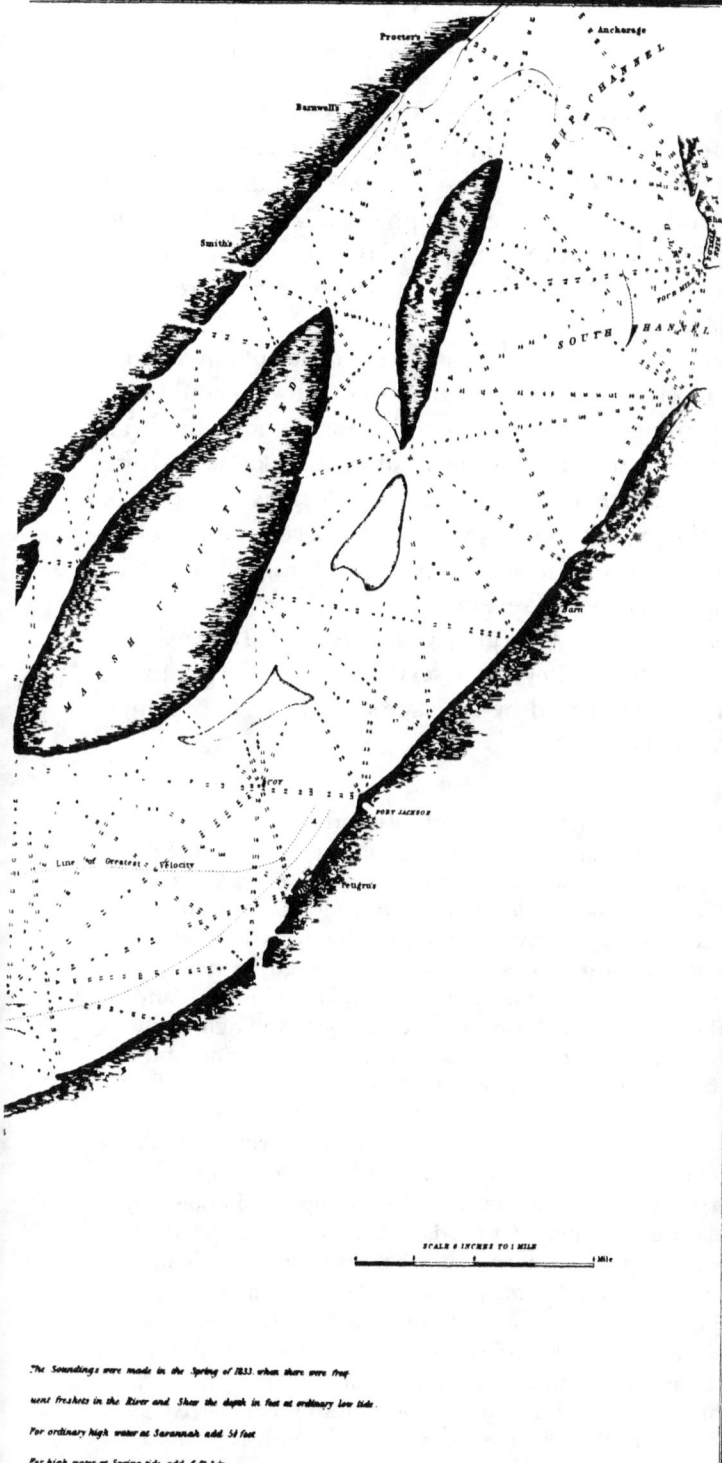

14B. "Chart of Part of the Savannah River, 1833, Surveyed & Drawn by Lieut. John Mackay, 2d Regt. Arty." Printed on two sheets, Lt. Mackay's map shows the Hutchinson and Barnwell islands area in considerable detail.

flow to benefit the city of Savannah's access to the sea. Dr. Daniell had expressed some fear of criticism in connection with his earlier attempt to block the channel between Hutchinson and Fig islands, but in that case, the Fig Island channel served simply as a shortcut between South Carolina plantations and Savannah. In the case of Cross Tides, the free navigation of the route clearly specified in the Treaty of Beaufort was being threatened.

In 1836 the governors of the two states were contacted by federal authorities in an effort to resolve the difficulty so that work could proceed on the improvement scheme. Georgia responded with a full grant of authority to proceed, but South Carolina appointed a commission to examine the site of the proposed obstruction and report to the governor on the expediency of granting the necessary authority. Lieutenant Mansfield was frustrated in trying to bring this commission to a meeting and action on several occasions.

In their official response, Georgia's Committee on Internal Improvement included the following observations on the Treaty of Beaufort, which were approved by the state's House of Representatives, Senate, and governor:

> That they cannot perceive that the treaty of Beaufort, made in 1787 . . . can be an obstacle to the proposed improvement in the navigation of the Savannah river; that the second section of that treaty reserves to the citizens of each State only equal privileges and equal exemptions from tolls, hindrances, etc. That it will be obvious from reading that section, it was intended to deny to the citizens of South Carolina the right to the use of the south channel of said river, lying to the south of Hutchinson's island; and so long as the south channel was so denied to them, the right to the use of the north channel (which branches from the south channel at the upper end of Hutchinson's island) was reserved to them. That after the adoption of the constitution of the United States, it was considered and understood that the citizens of Carolina were at liberty to use the south channel, and no objection being made, the north channel was seldom used by them, and more seldom still was the course laid down by that treaty for their use pursued. Upwards of twenty years since, an attempt was made to stop this northern channel of the river at the identical spot proposed; no objection was made from any quarter; a line of palisades was driven, and, had the work been successful, probably no objection would have been made. It was not so, however, and although the work thus done has caused such an accumulation of alluvial matter as nearly to prevent the use of this communication with the main river, it has not produced that effect on the main channel which is promised

from the proposed work. Your Committee, from an examination of the chart of the river, are satisfied that the obstruction proposed will improve the navigation of the river, and will do no injury to individuals; and that, therefore, the State of Georgia should cheerfully yield her consent to it. Nor can they believe that the Legislature of South Carolina will withhold her consent, when it is considered that her citizens now enjoy the use of the south channel on precisely an equal footing with the citizens of Georgia; that this communication of the north branch with the main channel is now become useless to its citizens from the accumulation before mentioned; that the proposed obstruction will improve the main channel of the river; that the back river and this northern branch will convey to the low or river lands, in Carolina, an ample supply of fresh water for irrigation. [Joseph K. F. Mansfield, "Report of the Progress Made in the Improvement of the Navigation of the Savannah River . . . the Year Ending the 30th of September, 1836 Inclusive," pp. 276–77]

Clearly, the Georgians considered that the commerce clause of the United States Constitution had nullified the situation that had earlier made Article 2 on navigation rights necessary in the Treaty of Beaufort. The committee also obviously was concerned about the accretion of alluvial matter that had resulted from the unfinished line of pilings placed in the Cross Tides channel several years before under the auspices of the commissioners of pilotage in 1812.

Finally, in 1838, the commissioners for South Carolina "decided against granting authority to make the obstruction between Hutchinson's and Argyle islands," and thereby frustrated, for the time being, "the plan for any permanent improvement in this river from the city of Savannah to its mouth" (Topographic Bureau, "Report for 1839," p. 58).

In December 1839, Captain Mackay submitted an improvement plan which he stated could not "injure any individual or public interest, nor can any one object to it under any law or treaty." He recommended "a system of piers be placed so as to diminish the breadth of the inlet and outlet of the back river, and thereby cause the water to be slightly checked in its course, both in flood and ebb tide, and at once turn it to the desired direction. . . . I would propose that these piers be made by driving two rows of piling ——— feet apart, tying them with capsills and crossties and filling in between them with old vessels, flats, stones, ballast etc." The result would be partial closures that could be progressively increased to achieve a desired degree of flow through the Front River channel to prevent the accumulation of sediment there and at the wrecks. He noted, "By placing obstructions at both ends of Hutchinson's Island, the river by the city of Savannah will feel the influence at once in both the ebb and flood tide, and there will be no tendency in the flood tide to force the water through the branch of the river on the north side of Argyle Island" (John Mackay, Captain, "Improvement of Savannah River, December 6, 1839," p. 145).

Significantly, Mackay realized that a more than partial closure would lead to accretion: "If the channel were diminished by a jetee, run out from each side, it would cause a tremendous deepening in the interval, and probably a bank would be formed somewhere below; but by dividing the obstruction across the river, I think the deposite would be less liable to be at any one point" (ibid.). His interrupted series of piers would be designed to "narrow the surface of the river at both points about a third of its width" (ibid.). Although he did not mention the analogy, Mackay's scheme is reminiscent of the medieval London Bridge, which formed a significant but interrupted barrier across the tidal Thames.

Mackay's plan was found acceptable, but no appropriation to fund its progress was forthcoming. In December 1845, the Savannah Chamber of Commerce was joined by several of the city's leading citizens in memorializing the U.S. Congress in an effort to stimulate passage of the necessary appropriation. Much of the memorial consisted of a documented account proving that the wrecks obstruction was indeed just that—an obstruction formed by the hulks of ships deliberately sunk by both sides in the revolutionary war. After they established the facts surrounding the origins of the wrecks, the Savannahians argued: "The fact of the sailing up of frigates and ships-of-war, and the necessity of an artificial obstruction to the approach, is irresistible evidence that there was no natural obstruction. A comparison of the depth of water, then of 18 feet, with that of some years after, of 12 or 13 feet, and now of 13½ to 14½ feet, caused by improvements by the commissioners of pilotage, is positive proof of the injury done to the navigation of the river [by the war]" (Savannah Chamber of Commerce, "Memorial of . . . Praying the Removal of Obstructions to the Navigation of the Savannah River," p. 3). Attention was also drawn to the fact that Congress had funded the removal of similar wartime obstructions opposite Fort McHenry near Baltimore.

Appended to the memorial was a sworn statement by Elijah

Broughton, who was described as having begun his career as a "pilot for the bar and river Savannah" in 1790. Broughton swore that his contemporaries in the pilotage forty-five years before had informed him that "previous to the sinking of the wrecks in the revolutionary war, they could readily navigate ships drawing eighteen feet water up to the city." He continued:

> That, at that time [1790?], the wrecks . . . below the city were perceptible, and impeded the passage of any vessel drawing over twelve feet water; that a freshet in the river had washed them round so that at that time, they lay fore-and-aft, up and down the channel; and that in 1796 the Yazoo freshet deepened the channel between the wrecks, so that by nice steering, with a favorable wind and tide, thirteen feet could be carried up and down; that, in 1799, the Commissioners of pilotage employed one Stephen Culver [Colver?], who raised three of the wrecks and removed them from the channel; that now fourteen and fourteen and a half feet (the result of the operations of the Commissioners of pilotage and freshets) can be carried up and down through a new channel washed near the bank which was created by the wrecks; and further states that the bar at the mouth of the Savannah river does not change; and that vessels drawing twenty-five feet can be navigated over it at high water. [Ibid., p. 5]

Captain Mackay's apparently well-conceived and innovative plan was never carried out. He left the Savannah area on sick leave in 1846, and his duties were assumed by Lieutenant M. L. Smith sometime later. Smith began a detailed survey of the same areas of the river above and below the city of Savannah that had been intensively studied by Mackay in 1832–33.

On November 6, 1849, Smith reported the completion of his survey to J. J. Abert, colonel of the Corps of Engineers. In his lengthy letter, Smith detailed his own plan for improving the Savannah's navigability. He stated that "the real bar of the river for all commercial purposes is . . . *the wrecks* . . . some sixteen miles from its mouth, since it determines the size of all trading vessels which reach its wharves" (M. L. Smith, Lieutenant, "Report and Plan of November 6, 1849," p. 2).

Smith's work in 1848–49 is particularly valuable because he carefully compared his survey findings with those of Mackay some sixteen years earlier. Thus his findings and chart can be of help in assessing the location and degree of morphological change that occurred between those surveys (Map 15). Smith wrote that "the greatest and

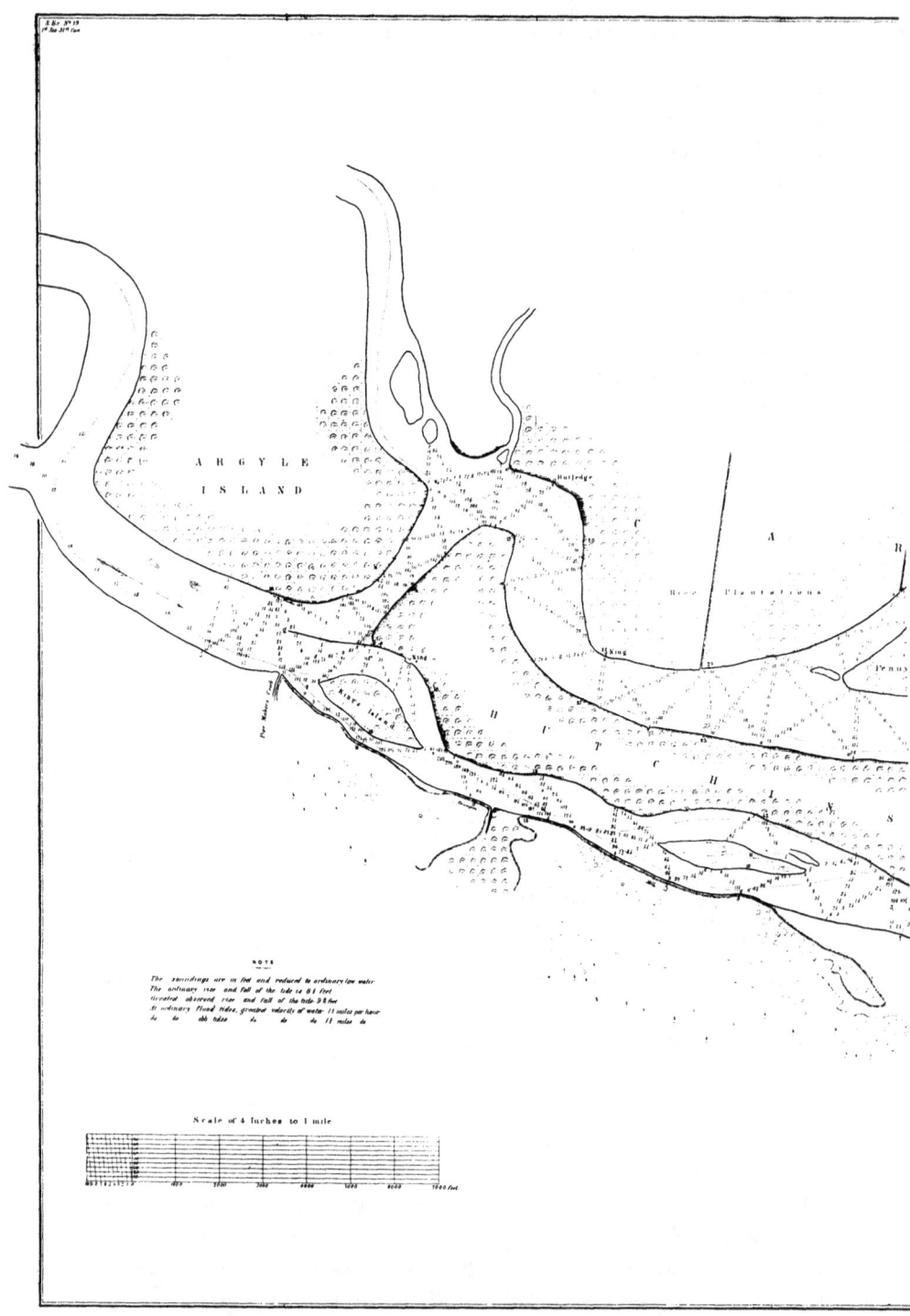

15. "Chart of a Portion of the Savannah River," by M. L. Smith, 1849. Lieutenant Smith succeeded John Mackay as the officer in charge of Savannah River improvement. His map is particularly valuable because he carefully

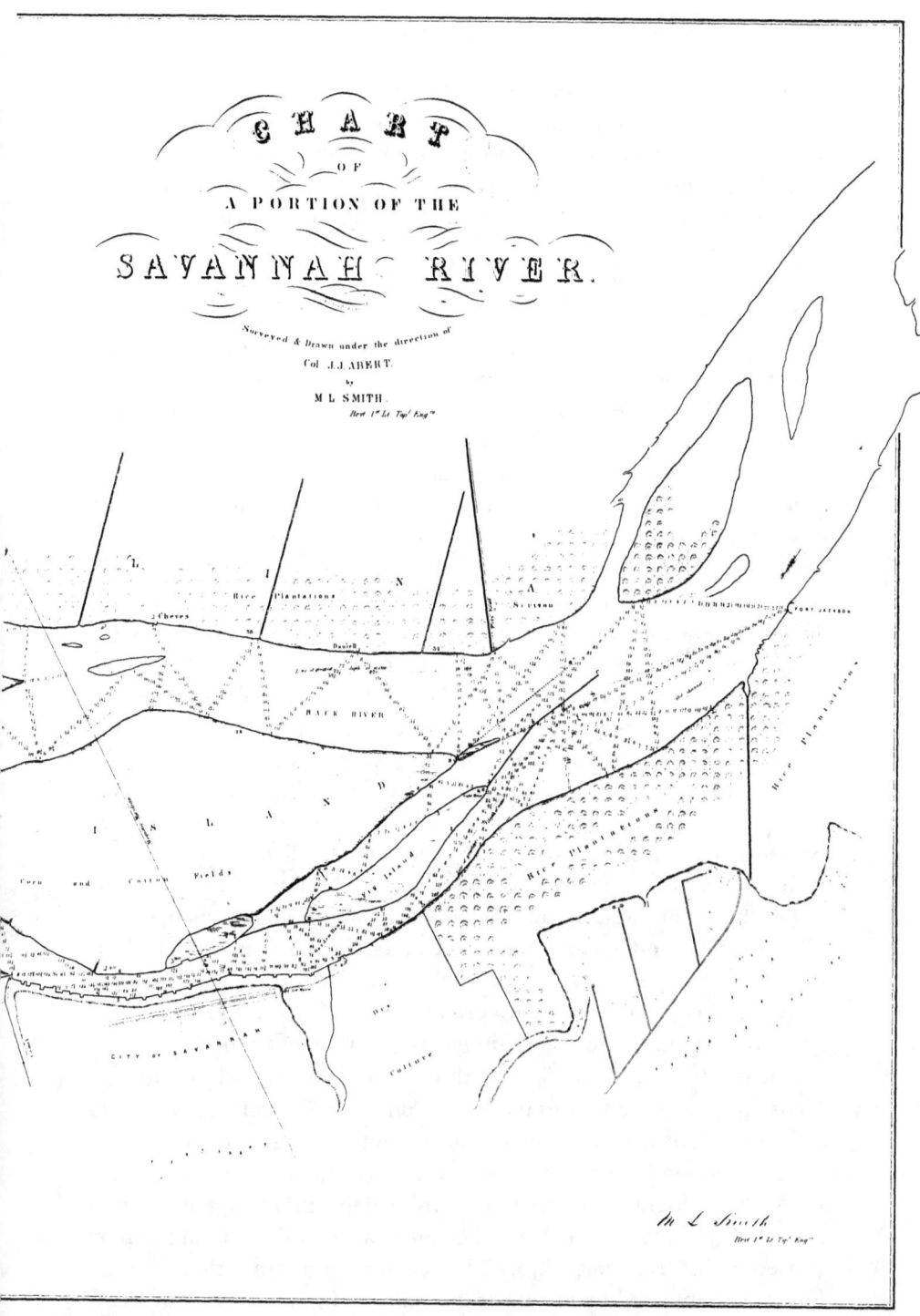

compared his survey findings with those gathered by Mackay sixteen years before.

most important change has taken place at *the wrecks*, the old channel across it having filled up, and a new one opened, passing nearer to the lower end of Fig island and uniting with that of the Back river sooner than the old one" (ibid.). No perceptible change in the island or bank morphology of the boundary stream Back River is indicated by Smith's careful work.

Smith's plan was designed to increase the flow through Front River at the expense of Back River by a long pier or jetty projecting upstream into the Front River from the northwestern point of Hutchinson Island. This jetty would in no way close the passage between the Front and Back rivers and thus could raise no objection from South Carolina. On the downstream end of Hutchinson the channel between it and Fig Island would be closed by another jetty. From the downstream point of Fig Island still another jetty would project downstream to a point below the wrecks. In effect, Hutchinson Island would be elongated by the jetties and ultimately assume a configuration much like its present one. Smith's far-sighted plan was not adopted, however, and it was several decades before works resembling those he proposed were undertaken.

Conflicting opinions among officials of the Savannah city government, the commissioners of pilotage, and other interested groups probably impeded the adoption of Smith's plan, and yet another survey was undertaken. Congress authorized formation of a commission of experts under the aegis of the War Department for the purpose of presenting a comprehensive plan for Savannah River improvement. Named to serve on the commission were Professor A. D. Bache, superintendent of the U.S. Coast Survey; Captain A. H. Bowman, Corps of Engineers; and Lieutenant J. F. Gilmer, Corps of Engineers. Gilmer appears to have conducted the actual survey. By the autumn of 1852, the Corps of Engineers were in charge of operations in the Savannah area and Lieutenant Gilmer was their chief agent.

During the 1840s, the Savannah city government had become increasingly concerned about navigation on the river. Railroad construction had a great impact on the hinterland of Savannah. Increasing volumes of goods were being delivered from the developing upcountry, making the need for harbor improvements more urgent. A committee of the Savannah City Council emphasized this point in a report presented in December 1840: "The constant communication with the interior maintained by means of the railroad has increased our prosperity, and we are now surprised at our former lethargy. Our energies have at length been aroused and we will not be laggards in the race for improvement." In reviewing some of the problems existing in the harbor, the council exhibited understanding of the physical processes operating in the river. For example, "The floods of rains which fall during the summer and fall months sweep large quantities of sand into the river which forming bars collect the floating rubbish and matter brought down by a rapid current from above. These two accumulate at the foot of the wharves and in the public docks so that wharves which formerly accommodated at all tides vessels of heavy tonnage are now dry at low water" (Quoted in Gamble, *History of the City Government of Savannah*, pp. 185–86). To overcome this problem they urged use of a dredge boat, "the cost of which will be considerable." To purchase a dredge, they recommended that $8,000 be raised by taxation.

In 1843, Mayor Richard D. Arnold of Savannah wrote to the secretary of the treasury to urge federal financial aid in river improvement efforts. To emphasize the severity of the problem at the wrecks, he pointed out that vessels drawing only 11 feet 9 inches or less could pass over, whereas only two years before 13 feet 6 inches of depth had been available there (ibid., p. 187). Six years later, in 1849, Lieutenant Smith reported a depth of only 9 feet 4 inches over the wrecks. Needless to say, the condition of Savannah's outlet to the sea had become critical by the mid-nineteenth century.

A commission "organized under the War Department, on the application of the Chamber of Commerce and Commissioners of Pilotage of Savannah, Georgia," drew up a detailed report in 1853 (J. F. Gilmer, A. D. Bache, and A. H. Bowman, "Report of the Commissioners on the Improvement of the Savannah River," p. 1). Following a lengthy description of the Savannah River basin and the economic life of the region, the report discussed the types and drafts of vessels engaged in Savannah's external commerce. It stated that vessels drawing over 14 or 14½ feet "cannot in the ordinary stages of the river go to sea from the city wharves" (ibid., p. 6). After taking on a portion of their cargoes at Savannah's wharves, these ships were required to "drop down to Venus Point, an anchorage about 7½ miles below and receive the remainder from Lighters" (ibid.). Such additional handling caused both delay and considerable expense, which could be avoided through the removal of the obstructions near the city.

Vessels with drafts of 17½ feet were able to "pass out of the River from . . . Venus Point in the ordinary stages of tide" (ibid., p. 14).

During spring tides, even larger vessels could be brought into the lower river. The Savannah's bar was "one of the best along the Southern coast of the U. States, and has a depth of 19 feet 6 inches at mean low water" (ibid., p. 20). The tidal range was about 8 feet on average, so that the depth at high water was 27 feet 6 inches on the bar. At any stage of the tide, vessels drawing 18 or 19 feet could "pass inside of Tybee Island to a good anchorage, where they are beyond the influence of the swell of the ocean" (ibid.).

The commissioners believed that the "outer obstructions or Sea-bar requires no improvements" (ibid. p. 21). They found the river's first obstruction requiring removal to be two and a half miles above Tybee Point. If this was removed, vessels of up to 20 or 22 feet could ascend to Venus Point, and the river "would . . . become a good harbor of refuge for vessels of war as well as merchantmen" (ibid.).

The Savannah's mouth and channel were described as follows:

> The entrance to the river is between Tybee Island on the South, and Hilton Head Island on the North; distant from each other about 5¼ miles: but the channel of deep water passes near the Northern point of Tybee. Going inside this point and ascending the river, it divides into two channels: the main or *North Channel*, and the *South Channel* separated by a succession of Islands, the principal of which are Cockspur, Long, York, and Elba Islands. At the upper end of the last named Island, about 4 miles below the City of Savannah, the North and South Channel unite: from this point there is but one channel until we ascend to the foot of Fig and Hutchinsons Islands, where another division occurs; the branch on the North is known as the *Back River*; the one between the Islands as *Fig Island Channel*; and the one to the South as the *Front River*. . . . The banks of the River and Island[s] are low, being either Salt Marsh or Rice lands, until we ascend to the Front River to the high bank or plateau, on which stands the City. [Ibid., pp. 21–22]

The islands and channels above the city were similarly described. The report continued with a detailed description of earlier river surveys and improvement projects.

In another section, the commissioners drew attention to the hydraulics of the Savannah River: "In the river the influence of the downward current upon the banks and bottom is the greater, and shoals and bars are generally formed by it. In most cases therefore works designed for the improvement of the channel, must be planned with a view to control and give proper direction to the descending currents. The shoals which offer the greatest impediments to the navigation show a downstream action; such is the character of Garden Bank; the wrecks; Four mile Point bar; and probably the shoals lower down" (ibid., p. 36). This principle was, of course, basic in all earlier as well as later schemes proposed for improving navigation depths in the river.

Like Captain Mackay and Lieutenant Smith some years earlier, Captain Gilmer and the other commissioners in 1853 were sensitive to the apparent constraints posed by the Treaty of Beaufort. On this topic, they stated, "The requisite deflecting works can be planned and located as not to infringe upon any rights secured by the Treaty of Beaufort" (ibid., p. 37). The deflecting works they proposed were very similar to those Lieutenant Smith had advocated in 1849. There would be no blockage of the Cross Tides channel, but the stream of Front River would be deflected away from it to ensure a greater volume and velocity along Savannah's front. A lower set of jetties would close the Fig Island channel and extend downstream beyond the island. Channel deepening and straightening "so far as to give uniformity of curvature" was also proposed in the Front River (ibid., p. 38). The possibility of "making a cut across the lower point of Isla Island and enlarging the existing cut across Drakees Point" (both upstream of Savannah) was included in the proposed project (ibid., p. 39).

Another provision in the proposal provides insight regarding the practice of dredge spoil disposal: "In order to facilitate the flow of the flood and the return of the Ebb tides—the dredging of the wrecks should be executed in such manner, as to diminish the curvature of the present channel, giving it in crossing the point of obstruction, a curvature equal to that of the South shore just above. The sand and mud removed to be deposited back of the lower point of Hutchinson Island or upon the wharves now constructing below the city, if proper arrangements can be made with the proprietors" (ibid., p. 40).[4]

In the lower reaches of the river, the commissioners found the need to increase depths in the channel over the knoll off Cockspur Island to be of the highest priority. To accomplish this and provide for safe passage of 20-foot-draft vessels to Venus Point, they proposed dredging a channel over the knoll 2 feet 2 inches into the accumulation. In their discussion of this topic, the commissioners provided an interesting view of the nature of much of Savannah's seaborne commerce in the mid-nineteenth century: "As most of the ranging timber exported, is taken from the rafts in the river, it could be shipped at [Venus] Point with nearly the same economy and convenience as in front of the city" (ibid., p. 45).

Unfortunately, the plan for Savannah River improvement which Captain Gilmer officially submitted to the secretary of war, Jefferson Davis, was deemed to exceed the provisions of the appropriation bill Congress had passed. Thus only the removal of the actual wrecks was to be allowed. Because of the decision to severely limit the scope of the federal project, the city petitioned the Georgia legislature for $25,000 to dredge through the knoll. The measure failed by a close vote. The city then sought to issue bonds in the amount of $160,000 to pay for improving the navigation of the river and harbor. This bold action took place in June 1856. In effect, the 1853 federal plan was being carried out with local money and with Captain Gilmer in charge. Thus the seemingly endless delays involved in the federal improvement program were overcome by local initiative.

By 1856, Captain Gilmer was able to report that considerable progress had been made in dredging the obstruction near Cockspur known as the knoll. He described a channel "three hundred feet wide and twenty-one and a half feet at mean high water," which he believed would make Savannah the best harbor south of Norfolk. In 1857 the jetty above Kings Island was constructed to divert the flow of Front River away from the Cross Tides channel above the city of Savannah. The Savannah mayor's report for 1858 announced the successful completion of dredging at the knoll. These works were continued in 1859–60 under the direction of Lieutenant W. H. C. Whiting, who replaced Gilmer as the supervising federal engineer at Savannah. By the time the Civil War broke out ships drawing 17½ feet could reach Savannah's wharves with favorable wind and tide conditions. In 1860, Mayor Arnold was pleased to note that even some vessels drawing 18 feet had berthed before the town.

During the early 1850s, another important agency of the federal government was focusing its energies in the lower Savannah River area. This was the U.S. Coast Survey under the leadership of its energetic and gifted superintendent, Alexander D. Bache. A primary mission of the Coast Survey was the production of detailed maps and charts of the nation's coasts and navigable waters. In the area of the lower Savannah River, their efforts resulted in several maps and sketches, which collectively provide an exceedingly accurate cartographic statement of riverbank and island configurations as they existed in the mid-1850s.

Of particular significance to any effort to recreate the riverbank and island morphology in the Savannah valley below the city of Savannah in the 1850s are two large-scale topographical surveys now in the archives of the National Ocean Survey. The first of these is titled "Map of Savannah River from Savannah City to Elba Island, U.S. Coast Survey A. D. Bache Supt. Topographical Survey made during January and February 1852." This detailed manuscript map is drawn at a scale of 1:5,000 and shows even individual buildings with fidelity. The second map was constructed at a scale of 1:10,000 and covers the river from the head of Elba Island to Cockspur Island. It is titled "Map of Savannah River from Fort Pulaski to Four-Mile Point U.S. Coast Survey A. D. Bache Supt. Topographical Survey made during parts of April and May 1852." These and a number of other sketches and trigonometrical surveys formed the data base for the first truly accurate published map of the Savannah River from its bar and mouth to the city and Argyle and Isla islands upstream.[5] This published map is titled "Preliminary Chart of Savannah River Georgia from a Trigonometrical Survey under the direction of A. D. Bache Superintendent of the Survey of the Coast of the United States . . . Scale 1:40,000 1855."

The foregoing evidence shows that all of the post-1787 engineering efforts in the lower Savannah River were directed at either the Front River close to Savannah or the knoll close to Cockspur Island. No significant changes in island or riverbank morphology appear to have taken place due to direct human action in "the most northern branch or stream of the River Savannah" prior to the preparation of the 1855 Coast Survey Preliminary Chart of the river. Consequently, this scientifically prepared chart may be taken as a largely correct statement of the Savannah's riverbank and island configurations as they had evolved through natural accretion or erosion in the period following the Treaty of Beaufort's signing and ratification in 1787.

The present-day National Ocean Survey (NOS) is the successor agency of the Coast Survey that produced the 1855 Preliminary Chart. In other instances, the National Ocean Survey has gone on record as accepting the cartographic work of their predecessor agency, the Coast Survey, as meeting present-day NOS standards of accuracy. Thus comparisons of Coast Survey charts with present-day NOS charts that show altered shoreline or island configurations can be interpreted as revealing real changes in the landscape concerned. The shoreline and island configuration differences that are revealed do not indicate merely apparent change due to surveying or mapping inaccuracies but, as stated above, real change caused by some natural or human agency. Thus a comparison of the 1855 Preliminary Chart (Map 16) of the Savannah River with a recent NOS chart of the same area and at the same scale can be employed to catalog the morphological change that had taken place through the intervening time period.

The Civil War caused a cessation of efforts to improve the Savannah's navigability and resulted in many actions intended to have a diametrically opposite effect. Numerous obstacles such as timber cribs loaded with brick and stone, iron shod snags, logs, piles, and torpedoes were strategically placed in the river to deny federal forces access to the port. In 1861, for example, two large ships and a smaller vessel were sunk in the navigation channel near Fort Pulaski. Other cribs and several vessels were sunk near the head of Elba Island to form what became known as the "Obstructions." The Confederate rams *Georgia* and *Ogeechee* were also scuttled and produced serious hazards when peace was restored.

According to Mary L. Granger, official chronicler of Savannah's harbor development, "These efforts not only blocked the channel but in deflecting the currents caused changes in their pattern. As a result there was a great amount of shoaling in the areas where the obstructions had been sunk. The minimum high water channel, which had been better than 17½ feet, was reduced to 13½ feet" (Granger, *Savannah Harbor*, p. 34).

Although some emergency clearing was undertaken by the U.S. Navy and Quartermaster Corps, the river remained in a deplorable condition when the war ended. In his annual report for 1867, Mayor Edward C. Anderson wrote:

> The hope expressed in the Mayor's Report of 1866 that the obstructions to the navigation of the river put down during the war, would be speedily removed under the Wells' contract, has not been realized. The iron clad gun boat Milledgeville, one sunken Light Ship, renovated and sold to the Government, and the hulks of four pilot boats, with some minor obstacles, have been taken up and disposed of, but the timber cribs obstructing the main ship channel remain intact, lightened in a measure

by the removal of the brick and stone which ballasted them, but still firmly embedded where they were originally sunk. No effort so far as I have been able to learn has been made by the Contractor to remove these impediments. They remain a hindrance to the easy access to the city, and a positive obstacle to the permanent improvement of the river, which at so much cost and labor has been carried on during the past season. The Commissioners of Pilotage, through the Mayor, addressed a remonstrance to the Secretary of the Treasury, calling his attention to the delay in the prosecution of the work, but were met with the response that the course of Mr. Wells in the premises was satisfactory to the Department, and it was hoped would be to the municipal authorities of Savannah. Mr. Wells' contract requires the removal of "all cribs, piles, boats, scows, vessels and other property obstructing the channel of the Savannah River," and is conditioned under a bond in the sum of $50,000 for the faithful performance of the provisions of his agreement. In the further hope of having these cribs removed, the Northern Agents of the steam lines running to this port have been appealed to with the view of enlisting the action of their Senators and Representatives in this work, and in the meantime application has been made to the Engineer Department at Washington, asking that skilled officers may be sent out at an early day to blow up with gun powder the cribs at Four Mile Point, the services of the City Dredge being proffered to remove the debris. [Edward C. Anderson, *Report of Edward C. Anderson, Mayor of the City of Savannah*, pp. 16–17]

The mayor also reported that a $20,000 patented dredge machine had been contracted for with Messrs. Morris and Cumming. This equipment was designed to excavate 1,000 cubic yards of mud in ten hours of operation. The terms of the contract with Morris and Cumming stipulated that "the city has the privilege of working their patent on the Savannah River from Augusta to Tybee bar—its approaches and tributaries, North to Broad River and Port Royal entrance, S.C., South to Ossabaw Sound and the Ogeechee River, and no other place" (ibid., p. 18). The city fathers of Savannah apparently construed their responsibilities and the extent of the Savannah River very broadly—Broad River and Port Royal entrance were far to the north of the southern tip of Hilton Head Island, the traditional northern headland of the Savannah's mouth.

As a result of the city's efforts through 1867, the mayor could report:

A channel has been dredged through the "Wrecks" of four hundred and fifty yards in length by one hundred and twenty feet in width, with a

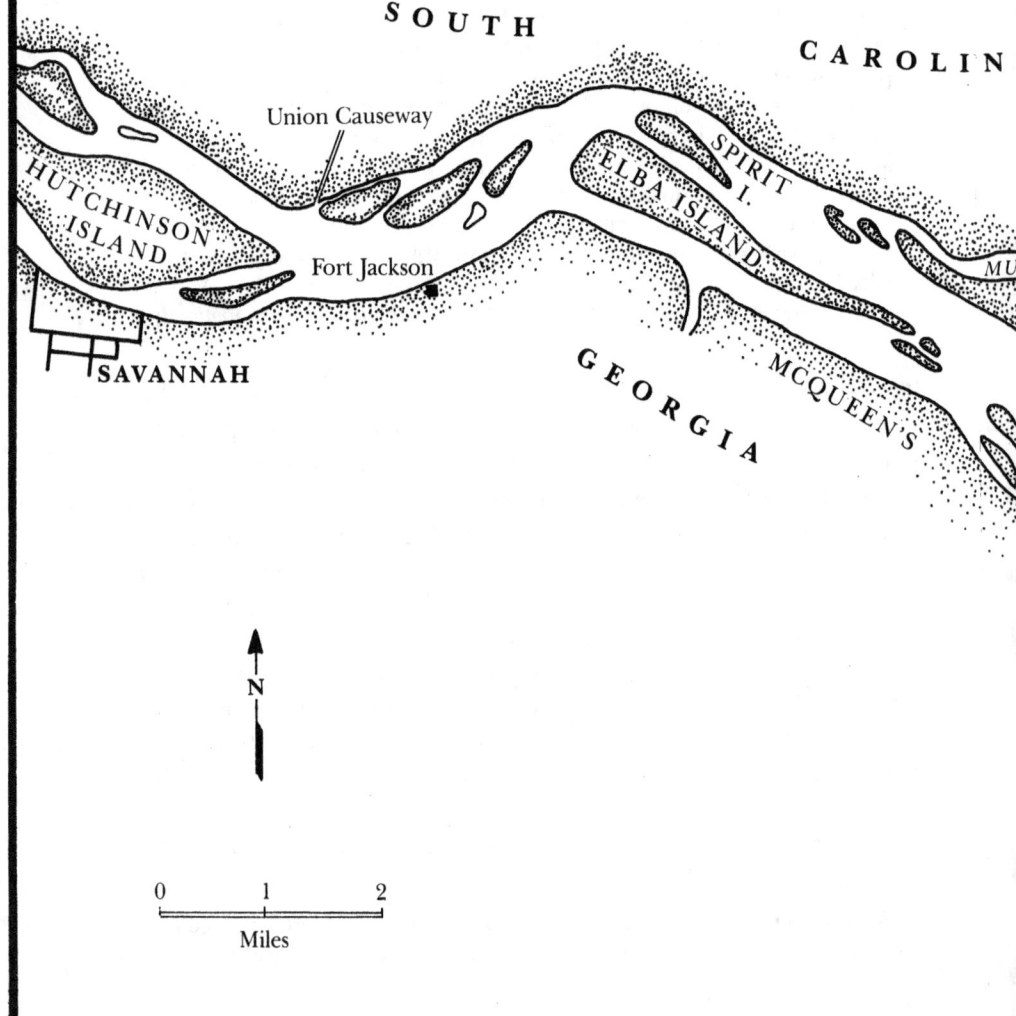

16. U.S. Coast Survey, Preliminary Chart of Savannah River, Georgia, 1855. The original from which this redrawing was prepared was the first scientifically prepared comprehensive map of the lower Savannah River area. It

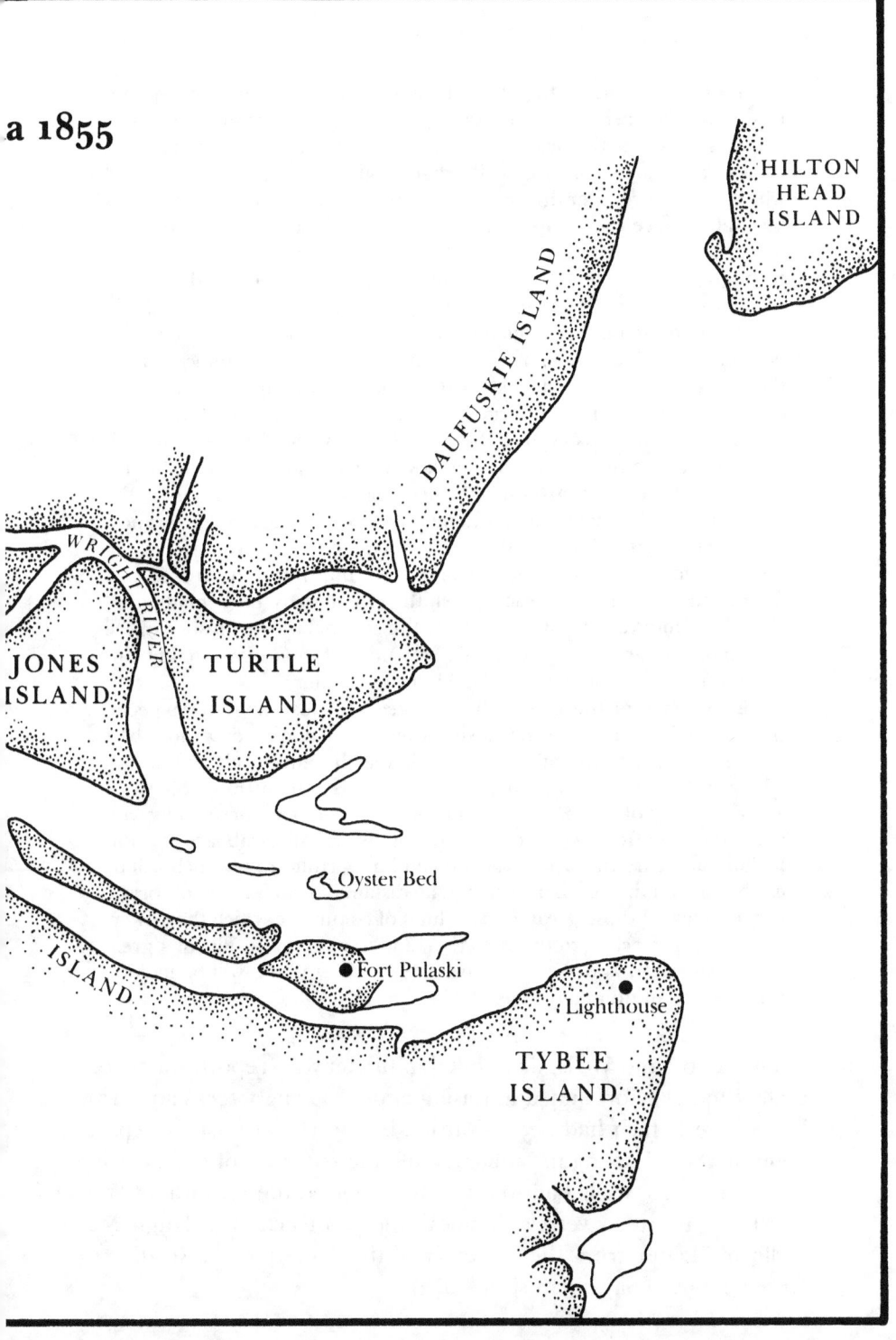

is invaluable in gaining an appreciation of the geography of the area before the massive river improvement works begun by the U.S. Army Corps of Engineers later in the nineteenth century.

depth of water at mean high tide of eighteen feet in the centre, and not less than seventeen feet on the margins, thus readily admitting to our wharves vessels of the heaviest burthen. The quantity of mud and sand removed is 34,000 cubic yards. The figures given in regard to depth and width are rather under than over the mark, and from subsequent soundings taken since the completion of the cut by Capt. J. S. Kennard, the officer in charge of the work, it is found that the sweep of the current through the excavated channel seems rather to have deepened than decreased it. As a guide to vessels passing to and from the City it will be necessary to establish prominent ranges on the shore, both above and below the cut. This probably will be done by the Hydrographic party of the U.S. Coast Survey, which is shortly expected out, and will operate in connexion with us. It is important likewise that a buoy should be placed at a point a few yards beyond the eastern end of the dredged channel. The natural channel of the river makes quite a bend here to the Southward, and vessels have grounded by keeping too near the margin on the South side. A channel of similar dimensions to the one completed is now being made through the mud bank immediately above the gap in the crib obstructions at Elba Island. The shoal is four hundred yards across. Three cuts of thirty feet each in width have already been made, and should no untoward delay occur the entire channel will be finished in the course of the next three weeks. The quantity of mud excavated at this point amounts to about 18,000 cubic yards, additional.

The working of the Dredge has realized the most sanguine expectations of its efficiency, and has insured the conviction among those best acquainted with its operations, that it will speedily and surely accomplish all the ends that induced its procurement. It has demonstrated the value and advantage of our harbor by enabling us to compete successfully with the strenuous efforts which other cities on the Atlantic Seaboard are now making to secure the large exporting and importing trade which will be established on the Southern Coast at no distant day; to fix a point for the convergence of those great internal lines of commerce which the powerful West is projecting in this direction, and to reap the profits of a great South American and West Indian trade which ere long will be looking for a lodgment upon our Coast. [Ibid., pp. 18–19]

The contract to Wells, mentioned in the mayor's report, was a federally funded effort aimed at raising and removing wrecks and cribs in the river which had been awarded by the U.S. Treasury Department in 1866. Writing in January 1868, the secretary of the treasury mentioned that Wells had to that date reported the removal of "the wrecks of fourteen vessels, besides other obstructions" (Hugh McCulloch, "Letter from the Secretary of the Treasury . . . Relative to Obstructions in Savannah river," p. 3).

In a letter addressed to the secretary of the treasury, C. P. Patterson, hydrographic inspector of the Coast Survey, provided an excellent resumé of post–Civil War river improvement efforts as they stood in January 1870:

> In 1865, immediately after the close of the war, a resurvey of the Savannah River, from the ocean to the city, was made by the Coast Survey, from which it was shown that but eight feet at mean low water, and fourteen feet at mean high water, could be taken over the bars below the city, irrespective of the obstructions placed during the war. These obstructions have apparently had no effect upon the channels and bars of the river except at their immediate locality.
>
> By correspondence with this office, and other means, the authorities of Savannah endeavored to induce the government to undertake the needed deepening of the channel over the bars. The only action, to our knowledge, taken by the government, was to make a contract with Henry S. Wells, of New York, to remove the obstructions placed during the war. This work was but partially executed, and I understand the contract is still alive, but not enforced.
>
> The government taking no action, the city of Savannah, unlike all other southern cities, with a wise liberality under the energetic lead of its mayor, undertook itself the work of deepening and straightening the channel from the city to the mouth of the river, and after the skillful expenditure of about $120,000, has succeeded in opening a channel by which twelve feet at mean low, and eighteen feet at mean high water can be carried up to the city. These depths, however, can be maintained only by further improvements of a more permanent character, and giving such depth to the channel as will enable vessels which can cross the outer bar going direct to the city. This depth is nineteen feet at mean low, and twenty-six feet at mean high water.
>
> The amount required for this purpose will probably not exceed $200,000. The small city of Savannah, with an amount of taxable real estate of less than $10,000,000 when this work was begun, has shown a liberality worthy of praise, and which should shame her richer sister cities of the South, not one of which has expended a dollar, as far as this office is informed, towards the improvement of its harbor.
>
> The tonnage freighting at Savannah is owned almost exclusively in the North, and the ship-owners are as deeply interested in this improvement as even Savannah itself. [C. P. Patterson, "Letter to George S. Boutwell, Secretary of the Treasury, January 25, 1870," p. 2]

Included with the annual report of the chief of engineers for 1888 is a detailed essay by Lieutenant Oberlin M. Carter titled "History of Past Work—Improvement of Savannah River and Harbor." Carter reviewed much of the material discussed above and arrived at very similar conclusions concerning the nature and location of eighteenth- and early nineteenth-century improvement projects on the river so there is no need to quote him on these matters.

His review of improvement efforts for the period 1868 through 1888, however, is extremely lucid and authoritative and is quoted in full as follows:

> In 1866 the work of removing the wrecks, cribs, and other obstructions in the river was begun by Mr. Henry S. Welles, under contracts with the United States Treasury Department of the dates of May 1 and July 5, 1866. Under these contracts which were annulled on January 18, 1870, there were removed twenty vessels, forty cribs, and one hundred and fifty piles, and a number of iron shod snags and torpedoes. By an act of Congress approved February 27, 1874, Mr. Welles was paid the sum of $193,132.96 for the work executed. The navigation of the river being seriously obstructed by the shoals, the city of Savannah assumed charge of its improvement in 1867 and dredged a channel 18 feet deep at mean high water through the Wrecks and began a channel at the Obstructions. In 1868 dredging was done at Marsh Island and at a projecting point of the Georgia shore opposite King's Island. In 1869 dredging was again done at the Wrecks and the channel north of the Oyster Beds, at that time 9½ feet deep at mean low water, was deepened. In 1870 the Wrecks Channel was deep enough to admit a draught of 17¾ feet, but the channel was very crooked and continued to shoal. The Garden Bank Shoal was dredged three times and the channel there was widened from 120 to 150 feet, but this improvement was not permanent. The shoal opposite the foot of West Broad street was also dredged in the same year. In 1871 an opening was dredged north of Marsh Island; 45 feet was cut off of the point below Pipemaker's Creek, and the channel widened from 45 to 60 feet.
>
> The channel at the Wrecks was also reopened. The total number of cubic yards dredged by the city from March, 1867, up to May, 1871, was 280,000 and the amount expended for dredge-boats, scows, steam-tugs, labor, and superintendence from the close of the war up to 1872, when the United States Engineer Department resumed charge of the improvement, was about $157,000, not including interest on the original outlay. From 1865 to 1875 there were removed from the river (mostly by Welles) sixty timber cribs, twenty-six wrecks of vessels, two hundred piles, and a number of logs, torpedoes, etc. One torpedo in good condition was removed from the channel as late as 1886. In 1872 the United States Engineer Department resumed charge of the improvement of the river and harbor and the appropriations for that year and for 1873—amounting to $100,000—were expended in removing from the channel six vessels, sixteen cribs, and one sunken lighter and in dredging 166,500 cubic

yards of material from various points between the city and the mouth of the river.

In 1873 a project for the establishment of a channel from Tybee Roads to the city of Savannah, practicable at high tide for vessels drawing 23 feet of water, was submitted by General Gillmore, of the Corps of Engineers. The essential features of this project, which was approved by the Department, were as follows:

(1) To construct a dam or a deflecting jetty, preferably the former, at the Cross Tides.

(2) To widen the water-way opposite the city front to 575 feet.

(3) To deepen the channel by dredging at various points between the city and Tybee Roads.

The cost of this improvement was estimated at $481,320, not including the cost of jetties and bulkheads, which might be found necessary at Fig Island and other points along the river. It was believed by the author of the project, that "if the construction of jetties should precede dredging, a large portion of the material would doubtless be removed by the increasing scouring effect of the ebb current—probably enough to cover the cost of the jetties."

A Board of Engineers, to whom this project was referred, recommended its adoption, and advised the removal of the old King's Island Jetty, and suggested that it might be found necessary to construct a jetty extending eastward from the lower end of Fig Island. In the fiscal year ending June 30, 1875, work under this project was begun. It consisted in dredging at the Garden Bank, Wrecks, Upper Flats, and Tybee Knoll, and in the removal of two cribs from the South Channel and one wreck (sunk during the Revolutionary war) from near the Gulf Railroad wharves. Some work was also done at the Obstructions.

In the next fiscal year it was decided to abandon the tortuous channel at the Wrecks, and to open a new and straight channel along the south shore of the river. The river was also widened and deepened between King's and Hutchinson's islands, and dredging was done at various points between Cross Tides and the sea. In February, 1876, the closing dam at Cross Tides was begun. This structure was to consist of two rows of piling braced together, the openings between the front row being closed by sliding shutters, capable of being adjusted so as to regulate the flow of water into Cross Tides. The piling was to extend entirely across the stream, but an opening was to be left in the middle deep enough to allow the passage of small boats.

The State of South Carolina objected to the construction of this dam, and on May 13, 1876, work was suspended in compliance with a temporary injunction granted by the Supreme Court of the United States.

This injunction was removed, and work was resumed in March of the next year. In April a freshet carried away 186 feet of the outer end of the dam. The structure was so much injured that it was deemed best to suspend operations in order to consider the question of a modification of the original design of the dam. The engineer in charge, moreover, considered it inexpedient to resume work upon the dam until the waterway below should have been enlarged, so as to afford a free passage for the increased volume of water diverted into Front River by the dam.

In 1878, beyond dredging at the Oyster Beds and on the Knoll, the only work done was the removal of ten piles obstructing navigation at the Cross Tides.

During the next fiscal year dredging was done between Cross Tides and the Gulf Railroad Wharf in order to facilitate the entrance of the flood tide, and a new dam was begun at the Cross Tides. This dam was built 273 feet above the abandoned pile structure, and was composed of a compact mattress of brush and cane overlaid with riprap stone.

About two-thirds of the foundation was laid during the year. The appropriations from the beginning of the work in 1874 having been small, the urgent demands of commerce had required the expenditure of the greater part of the funds for dredging. In 1879 an enlarged project of improvement was submitted by General Gillmore, retaining the features of the project of 1873, but recommending the definite adoption of the north instead of the south channel, which involved the construction of a submerged dam across the South Channel, and the closing of all lateral channels from the head of Elba Island to Fort Pulaski. It also provided for shore protection at various points along the river where needed, as well as for dredging, a feature which was essentially embraced in the previous project. The eventual necessity of a jetty extending downstream from Fig Island, and the contraction of the channel from Elba to Cockspur islands was recognized, but no estimates were given for this work.

In 1880 the foundation of the Cross Tides Dam was completed, and its crest brought up with riprap stone to about 4 feet below mean low water. Part of the foundation course of the South Channel Dam was also laid in that year. It was built of log and brush mattresses, loaded with riprap stone. Dredging was done between the city and Cross Tides, and at the Garden Bank, Wrecks, and Obstructions, and a cut about 35 feet wide was made in the King's Island Jetty.

In the next fiscal year the Cross Tides Dam was completed. In many places its crest rose to mean low water, but near the Argyle Island end for a length of about 100 feet there was from 6 feet to 8 feet at low water over the dam. The changes produced in the river bed by this dam were very marked. In 1874, on a line 60 feet below the dam, the average depth at mean low water was 8 feet, the maximum depth being 16 feet. In 1881, the average depth on this line was 15 feet, with maximum depths of 36.5 feet.

In the same year the shore of Argyle Island adjacent to the Cross Tides Dam was protected against erosion, and the gap in the King's Island Jetty was enlarged to 70 feet.

Fig Island Point and Screven's Point were cut off. The bottom course of the South Channel Dam, 1,460 feet in length, was completed, and 394 feet of the second course was laid. Over a quarter of a million cubic yards were dredged at various points between Cross Tides and the Knoll.

In 1882 another modification of the original project of improvement was submitted. It retained all of the principal features of the two preceding projects, but provided in addition for a number of works designed to render the further improvement of the channel permanent.

The details of this project were:

(1) To raise the Cross Tides Dam to mean high water.

(2) To regulate the width of the river along the city front by enlarging the waterway at certain points and by contracting it by wing-dams at Garden Bank, where the widths are excessive.

(3) To construct a training wall extending from the lower end of Fig Island eastward about 1 mile, its crest to be about 3 feet above mean low water.

(4) To close the channels between Barnwell islands, to raise the South Channel Dam and to contract the river by wing-dams at various points between the head of Elba Island and Fort Pulaski.

Shore protection was alone provided for at various points along the river, as well as dredging upon all the shoals between the city and the sea.

The cost of this project was estimated at $730,000 making the total cost of improvement $1,212,000.

In the same year the Cross Tides Dam was raised to 3 feet above mean low water by brush mattresses and riprap stone, and the adjacent shore was revetted by log mattresses to protect it from scour. Two wing-dams were built at Garden Bank, reducing the width of the water-way from about 1,000 feet to 600 feet. A training wall with its crest 3 feet above mean low water, was built from the lower end of Fig Island 5,000 feet eastward; closing-dams were built at Philbrick's Cut, Big Gap, and Dutch Gap. All of these dams were built of log and brush mattresses, loaded with riprap stone. Over 100,000 cubic yards were dredged during the year between Cross Tides and Tybee Knoll.

In the following year it was found that the Cross Tides Dam had settled badly, its crest being in places from 4 to 6 feet below mean low water. About 700 cubic yards of stone were distributed over the work during the year. A third wing-dam was built at Garden Bank. A wing-dam was built just above the Fig Island training-wall, and the latter was extended 1,000 feet. The width of the bottom course of the original work varied from 20 to 40 feet, but as this had settled badly in places—especially at the Old Ship-channel Crossing—the width of the foundation course of the extension was made from 55 to 70 feet. Some stone was placed on the crest of the work to bring it to a uniform height, and eleven spurs were built on the channel side, making the width of the water-way between the end of the spur heads and mean low water on the opposite shore vary from 680 feet at the upper end to 740 feet at the lower end.

The Barnwells Island closing dams were constructed. A dam was built at the Obstructions, reducing the width of the channel to 1,000 feet, and four dams were built at the Upper Flats, reducing the low-water width of the channel at this point to from 1,050 feet to 1,100 feet.

The dams at Philbrick's Cut and at Big Gap had settled several feet at some points, and some stone was placed on these to bring their crests to a uniform height.

During the fiscal year ending 1884 wing-dams for the improvement of the Lower Flats Crossing were partly built. Some stone was put on the dam at Philbrick's Cut and dredging was done between the city and the Lower Flats.

In 1885 the Cross-Tides Dam, which had settled badly, was raised to mean high water by building above or on the up-stream side of its crest, the original crest being too narrow to be built upon. A wide apron mattress was sunk against its down-stream face to protect it against undermining. The log mattresses which were used settled some, and the gaps were filled with brush fascines and stone. Two wing-dams were built at the lower end of the Upper Flats Crossing, and the dams at the Lower Flats, the foundations of which were laid in 1883–'84, were completed. Two wing-dams were built at the Long Island Crossing, reducing the width of the river from 3,100 feet to 1,300 feet. The Oyster Bed Dam was begun, and dredging was done at various points between the city and Fort Pulaski.

In the fiscal year ending June 30, 1886, the Cross Tides Dam, which had settled in some places, was again brought up to mean high water. The crest of the Fig Island training wall was brought up to 5 feet above mean low water throughout. Some gaps in the dams at the Upper Flats were filled with brush fascines and stone. The dams at the Long Island Crossing, which had settled in a few places, were brought to an even crest with brush fascines and stone.

The crest of the Oyster Bed Dam was brought to about mean low water. The gaps in the Philbrick's Cut and Big Gap dams were filled with brush fascines and stone.

Dredging was done between the city and the Lower Flats. During the next fiscal year the Fig Island jetty was raised to mean high water and extended 750 feet. A small gap in Dam No. 25 was filled with brush fascines and stone; the dams at the lower flats and at the Long Island crossing, which were injured by the cyclone of 1885, were repaired; two wing-dams were built at the lower end of the Long Island crossing, reducing the width of the river to 1,350 feet, and the crossing dams at Philbrick's Cut and Big Gap were brought up to mean high water.

All of the dams upon the river are built of log mattresses of an average thickness of 15 inches. The mats are covered with from 4 to 9 inches of brush, and loaded with from 5 to 9 inches of stone, the top course receiving about 13 inches. In profile the shore ends of the dams are at high-water level, or at the height of the adjacent shore. The crest then slopes down to about 5 feet above mean low water, which height is maintained to within about 200 feet of the outer end of the dam; the crest then falls gradually to the outer end, where a toe or a wider lower mat is placed. Repairs, when needed, have in general been made by filling the holes with brush fascines loaded with riprap stone. [Pp. 1017–21]

For locations of the features mentioned by Carter, see Map 17, "Savannah Harbor, Ga., Showing Progress of Improvement to June 30, 1888," which was included with the 1888 report.

Although Lieutenant Carter's report is clear, a few items require further comment. He writes of dredging done in 1869 at "the channel north of the Oyster Beds," implying that the Oyster Beds were still being construed as a shoal or shallow area and not as an island.

It is also significant that the construction of a dam at Cross Tides was again objected to by South Carolina in the mid-1870s. The U.S. Supreme Court considered the complaint of South Carolina as a bill in equity "praying for an injunction restraining the State of Georgia, Alonzo Taft (Secretary of War), A. A. Humphries (Chief of the Corps of Engineers United States army), Q. A. Gilmore (lieutenant-colonel of that corps), and their agent and subordinates from 'obstructing or interrupting' the navigation of the Savannah River, in violation of the compact entered into between the States of South Carolina and Georgia on the twenty-fourth day of April, 1787" (93 U.S. 4 [1876], p. 5). The Court found that the defendants were not threatening the navigation of the river and pointed out that the two channels on either side of Hutchinson Island were parts of the same river and not separate entities. The closing of one to improve navigation in the other could not be construed as destroying or impeding the river's navigation. Further, the Court pointed out that the second article in the Beaufort Treaty had been nullified by the commerce clause of the U.S. Constitution to which both states were subject.[6]

Also of interest in Lieutenant Carter's 1888 report is the mention of a proposal in 1879 to adopt the north channel of the Savannah from the head of Elba Island to Fort Pulaski. This proposal involved the construction of a submerged dam across the south channel and closing all intervening lateral channels between the islands. The numerous subsequent projects that culminated in the carefully engineered and controlled lineaments that characterize the lower Savannah River of the present era resulted from those early decisions. From about 1880 onward, the course and flow of the river dramatically changed as the result of deliberate engineering efforts proposed and carried through by the Corps of Engineers.

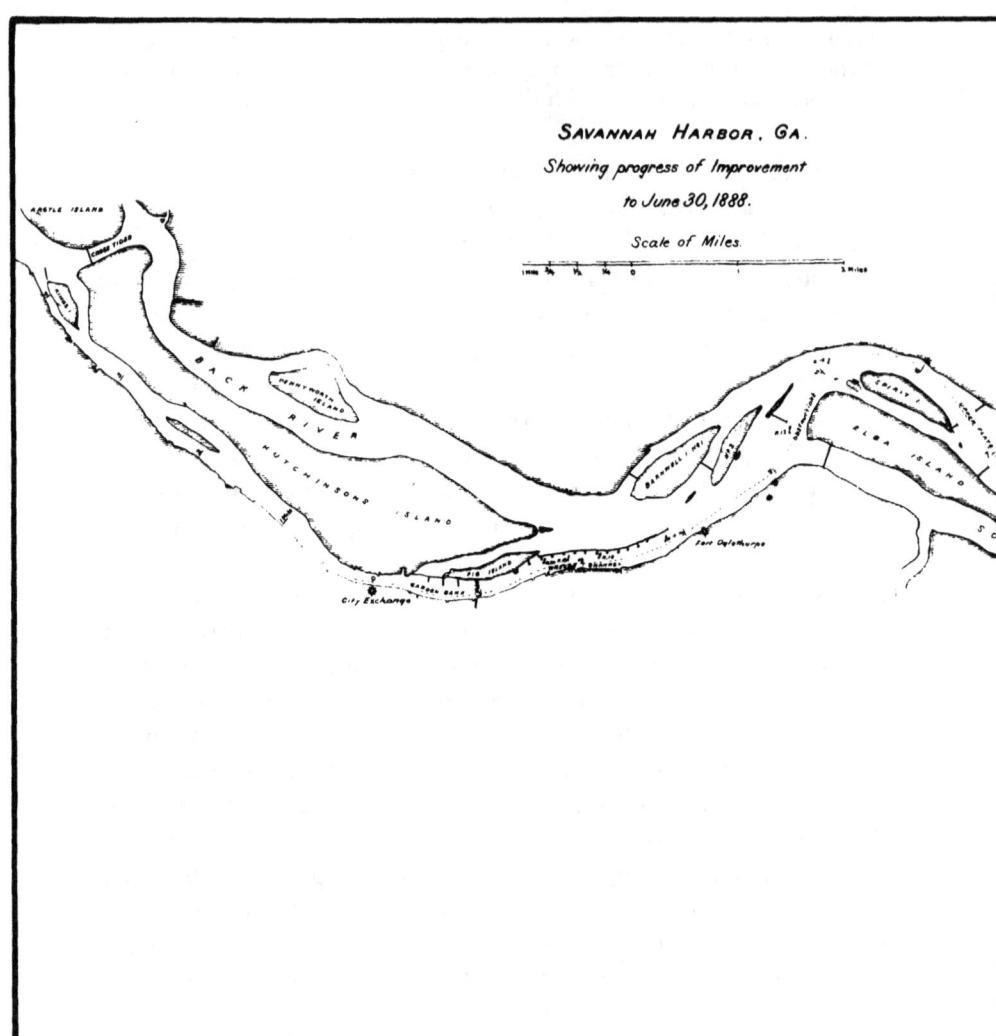

17. "Savannah Harbor, Ga., Showing Progress of Improvement to June 30, 1888." This map shows many of the dams and training walls built by the U.S. Army Corps of Engineers in the late nineteenth century.

The 1882 modification of the plan was to have a dramatic effect on conditions insofar as the boundary between Georgia and South Carolina was concerned. Included in the projects subsequent to this date were the intentional closing of "the channels between Barnwell islands" and the contracting or narrowing of the river "by wing-dams at various points between the head of Elba Island and Fort Pulaski." Such changes in island and bank morphology would be clearly avulsive in nature.

The construction of dams in the area known as the Upper Flats brought the northern bank of the river far to the south and sealed the already badly silted mouth of Mud River. Mud River had clearly been a branch of the lower Savannah from the earliest period through the Civil War, when it was utilized by Union forces in their siege of Fort Pulaski. Jones Island thus lost for a time its island character. When the Mud River Cut was excavated at a later date it once again took on the traditional characteristics of an island surrounded by water at all tidal stages.

The shoal area traditionally known as the Oyster Bed became the focus for a major current diversion dam and began to emerge as an island. Later enlargements and extensions of Oyster Bed training wall and other structures were to tie the island to the larger mass of Jones Island and eventually form the bulky peninsula now occupied by the U.S. Wildlife Refuge.

Through the use of better equipment and the application of refined theories of river development in the post–Civil War period profound changes were made in the morphology of the lower Savannah. More and more the area took on the character of a man-fashioned or engineered landscape. These efforts were extensively reported in both verbal and cartographic terms by the engineers involved. A detailed, step-by-step account of the changing morphology of islands and shorelines in the lowermost Savannah valley is thus included in the voluminous files of the Corps of Engineers, who came to assume the full responsibility for the river's improvement. Because much of this full account is readily accessible in the published annual reports of the corps from the late 1870s onward, only selected aspects of their work will be discussed through the remainder of this book.

Of particular value in clarifying and precisely locating the engineering efforts reviewed by Lieutenant Carter in his 1888 report are a number of maps and sketches dating from the 1870s and 1880s. Be-

Changes in the Lower Savannah River Area, 1787–1900 137

cause of their extremely large size it was not feasible to include most of these maps in this book. Maps 17 and 18 will be helpful in following the discussions of those maps omitted.

1871—"Sketch Showing Examination of the North Savannah River, Opposite Fort Pulaski. Made under the Direction of Major Q. A. Gillmore, Bvt. Maj. Gen'l. U.S.A. by Capt. William Ludlow, U.S. Engineers, Assisted by F. M. Eppley & C. Guerro. May 1871. Scale 1:5000" (Ms. notation on face of map—"Sent to the Chief of Engineers with letter of this date. New York Dec. 21, 1871. Q. A. Gillmore Maj. Egr. Bvt. Maj. Genl.")

This sketch of Fort Pulaski and the Oyster Bed directly north of it was designed to show the channel passing to the north of the Oyster Bed. Depth lines and soundings give a detailed statement of depths in this channel, which Lieutenant Carter had mentioned as being dredged in 1869. The Oyster Bed is indicated by a light dotted line probably intended to indicate a shoal area and not a shoreline as shown on Cockspur nearby.

1874—"U.S. Coast Survey Carlile P. Patterson Supdt. ENTRANCE TO SAVANNAH RIVER GEORGIA Surveyed in April 1874 Under the direction of Charles Hosmer Assistant By Wm. E. McClintock, Aid. Scale 1:5000"

This large manuscript chart is held in the file of the National Ocean Survey, Washington, D.C., under Register No. 1349. It is a very detailed sketch of the northern shoreline of Tybee Island, Cockspur Island, and the eastern tip of Long Island. Channel buoys and shoal areas are indicated. The area of the Oyster Bed shoal is depicted with a fine dotted outline shaped approximately as it was on the 1871 sketch. Additional features within the outline include "Oyster Bank Lt. Ho." on the upstream side and a "Stake with 2 Barrels" located with a heavy dot symbol. Written across the central portion is the caption "Sand & Shell Banks," providing a clue as to the origin and nature of the area outlined. Most significant is the placement of a pattern of symbols representing marsh vegetation along much of the northern portion of the area. If the evidence presented on these two maps is accepted as being essentially correct, it would seem that some marsh grass vegetation had begun to occupy the shallowest portions of the Oyster Bed by spring 1874 when the second survey was made.

1874—"U.S. Coast Survey Carlile P. Patterson Supdt. PART OF SAVANNAH RIVER GEORGIA Surveyed in April 1874 Under the directions of Charles Hosmer Assistant By John de Wolf. Scale 1:5000"

Located in the NOS file as Register No. 1348^b, this chart is an upriver continuation of the effort that produced the immediately preceding one. Stylistically it is similar, and it could easily be joined to the manuscript sheets to show the upstream and downstream areas adjoining. Bird Island and the upstream portion of Long Island plus two smaller unnamed islands are shown, as is the entrance of Wright River, but Jones Island is not named and appears only as the northern bankline of the Savannah. Shoreline and island configurations appear to be very carefully done and would make these maps valuable in plotting such features as political boundaries in the areas covered. They would also be valuable in assessing the local impact of a number of Corps of Engineers projects built in the succeeding years.

1874—"U.S. Coast Survey Carlile P. Patterson Supdt. ELBA ISLAND SAVANNAH RIVER GEORGIA Surveyed in April 1874 Under the directions of Charles Hosmer Assistant By Wm. E. McClintock, Aid. Scale 1:5000"

This detailed manuscript is in the files of the National Ocean Survey in Washington. Elba and an unlabeled Spirit Island and some smaller islands are the chief features on this sheet. The large scale permits identification of the dikes marking rice fields along the Savannah's shoreline from the mouth of St. Augustine Creek upstream. Of particular interest is the indication of the mouth of Mud River along the north shore.

1875—"Chatham County State of Georgia Compiled Exclusively From certified plats and maps of the most eminent local Surveyors Charles G. Platen . . . 1875"

Unlike the maps discussed above, this is a commercially produced effort. Although lacking in fine detail, it gives a reasonably accurate view of the lower Savannah River. Of particular interest is the depiction of Barnwell (here named Smiths) Island. A dam or causeway-type structure blocks the channel behind Smiths Island and connects it to another island that can be identified as the forty-six-acre Barnwell Island, which had been platted even before the Treaty of Beaufort was signed in 1787 (see Map 21 and discussion in Part IV). Mud River is shown flowing so as to make Jones Island an island in the Savannah River. The Oyster Bed shoal is north of Cockspur but is unnamed. A "Beacon" is located within the light dotted line indicating the shoal. Several Civil War fortifications in the Savannah area also appear on this map, including Fort Tatnall in the river near Smiths Island.

> 1879—"Chart of the Savannah River, Ga., from Barnwell Island to Tybee Roads, Accompanying project of improvement. Sent to the Chief of Engineers with my letter dated New York, March 19, 1879. Q. A. Gillmore Lieut. Col. Egns. Bt. Maj. Genl. U.S.A." (bar scale).

An important feature of this chart is the indication of the existing channel and the proposed channel in the river with heavy dashed line symbols. These lines show the existing navigation channel in 1879 and Gilmer's proposed straighter channel. Dams are in positions that would block the old south channel from Four Mile point down to Cockspur and Tybee. Other dams link Elba, Bird, Long, and Cockspur into a continuous division between the old, shallow south channel and the engineered north channel.

> 1880—"Chart of the Savannah River, Ga. from Savannah City to Tybee Roads Showing location of work of improvement now in progress accompanying annual report dated July 1, 1880."

This detailed chart is very similar to the one Gilmore forwarded in 1879. It, too, uses dashed lines to indicate the shift in the channel from the northern side of the Oyster Bed to the southern side abreast of Cockspur Island. Taken together the 1879 and 1880 charts provide a good view of conditions existing in the lower Savannah area at the close of the 1870s. On the 1880 chart, Colonel Gillmore included detailed sketches of the stone, log, and timber dams that were under construction at that time. These sketches are very helpful in clarifying the exact nature of the work referred to in several narrative reports.

During the 1880s, sketches and maps similar to those discussed above continued to be produced by the Corps of Engineers as they pursued their projected improvements in the Savannah River. The following are of particular value.

> 1883—"Progress Sheet No. 3 Showing Works Constructed Between Barnwell Island and Long Island To June 30, 1883. Under the Direction of Colonel Q. A. Gillmore, Corps of Engineers, Bvt. Maj. Gen. U.S.A. First Lieut. Thos. N. Bailey, U.S. Corps of Engineers, in local charge. T. H. Fisher, Asst. Eng." Scale of feet. Accompanying Annual Report of July 30th 1883, for the fiscal year ending June 30, 1883.

The dams connecting the Barnwell islands are numbered and dated 1883. A long jetty extends toward Elba Island from Barnwell No. 3 and is numbered No. 15 and dated 1883. Other wing dams are shown built out from opposite shores to constrict the river's flow to a gently curving channel or thalweg of even width up to the city of Savannah. The legend explains that soundings "are expressed in feet and tenths and are reduced to Mean Low Water." Soundings were either obtained by the engineers in 1882 or 1883 or taken from the Coast Survey chart of 1882. The twelve- and eighteen-foot depth curves are shown by line symbols as are the borders of the channel. This and similar progress sheets would be valuable in gauging the eventual impact of the works on the shore and island morphology as time passed.

> 1887—"Chart of the Savannah River, Ga. From Cross Tides to the Sea. From Surveys Made Under the Direction of Colonel Q. A. Gillmore, Corps of Engineers, Bvt. Maj. Gen. U.S.A. April–July 1887" (In three joining sheets marked "Accompanying my report of August 25, 1887 O. M. Carter 1st Lt. Corps of Engineers, U.S.A.").

As on similar preceding sheets, the dams, wing dams, and jetties built to confine the Savannah in a gently curving channel of even width down the length of the old North Channel and through the opening between the Oyster Bed and Cockspur Island are the dominant features. The dams are all numbered and dated. Soundings are numerous and expressed in feet and tenths in the river. A note in the legend indicates that "shore lines are taken from previous surveys." Dam 31 extends northwest from Oyster Bed toward a shoal area south of Turtle Island. Oyster Bed has a definite shoreline, and a set of symbols apparently indicating a pier and building are identified as "Quarantine." A small figure near the southern edge of Oyster Bed resembles "+2.2" and may indicate an elevation of 2.2 feet above mean low water here. A better copy of this sheet should be studied to verify this interpretation. The indications are that Oyster Bed was an island or considered nearly so by the engineers working there in 1887. Another interesting feature of Sheet III in this set is the presence of three long piers or works projecting out from the northern side of Tybee Island.

> 1887—"Chart of the Savannah River, Ga. from the head of Isla Island to the Sea. Accompanying report of First Lieut. O. M. Carter, Corps of Engineers, U.S.A. dated August 25, 1887."

This is a much smaller-scale chart and hence much less detailed than the set discussed above. Its main value is in presenting a good general view of the corps's efforts in controlling the Savannah's channel width and direction during this period. A note explains that the base map for this chart was the U.S. Coast Survey chart of 1867, so island and other configurations probably reflect that date rather than 1887.

> 1888—"Savannah Harbor, Ga., Showing Progress of Improvement to June 30, 1888."

This small-scale sketch accompanied Lieutenant O. M. Carter's report of 1888 and will help clarify much of that material discussed above at length (Map 17). Although still named simply Oyster Bed, the former shoal now has a definite outline, indicating that it is regarded differently from other shoals nearby.

In 1890, Lieutenant O. M. Carter's "revised project of improvement for Savannah Harbor and River with a view to obtaining a channel depth of 26 feet at mean high water from the city to the sea" was included with the corps annual report. Carter explained that this revision was based on information derived from surveys he directed in 1889 and 1890. The extremely detailed results of these surveys are fully reproduced as a lengthy appendix to the annual report of the chief of engineers of 1890. Of particular interest in the 1889–90 surveys is the data on tidal flow into and out of the river. Several gauging stations were established and a mass of data were collected so that solid empirical evidence could replace the theoretical assumptions that had underlain much of the earlier improvement work.

Typical of the insights these data provided are the following paragraphs quoted from Carter's report:

> The effect of Cross Tides Dam is strikingly illustrated. . . . Previous to its construction two-thirds of the entire volume of Savannah River passed through Cross Tides into Back River, and only one-third passed down Front River. Now the situation is precisely reversed.
>
> The relative size of volumes passing north and south of Oyster Bed is somewhat of a surprise, the importance of the northern opening being demonstrated by the survey to be much greater than was supposed. We should then proceed cautiously in the construction of such works as may be intended to partially close this opening.
>
> The results of the survey appear to indicate that a mean ebb velocity of about 2 feet per second is required to secure permanence of the channel. The general aim of the revised project will be to mold the riverbed from Cross Tides to the Sea in such a way as to allow the free ascent of the flood-tide, and to secure throughout, as far as practicable the above uniform mean velocity of ebb flow. [Oberlin M. Carter, "Project of Lieutenant O. M. Carter," p. 1260]

Among other provisions included in his revised plan of 1890, Carter recommended the construction of "training-walls and shore protection between the Lower Flats and Oyster Bed." The Lower Flats is the area adjacent to the upstream end of Jones Island. Carter also recommended "dredging south of Oyster Bed with a view of obtaining cross sectional areas of about 45,000 square feet for mean ebb outflow, in order to induce a stronger flow through the southern opening and thence over Tybee Knoll" (ibid., p. 1261).

The present-day configuration of the area of Cockspur Island and Oyster Bed Island is presaged in his observation that "it may become necessary to close the northern opening either by continuing the present jetty, No. 31, to the shore, or by building a training-wall from Long Island Flats to Oyster Bed; further to construct a training-wall running easterly from the lower end of Cockspur Island and finally to extend and raise the Oyster Bed training-wall" (ibid.). Clearly, the engineers were launched on a massive plan to refashion the shoreline and island configurations in the lowermost Savannah River as the 1890s began.

During the 1890s, interest in a possible steamboat channel between Beaufort, South Carolina, and Savannah, Georgia, drew the attention of the Corps of Engineers to a heretofore seldom mentioned area of the Savannah delta. This was the navigable distributary channel known as Mud River, which had bounded Jones Island until it began to silt in badly in the post–Civil War period.

By the existing route that ran through Walls Cut and Wright River and around the eastern end of Jones Island, the distance from Beaufort to Savannah was fifty-two statute miles. In his report dated January 22, 1895, Captain O. M. Carter wrote of the waterway known as Wright River as "shoaling and will soon be closed." Carter proposed two possible routes for development in the future. The first of these ran "from Walls Cut up Wrights River into Mud River and thence by a cut about 3000 feet long through the marsh into Savannah River. The distance from Beaufort to Savannah by this route will be 49 statute miles." A second possible route was "from Walls Cut down Wrights River along Dam No. 31 into Savannah River. The distance from Beaufort to Savannah by this route will be 54 statute miles." In his discussion of the shorter Mud River route, Carter observed: "The opening of that route will change materially the conditions now existing in that locality. Mud River will become a connecting channel between Savannah River and Wrights River, and the tidal conditions show that the ebb current will flow from the former into the latter, the flood current flowing in the opposite direction" (Oberlin M. Carter, "Survey for Steamboat Channel, Seven Feet Deep at Mean Low Water, between Beaufort, S.C., and Savannah, Ga.," p. 3). Carter supported this contention with specific hydraulic data. He further emphasized that a reopened Mud River would drain off a significant volume of the Savannah River's discharge and possibly prove injurious to the dredged channels and other works between Mud River's mouth and Tybee. During the Savannah's periodic freshets, he argued, there was the further possibility that "large volumes of Savannah River sediment will be carried through Mud River and be deposited in Wrights River" (ibid.). A review of Carter's findings leaves little room for doubt concerning the nature and function of Mud River as a distributary of the Savannah River. In the terms of the Treaty of Beaufort, it is correctly to be construed as "the most northern branch or stream of the River Savannah" immediately within the "mouth" formed by Hilton Head and Tybee islands. In 1787 water from the Savannah drainage basin flowed through it just as it did Back River some miles upstream.

In a letter dated December 20, 1894, several members of Savannah's Cotton Exchange and Board of Trade wrote in favor of a reopened Mud River route: "The old and much used route via Mud River was closed about 1861, but basing our ideas upon its reopening and improvement, thus making a route both safer and shorter we present the following (ibid., p. 4).

The 1861 date for the abandonment of the Mud River as a commercial routeway may be early. In the spring of 1862, intense military operations began in the lower Savannah, chief among them the siege of Fort Pulaski. In his report on the siege, General Q. A. Gillmore noted with reference to Jones Island and Mud River:

> 18. It was known to General Sherman before that time [January 1862], that gunboats of medium draught could enter the river above Fort Pulaski, without encountering any batteries; on the south side through Wassaw Sound, Wilmington Narrows (or Freeborn's Cut), and St. Augustine Creek; and on the north side, through New River, Wall's "Cut," and either Wright or Mud River.
>
> 20. Mud River is navigable, at high spring tide, for vessels of eight and a half to nine feet draught. Wright River bar has about eleven and a half feet of water at ordinary high tide.
>
> 29. Jones Island is nothing but a mud marsh, covered with reeds and tall grass. The general surface is about on the level of ordinary high tide. There are a few spots of limited area, Venus Point being one of them, that are submerged only by spring tides, or by ordinary tides favored by the wind; but the character of the soil is the same over the whole Island. It is a soft, unctuous mud, free of grit or sand, and incapable of supporting a heavy weight. Even in the most elevated places, the partially dry crust is but three or four inches in depth, the substratum being a semifluid mud, which is agitated like jelly by the falling of even small bodies upon it, like the jumping of men, or ramming of earth. A pole or an oar

can be forced into it with ease, to a depth of twelve or fifteen feet. In most places the resistance diminishes with increase of penetration. Men walking over it are partially sustained by the roots of reeds and grass, and sink in only five or six inches. When this top support gives way, they go down from two to two and one-half feet, and in some places much further. [Gillmore, *Official Report . . . of the Siege and Reduction of Fort Pulaski*, pp. 11–14]

General Gillmore provided much additional information on Jones Island and Mud River in the form of extracts from his personal journal. Naval officers found that "Mud River has about one and one-half feet of water in it at extreme low tide, with a very soft, almost semifluid bottom" (ibid., p. 16). Vegetation on the northern part of Jones Island was cut to lessen the danger of fire when a wharf and causeway were built for moving guns and material to Venus Point. Prodigious efforts were involved in this phase of the Pulaski siege.

At about the same time that he was supervising the investigation of the possible inland passage from Beaufort to Savannah, Captain Carter was also looking into the need for improved anchorages in Tybee Roads. The Savannah Cotton Exchange and Board of Trade had informed the state's congressional delegation of the pressing need for protected anchorages in the Tybee Roads area. As a result, the 1894 River and Harbor Act included the requirement for a report on the probable effectiveness of the works then in progress for achieving that end.

Carter found that these works included no provisions "for the sheltering of that anchorage" (Oberlin M. Carter, "Modified Project of Improvement of Harbor at Savannah, Ga.," p. 3). The Oyster Bed and Cockspur training walls were designed to ensure only a navigable channel and not a protected anchorage for ships waiting to pass up the river to Savannah's busy wharves. By examining available records, Carter determined that one-third of all the winds observed in the area over a sixteen-year period "were from the northeast and east, while all of the severe storms during that period were from the same direction" (ibid.). The value of shipping annually anchoring in exposed Tybee Roads was placed at $32,000,000. In addition to protecting this shipping, Carter felt that additional protective works would be necessary to maintain channel depths, which were vulnerable to serious silting during storm periods.

To provide the desired protected anchorage ground to the north-

northeast of Tybee Island, Carter proposed to extend the Oyster Bed training wall and build a detached training wall segment "parallel to the currents along the axis of the shoal between Tybee Roads and Calibogue Sound" (ibid.). This detached training wall was built and can be seen on the 1971 U.S. Geological Survey's map "Savannah Beach North," scale 1:24,000. On the USGS map the feature is approximately a mile and a quarter long, lying to the north of Tybee Roads and marked "Submerged Breakwater."

An interesting feature of the corps's 1895 annual report is Carter's "Index Map of Savannah Harbor Georgia Showing Progress of Improvements to June 30, 1895" (Map 18). Included with the map is a "Profile of Savannah River from Cross Tides to the Sea," which graphically demonstrates the changes in channel depth along the thalweg from 1884 to 1895. It forms a dramatic statement of the effectiveness of the corps's programs during that decade of intense channel improvement effort.

In the annual report for 1896, however, some doubt was expressed concerning the long-term effectiveness of the project in maintaining the desired depth. In Carter's words, the Savannah's bed had "failed to make up in depth for what it has lost in width through the works of contraction." It appeared that the decrease in the size of the riverbed being achieved had in turn caused a decrease of tidal volume moving in and out of the system. In discussing this condition, Carter drew attention to the Barnwell islands area: "At Obstructions the ebb volume is somewhat more than 900,000,000 cubic feet, an increase as compared with former conditions, which was brought about through the closing of the various Barnwell Island channels and to which is due the present much greater stability of the channel in this region" (Oberlin M. Carter, "Improvement of Rivers and Harbors in Eastern Georgia," p. 1222). The dams connecting the three Barnwell islands to the relict forty-six-acre island and the Barnwell Island training wall linking the whole to the South Carolina shore opposite the head of Elba Island were obviously proving to be effective insofar as adjacent channel depth was concerned. Although not of immediate interest to the engineers, these works, like the North Elba Island training wall, Jones Island spur dams, North Long Island training wall, and Oyster Bed training walls, were combining to create major realignments in the course and width of the lower Savannah River. These realignments in turn would result in a serious potential for misunderstanding and controversy concerning the correct location of the Georgia–South Carolina boundary as human interest in the area increased in the twentieth century.

The 1900 annual report of the corps included a comprehensive review and evaluation of the Savannah Harbor improvement efforts of the preceding decade. The board of examining engineers found the projects begun in 1890 to be generally successful. They did, however, suggest that certain changes were needed. The following extract formed the final section of their report and provides a view of the direction efforts would take in the pre–World War I period:

SUMMARY OF CHANGES SUGGESTED

The changes suggested in the present project may therefore be briefly summarized as follows:

The removal of the old Cross Tides dam; the change of the general project so as to provide a channel for boats drawing 24 feet instead of providing for a channel depth of 26 feet; the substitution of dredging between training walls and outside their ends and on the ocean bar, and the dredging of three up-river mooring basins and establishment of mooring posts or dolphins at the same instead of the removal of the quarantine middle-ground shoal and of the construction of the attached and detached extensions of the Oyster Bed training wall; the substitution of route No. 1 from Wrights River, through Mud River, instead of the unfinished portion of route No. 2; the opening of a new smallboat passage through the dikes and training walls near the foot of Elba Island; and the prohibition of all future dumpage in Savannah River below Cross Tides dam, except where needed for harbor improvement.

By the adoption of the changes suggested above, the project for the further improvement of Savannah Harbor and the steamboat channel from Beaufort, S.C., to Savannah, Ga., would be as follows:

To remove Cross Tides dam; to maintain all other existing training walls, dams, and dikes; to do the necessary work of dredging to obtain and maintain a channel from Savannah to the sea suitable for vessels of 24 feet draft at mean high water, depositing all dredged material outside the limits of the river; to establish and maintain three mooring stations between Savannah and the sea; to open and maintain a steamboat channel of sufficient width and 7 feet draft at low water from Beaufort, S.C., to Savannah, Ga., by way of Mud River;[7] and to open and maintain a small-boat passage of 20 feet width and 3 feet length at low water through the dikes and training walls near the foot of Elba Island. [Clinton B. Sears, W. H. Bixby, and Thomas W. Symons, "Report of Board of Engineers on Project for Improvement of Savannah Harbor," p. 1927]

Hurricanes, storm tidal surges, freshets, local floods, and tornadoes visited the lower Savannah on several occasions in the years following

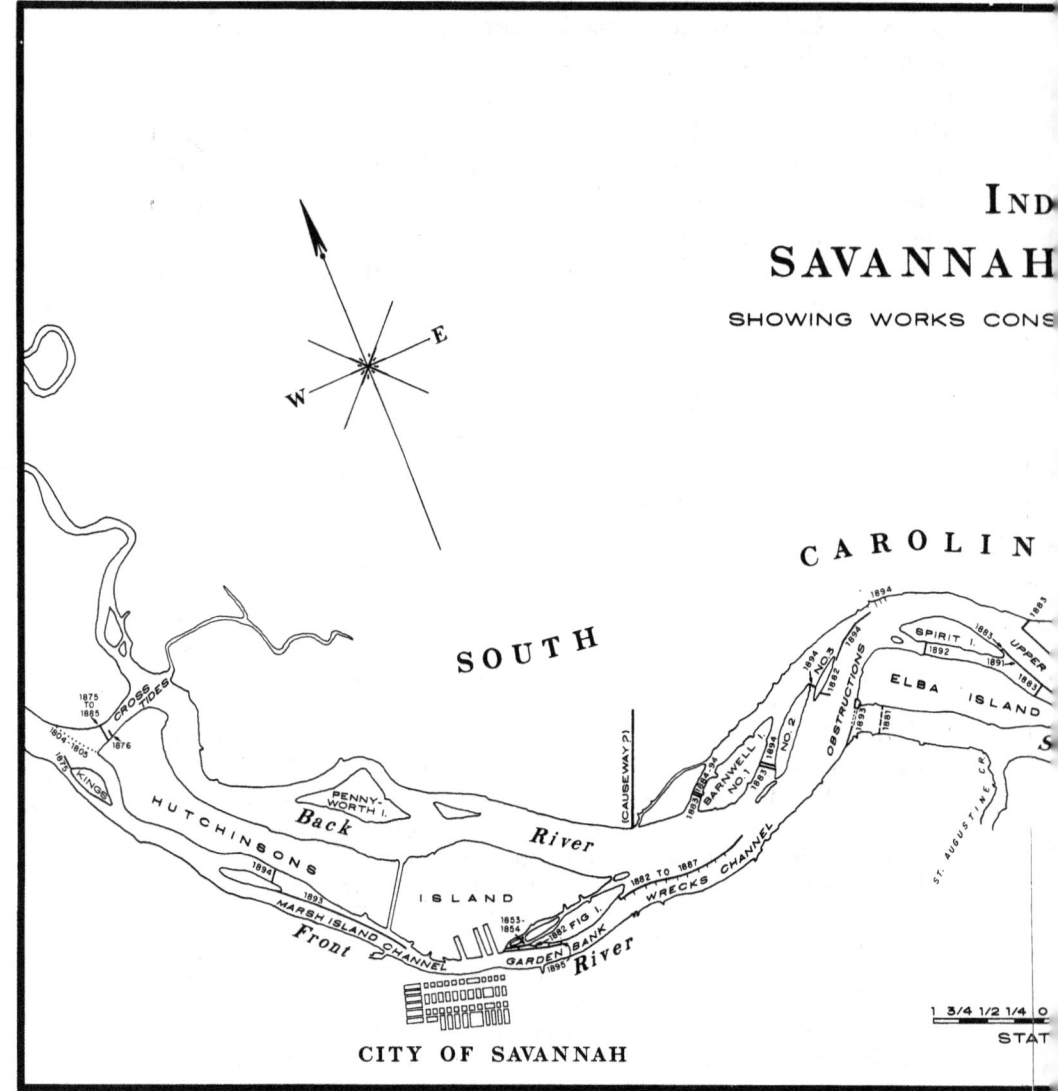

18. Index Map, Savannah River, Georgia, showing works constructed from 1804 to 1896. This map was redrawn from an original done by the U.S. Army Corps of Engineers. Here one can see when the dams, training walls, jetties, and other works that radically altered the lower Savannah River were built.

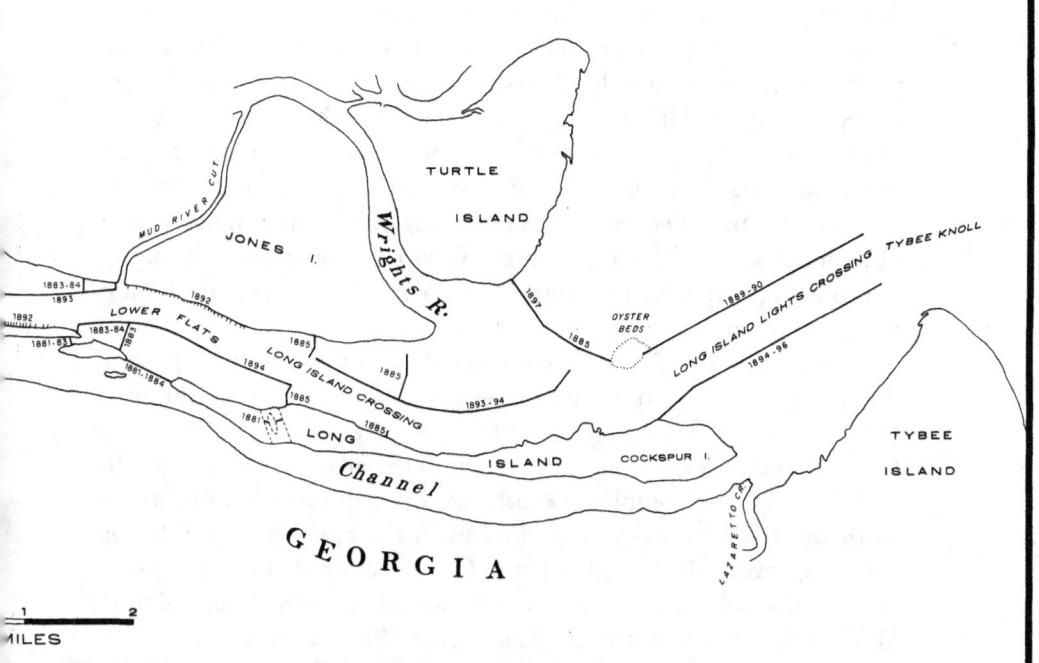

the signing of the Treaty of Beaufort. No systematic record of these events seems to have been kept, and references to them are noticeably few in the published reports of the Corps of Engineers. In an attempt to gain some appreciation of the possible effects of these violent natural phenomena in the lower Savannah area, local newspapers and other historical sources were searched. Although the results of this effort are not entirely satisfactory, they do indicate that natural catastrophes occurred with sufficient force to cause possible changes in the island and riverbank morphology of the area during the period from 1787 to about 1900. Unfortunately, the style of eighteenth-century journalism was such that few local happenings were reported even though political events in remote corners of Europe were often exhaustively discussed. The small size of the community being served probably ensured that all local news was learned firsthand and did not require formal publication in the gazettes. One should conclude that some natural events of catastrophic dimensions may have visited the lower Savannah area but went unreported in the press during the postrevolutionary decade. In the early nineteenth century, the growth of national self-interest and community size probably led to a change in reporting emphasis, and local events began to receive considerably more attention.

On the morning of September 8, 1804, Savannah citizens witnessed the worst hurricane to strike the Georgia coast since the founding of the colony in 1733. According to the *Georgia Republican and State Intelligencer*'s eyewitness account, the storm raged all day and late into the night. A scene of complete devastation greeted those who ventured forth the following day. Many houses in the city were mere heaps, chimneys everywhere had collapsed and scattered themselves over the general debris, the wharves and business houses along the town bluff were entirely destroyed, fallen trees blocked every main street, the walls of old Christ Church showed signs of splitting, and the Presbyterian Church steeple lay in pieces in the street. Further investigation indicated that the river had suffered equally from the onslaught. Every ship in the harbor had been wrecked, and the rice fields along the river were flooded and ruined by the saltwater. A complete submersion of Hutchinson Island had drowned nearly one hundred slaves on plantations there. One newspaper editor ventured as far as Cockspur Island to examine the storm's effects. His report hints at the hurricane's tremendous alterations of various riverine features:

"Some idea may be formed of the force and violence of the late storm from the traces it has left at Cockspur. On the island not a vestige of the former buildings is remaining, and the surface is much below its former height" (*Georgia Republican and State Intelligencer*, September 14, 1804). The former buildings mentioned in this news account were probably associated with Fort Greene, which had been built in 1794–95 as a part of President George Washington's national defense policy. The fort was totally destroyed and several of the garrison were killed in the hurricane.

The year following the great storm of 1804, another less severe hurricane hit the Georgia coast and destroyed portions of Bethesda Orphanage, just south of Savannah. The city again experienced the effects of a powerful storm in October 1824. Several tempests swept over Savannah during the next thirty years, including the "severe storm of wind and rain" that "visited" the coastal area in August 1851, lifting rooftops into the air "like sheets of tissue paper" (*Daily Morning News*, August 25, 1851, 2/2). However, the immensely destructive gale of 1854 overshadowed the damage caused by these milder disturbances.

A stiff breeze and heavy rain ushered the 1854 storm into Savannah on September 8. The wind velocity increased that evening and wreaked havoc on the town and river throughout the night. The *Savannah Morning News* printed a full report of the hurricane the following day:

> We noticed in a short paragraph in yesterday's *News*, the prevalence of a strong northeasterly wind which continued during the entire day and up to 10 o'clock at night, when we made our notice of it. But little did we think at the time that it was the precursor of the severest and most destructive storm that has visited our city since October, 1824. It may be regarded as a singular coincidence, that on the 8th of September, 1804, just fifty years ago, a like storm prevailed and continued, unabated, for three days. Then a large amount of property was destroyed in crops, building, and cattle. We understand from those whose memories extend back to that period, that large numbers of negroes were lost to the plantations to the southward.
>
> Whilst we would feign be hopeful that the present storm would deal less harshly with our city and the country wherever its ravages may extend, we see but little grounds for hope. At eleven o'clock yesterday forenoon, what we regard as the most serious damage that could result to Savannah, from the storm, was completed. Hutchinson's Island at that time was entirely submerged; and as far as the eye could reach, looking

north and east from an elevated point on the bay, the rice plantations in South Carolina were in like condition. It is estimated that the depth of water on Hutchinson's Island and the plantations north of it must have been from six to eight feet. The rice plantations below the city must also have been inundated and to a greater depth than those directly opposite the city. The loss to the owners of these plantations, by the total destruction of their crops, can scarcely be computed. . . .

At 2 o'clock, P.M., the wind increased to a hurricane, and was accomplished by a heavy driving rain. In the eastern part of the city, the wharves and cotton yards were covered with water to the depth of several feet, and we learn a large amount of goods stored there has been damaged by the water. The large brick wall of the old Georgia Steamboat Company Yard is blown down. . . .

Great fears are entertained for the safety of the negroes on Hutchinson's Island. The water rose so rapidly, that it is believed many of them have perished. To send them aid from this side was impossible, no boat could live five minutes in the seas. We learn that several attempts were made to launch life boats, but in every instance they were immediately filled. A gentleman informs us that with the use of a spy-glass, he saw a negro house blown down. All the cattle on the island supposed to number upwards of a thousand head, have no doubt perished—a number was seen carried off by the force of the water. This island, but a day or two since, presented a beautiful appearance, being in a high state of cultivation. Yesterday it presented the appearance of an inland sea violently agitated whose waves were driven in every direction by the high wind. Nothing could be seen on it but the houses and large trees. . . .

The shipping along our wharves must have suffered to some extent. During the day several vessels broke from their moorings and drifted up the river. Their names we could not learn, nor the extent of damage which they sustained. The brig *Amelia*, just discharged, was nearly blown upon the wharf and lays in a dangerous situation. It is feared that the shipping at Tybee has sustained serious injury. Among the vessels at that place is the British ship *Lady Westmoreland*, from Cardiff, Wales, with railroad iron, just arrived.

The damage to the rice crop must be very great. A considerable quantity had been harvested, but the high water on the plantations has no doubt destroyed a large amount in the graneries. Much anxiety is felt for the safety of the negroes on the plantations in South Carolina opposite the city. As far as we could see they (the plantations) are all covered with water. . . .

The reader at a distance will be able to form some ideas of the gale, when we state that the Savannah Dry Dock parted from her moorings and floated up the river. She ran afoul of the schooner *Manhasrett*, lying at Habersham's wharf, and into the ship *Hartford*, bark *Flight* and brig *Joseph*. What damage, if any, these vessels sustained, we could not learn. The Dry Dock, by great effort, was finally made fast to the wharf.

Major Stark's Saw Mill on Fig Island was unroofed, and a large amount of timber floated off.

If anything further was wanted to give the reader at a distance an idea of the great and destructive gale which swept over our city yesterday, it will suffice to state, that the Light House on the eastern end of Fig Island, known as Fig Island Light, was swept off about 1 o'clock in the afternoon. It is feared that the keeper was carried off with this building, and apprehensions for his safety are felt. He raised a flag of distress during the afternoon, and the flag was flying on the building when it was washed away. We could not learn any further intelligence in relation to this subject. . . .

Up to 12 o'clock last night, at the time of closing this article, the gale still prevailed, but at that time seemed to lull at times, as if old Boreas was satisfied with his destruction, and desirous to take repose. Thus we close a hurried account of one of the most disastrous gales ever felt on the coast of Georgia. May He who holds our destinies in his hand, stay the tempest and the pestilence which now afflict and surrounds us. [*Savannah Morning News*, September 9, 1854]

The destructive 1854 hurricane seemed to herald an onslaught of storms throughout the remainder of the decade. The gale of 1858 proved especially disastrous. The local newspaper claimed the accompanying wind and rain "to have been the heaviest blow experienced in Savannah since 1854" (ibid., August 14, 1858, 2/1). Following the Civil War, reports of storms, gales, and cyclones became a common feature in the *Savannah Morning News*. Available evidence does not indicate whether the magnitude and frequency of these occurrences were a phenomenon peculiar to the last half of the nineteenth century along the Atlantic coast, or whether many storms in the early part of the century simply went unreported in the local newspapers. In any event, the journalists of the 1870s, 1880s, and 1890s wrote of the recurring disasters in great detail and left an excellent record of the natural forces that may have altered the morphology of the Savannah River during this period.

An unusually high spring freshet flooded the river and plantations around Savannah in March 1870. On March 28, the *Savannah Morning News* announced that the water had seriously interfered with "planting operations" and in some cases had drastically hurt "the rice prospect for the coming year." Troublesome as the freshet seemed, the series of storms in the summer of 1871 brought absolute catastrophe. The first storm of wind and rain passed over Savannah on July 17, raising huge sand and dust clouds. The *Morning News* observed on the eighteenth that "female pedestrians who were caught out on the streets were seen in deplorable plight. Crinoline could not be forced to obey the laws of gravity."

The next summer squall blew into Savannah on August 18, 1871. By the following day entire portions of the town lay under water, and the *Morning News* reported "several persons taking a swim about the Baptist Church." The storm worsened and still raged on August 21. The *Morning News* undertook to describe the "nights of horror" as best it could. The ground floor of almost every structure in Savannah lay submerged. The railroad yards and plantations west of the city gave the appearance of a gushing "millrace." A number of railroad bridges and culverts collapsed. Ships on the river were sunk or drifting, and the wharf area was a tangle of flooded debris. The river appeared more swollen than ever before "in the history of Savannah." Two days later, another fierce wind and driving rains paralyzed the city. The extremely high tides in the river broke several key dams and flooded hundreds of dry-culture areas (ibid., August 23, 1871, 3/1).

The year 1874 brought another rash of storms. A cyclone or tornado roared through downtown Savannah on July 5 (ibid., July 6, 1874, 3/1), and a powerful electrical storm produced panic among the citizenry in September (ibid., September 18, 1874, 3/3). The lightning was followed several days later by devastating wind, rain, and high tides. On September 30 the *Morning News* reported on the storm's complete destruction of Tybee Island:

> A special telegram to the *Morning News* from Tybee gives the following information in regard to the gale, at that point. The day commenced with a very heavy rain and blowing a gale from the eastward. The tide rose so high that the island from the beacon light to the west end was flooded to the depth of three feet. About ten o'clock the wind changed suddenly to the westward and blew about fifty miles an hour with heavy rain and hail. . . . The tide made a clean sweep from the beach to the marsh in the rear. . . .
>
> It is believed that if the wind had continued in the same direction, and with the same velocity half an hour longer, the entire island would have been submerged. The east end was washed away about fifty feet, and the high hills were levelled. The Light House shook fearfully.

Savannah was again submerged in September 1878 with the arrival of a terrific gale that "had had no parallel since the fearfully destructive gale of September 8, 1854" (ibid., September 13, 1873, 3/3). Extremely high tides flooded most plantations along the Savannah and Back rivers. On the day following the storm the newspaper printed an account of the damage caused by the flooding:

> The destructive storm which had been working up since last Friday along the Gulf coast, and culminated at Savannah on Wednesday in a terrific gale and heavy rain, entailed, as was expected, great loss upon the rice planters along the Savannah, Back, and Ogeechee rivers. . . .
>
> Yesterday morning early all the planters left the city for their respective plantations to ascertain the extent of the damage and take such measures as were necessary to save what had been left of their crops. They returned last evening with the information that scarcely a plantation in this section had escaped, many of them being under two and three feet of water. In conversation with several of these gentlemen last night we ascertained that whilst the individual losses occasioned by the storm of 1874 were possibly greater, yet the present disaster is more general, the entire rice interest suffering, and the aggregate loss will be heavier.
>
> On the Savannah and Back rivers there are in all 11,000 acres under rice cultivation, whilst on the Ogeechee there are 4,000 acres.
>
> The plantations opposite Fort Jackson were completely submerged, the water extending from the highland on the Carolina side to the highland on this side, the river at that point being fully six miles wide. . . .
>
> About three hundred yards of bank on Mr. C. F. Stubb's place, on Hutchinson's Island, were washed out.
>
> Some damage is also reported to the banks of the city's land on the island, but we are informed that none of these breaks are very serious, and can be repaired without great expense. [Ibid., September 13, 1878, 3/3]

In a subsequent report on the state of Tybee Island, the *Morning News* provided striking evidence of the rapid effects of erosion on that island: "Sixteen years ago the old 'Little Light' on Tybee was inside of the sand hills, now its foundations can just be seen at low water. . . . The continued washing away of this end of the island must inevitably affect our bar channel" (ibid., September 16, 1878, 3/3). A fierce gale in August 1881 further damaged Tybee Island, as well as Savannah proper. According to the *Morning News* of September 5, "The slew which was made through the sand hills into Beacon Pond during the terrific storm of Saturday night, is increasing in width and threatens to cut off a part of the eastern beach from the Island. . . . This part of Tybee includes land of the Government. Unless something is done about it, it will soon be entirely inundated."

The 1880s saw the beginning of severe spring and fall floods on the

Savannah River. On August 14, 1887, a seventy-year-old gentleman addressed the *Morning News* "on the subject of the recent floods that caused so much destruction in this State." He cited the present floods as "greater and more destructive" than past floods "because the trees that once lined the banks of the stream have, in large measures, been cut away." The newspaper editor agreed that the destructiveness of the annual floods had indeed increased "in proportion to the removal of the forest."

The *Morning News* reported that during the freshet in August 1887, the exess water, in addition to flooding the lowlands and plantations around the river, was "finding outlets in New river, South Carolina" (ibid., August 15, 1887, 8/1). When the even higher September floods of 1888 came, the Savannah again found an outlet in the South Carolina marshlands. On September 19, 1888, the *Morning News* reported: "Savannah river crossed the country between Ferrebeeville and Hardeeville and poured a volume of water three miles into New River, it may prove disastrous to crops there. This cut off had much to do with lowering the height of the water here. The danger to the banks will be irreparable until the water recedes entirely from fields." The river continued to rise for several days, and a heavy rain also fell in Savannah. The local newspaper described the impressive scene: "Looking over the vast expanse of water fronting the city one can not form an idea of the ravages of the flood. . . . An immense lake spread out for miles where less than a week ago were thousands of acres of rice. . . . The river is five miles wide at Mulberry Grove" (ibid., September 22, 1888, 8/1).

The terrible 1888 flood, typical of what Savannahians were beginning to expect on an annual basis, inspired an editorial in the *Morning News*. In outlining the causes of the flood, the editor expressed his feeling toward federal improvements on the river:

> What caused the damage of the recent freshet which resulted in such disaster to the planters on the Savannah River, is worthy of investigation of the representatives in Congress whose constituencies are the sufferers by its devastations. That the greater part of the rice crop destruction was caused by the improvements made by the government for the benefit of the commerce of our country is capable of proof. Competent parties observed the freshet had no dangerous effect upon the Front River, as the water did not attain a height greater than an ordinary spring tide. It would appear from this that the volume of water found its exit else-

where. It was backed up by the crosstides dam at the upper end of Hutchinson's Island until it attained a height and volume sufficient to go over the rice field dams, and the river left its natural channels, and swept in one immense sheet over the plantations below, and also backed up the water on the places above. Year after year, the planters of Georgia and South Carolina lost their crops and were made bankrupt by the damming of the main channels of the river, above the city. The planters protested against the building of the cross-tides dams because they feared the water from the Back river would be entirely diverted to the Front river. The river has been diverted but not in that direction. The narrow channel left for the exit of its waters is not sufficient during a freshet, and the pent up flood is diverted and rushes madly over all the low-lands on its way to the Ocean. Sweeping before it, hundreds of thousands of dollars worth of property. The government had the power to remedy these disasters by building a levee along the river. . . . No question is more important to the constituents of the Congressmen from Georgia and South Carolina than that here presented. [Ibid., September 22, 1888, 4/1]

The construction of a levee by the U.S. Corps of Engineers did alleviate future disasters resulting from high freshets, but no amount of improvements could arrest nature. The hurricanes of 1893 and 1896 were long remembered in coastal Georgia for their destruction of life and property. Then in 1898 two cyclones struck Savannah, the first flooding the surrounding country "for fifty miles" and the second covering Hutchinson Island with a sheet of water (A. E. Scholes, *Chronological History of Savannah*, pp. 95, 104, 113). Each of these disasters occurred in spite of all precautions taken along the river to prevent flooding.

During these storms, as in every flood and gale since 1804, tremendous amounts of sediment were redistributed and channels modified. The effects on island and bank morphology are nearly impossible to determine with any degree of precision from the evidence available. It does appear, however, that natural phenomena such as those discussed here should be kept in mind as any effort to reconstruct past island and riverbank patterns is undertaken.

NOTES

1. Other dredge operators appear to have done the same thing here. Writing in 1854, First Lieutenant John Newton mentioned that dredge spoil being removed at the wrecks and Garden Banks had been "dropped in a pocked

channel existing on the wreck bank" (John E. Ward, *Report of John E. Ward, Mayor of the City of Savannah for the Year Ending 31st October 1854*, p. 15).

2. It is uncertain whether this area coincides with the Oyster Bed shoal, which evolved later into Oyster Bed Island and peninsula. If it is the same area, this statement may assist in gauging the rate of deposition which took place here in the past.

3. Gibbet was an early name for present day Elba Island (see Map 13).

4. The disposal of the mud and sand from the dredging sites drew considerable attention for a reason that seems unusual in present-day terms. During the mid-nineteenth century, ideas other than the germ theory were employed in efforts to explain the cause and spread of disease, especially the seasonal febrile maladies that had become epidemic. The Savannah mayor's report for 1854 included the following two letters, which are worthy of full quotation here:

Charleston, S.C. 9th November, 1854

Hon. John E. Ward, Mayor.

Dear Sir—In reply to your letter just received, I have to state, (without opportunity of looking over returns), that about 90,000 cubic yards have been taken out of the channels over the Garden Banks and the Wrecks.

All the material from the bottom was deposited until July on the S.C. shore, near Hog Island, distant about four or five miles from Savannah. After that time they were dropped in a pocked channel existing on the wreck bank, and have never, I believe, been exposed for a moment to the air. I regard the assumption of sickness eminating from such cause, as the most unwarranted possible. Capt. Cercopely can give you the most minute information on this subject if you require more.

I am Sir, your most respectfully,

John Newton, First Lieut. Engineers

Hon. John E. Ward, Mayor.

Dear Sir—As you wish information from me, in regard to dredging done in Savannah River, I will comply with your request as near as possible. I have been Inspector of the dredging under Capt. Gilmer and Lieut. Newton's instructions, and I must in the first place say, that the material taken from the bottom of the river, has never been deposited on any of the wharves. All the material has been deposited, at different places, generally in back river, and points near the Carolina shore, as directed by the officers, about four or five miles from the City, and have never for a moment been exposed to the air, excepting at the time the Scows were loading, and when loaded they were immediately towed to the places above mentioned, and the mud dropped in six or seven feet water.

Your wish to understand how the Scows are constructed, they are so constructed, that by the means of a trap door the material drops through the bottom. (As regards the assumption of sickness originating from such a cause), it is in my opinion very absurd and inconsistent. Why did we not have yellow fever last year, when dredging was in operation from about June to November.

I am yours, etc.,

Frances J. Gercopely.

5. For a review of these activities, see Department of Commerce, U.S. Coast and Geodetic Survey, *Descriptions of Triangulation Stations in Georgia*, by Clarence H. Swick, Special Publication No. 45 (Washington, 1917).

6. See *South Carolina v. Georgia et al.*, Supreme Court, October 1876 (93 U.S. 4), pp. 4–14.

7. An undated map in the files of the Savannah District Office of the U.S. Corps of Engineers shows the "New Dredged Cut Mud River." The map is titled "Part of Inside Route Savannah Ga. to Beaufort S.C. Showing Cut through Mud River." The map was endorsed by "Cassius E. Gillette, Capt. of Engrs."

PART FOUR

Concluding
Observations

THE BEST CONCLUSION FOR THIS STUDY comes in the form of a map overlay (Map 19) that has been constructed by overlaying the 1855 U.S. Coast Survey chart of the lower Savannah River area on a 1976 National Ocean Survey chart of the same area. As pointed out in the preceding part, any differences in riverbank and island configuration that are revealed are attributable to changes through the years between 1855 and the modern survey. Thus, the overlay represents a cartographic inventory of the exact amount and precise location of landscape change in the lower Savannah River area. It is also very useful when attempting to fix the correct location of the Georgia–South Carolina boundary here as it was delineated by the U.S. Supreme Court in 1922. The Court's 1922 decision placed the boundary as follows:

(1) Where there are no islands in the boundary rivers the location of the line between the two states, is on the water, midway between the main banks of the river, when the water is at ordinary stage;

(2) where there are islands, the line is midway between the island bank and the South Carolina shore when the water is at ordinary stage. [*Georgia* v. *South Carolina*, 257 U.S. 516 (1922)]

Before discussing Map 19, it is necessary to consider some background information. First, the latitude-longitude graticules differ on the two charts. This results from the fact that U.S. mapping agencies adopted a new datum base in 1927, as noted on the 1976 NOS sheet in the caption, "North American 1927 Datum." The two graticules can easily be resolved, so this difference poses no serious problem in interpretation. More important than the latitude-longitude graticules for the purpose of keying the 1855 overlay to the 1976 base are a

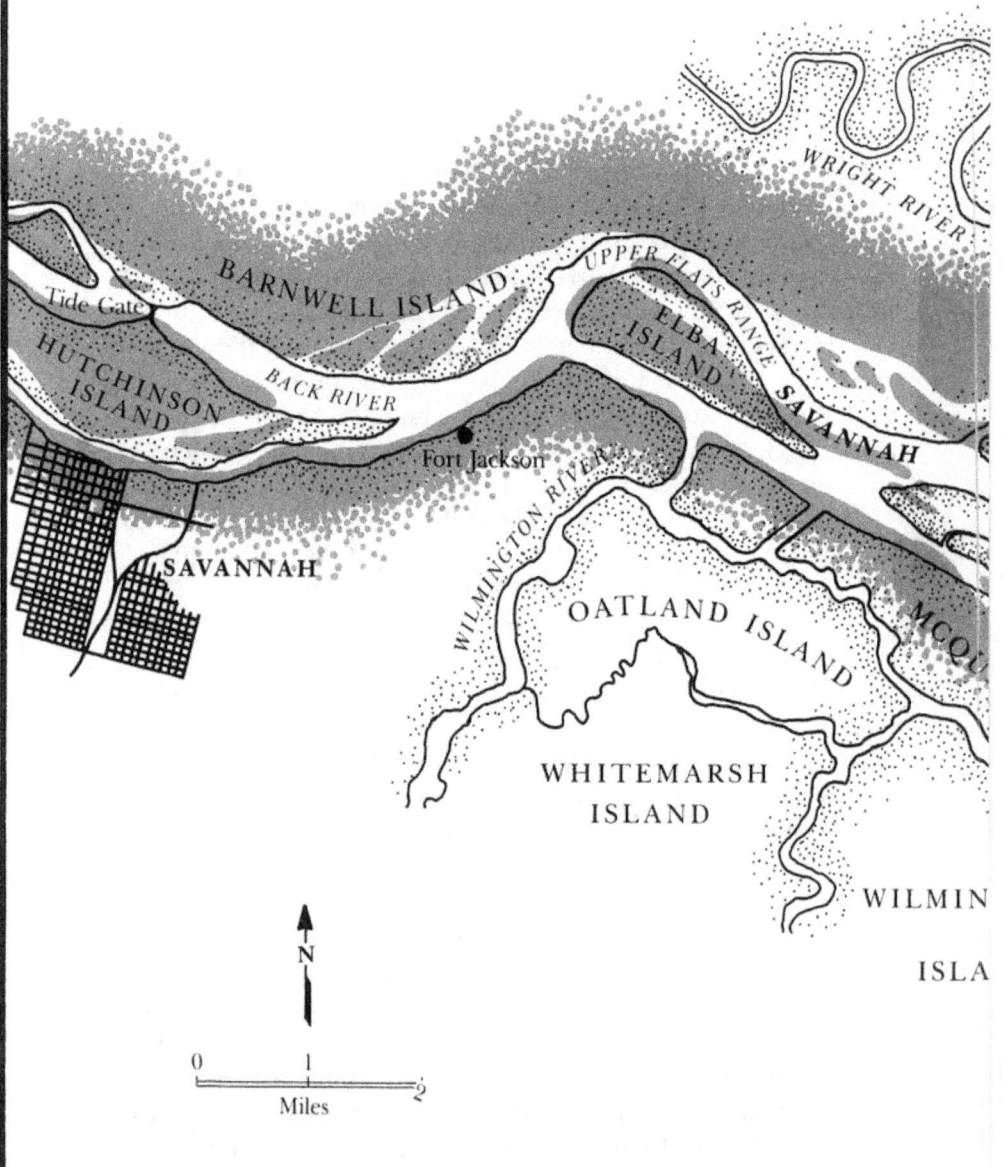

19. Section of U.S. Coast Survey, Preliminary Chart of Savannah River, Georgia, 1855, overlaid on a 1976 U.S. Department of Commerce Map of Savannah River. With this overlay it is possible to make some assessment of

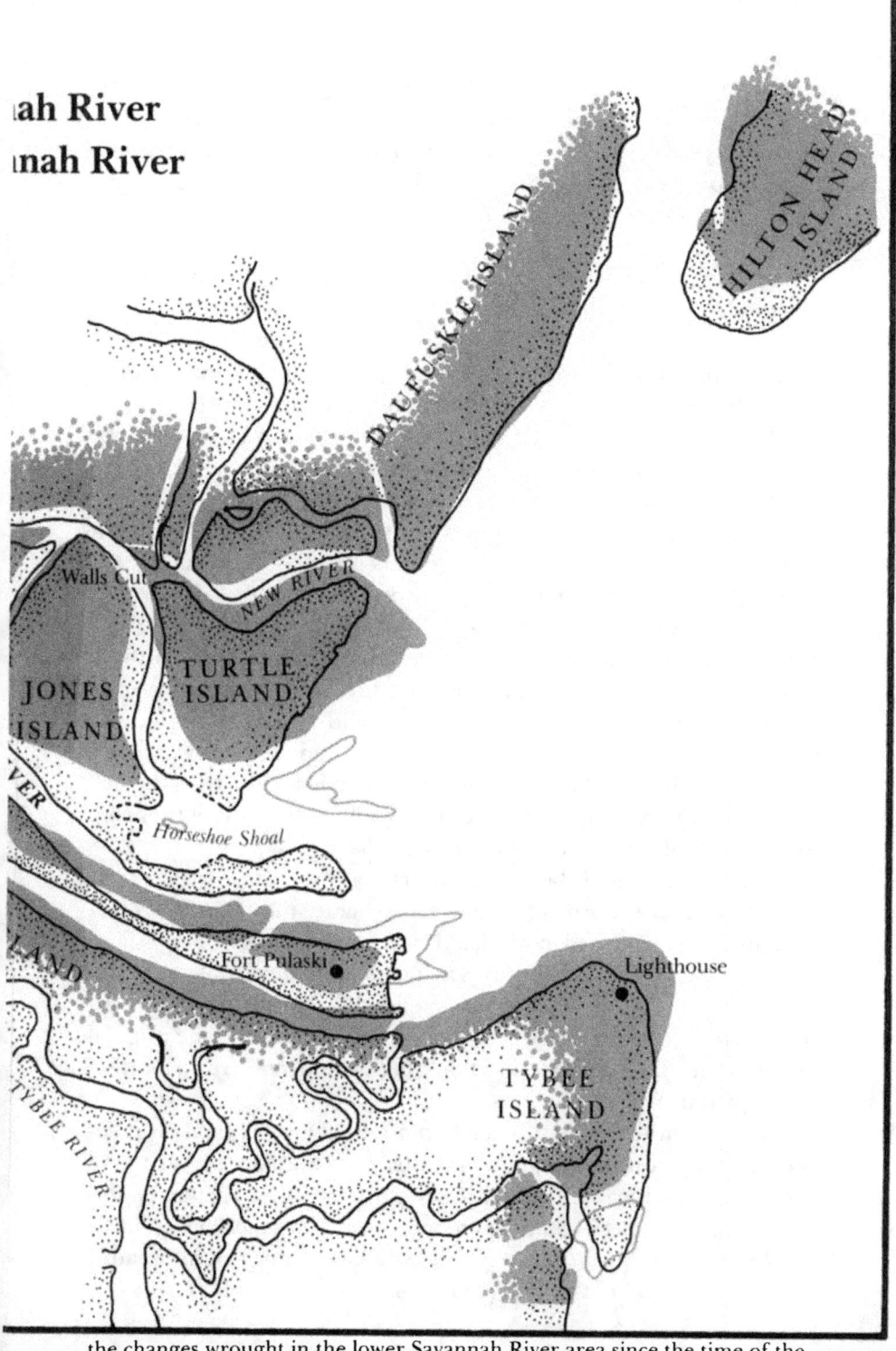

the changes wrought in the lower Savannah River area since the time of the first complete scientific survey and chart. Both maps have been redrawn from published originals for clarity.

number of points and landscape features common to both. In keying the overlay, these common features serve to guarantee the accuracy of the overlay's fit and scale properties. The Tybee Lighthouse, Fort Pulaski, Fort Jackson, and the Savannah city street grid form excellent common reference points and are used to key one chart to the other with accuracy.

Beginning at the western or left-hand margin of Map 19, one can observe very clearly the conditions along the northern stream of the Savannah River, wherein lies the boundary between Georgia and South Carolina. Pennyworth Island has grown slightly through apparent accretion along its upstream and northern shoreline. The South Carolina bank, however, has remained remarkably stable opposite to the island. Unless further information can be found to indicate that the growth of Pennyworth is due to some avulsive factor or agency, it would appear that the boundary has migrated here through natural accretion to the amount of from 500 to 750 yards since 1855. Immediately downstream from Pennyworth Island is the site of a tide gate structure constructed under the auspices of the Corps of Engineers. A small, elongated, marshy island was located here in 1855. Unless it can be shown that this island was formed through some early avulsive action, the political boundary would appear to be located midway between the former island's position and the South Carolina bank. Depending on the precise definition applied to the term "bank," the boundary probably runs somewhere well to the north of the levee to the north of the tide gate on the 1976 chart.

In the lower area of Back River, which has been designated a sediment trap in the Corps of Engineers' scheme, the South Carolina shoreline has remained remarkably stable. The Hutchinson Island shoreline has accreted slightly on the north, and the downstream end of the island has been deliberately extended far downstream through the construction of training walls. The boundary abreast the original Hutchinson Island remains essentially in the same midstream location it occupied in 1855.

Downstream from the southern tip of Hutchinson Island, as it existed in 1855, a difficult situation exists. This is an area of fast land now known as Barnwell Island. During the 1950s, a portion of this area was the subject of a litigation known as *United States v. 450 acres . . . Known as Barnwell Island. . . .* The details of this suit are readily accessible and will not be repeated here.

Concluding Observations 167

A close study of the Barnwell Island situation is doubly imperative because it appears that the political boundary information shown on the 1971 edition of the U.S. Geological Survey's 1:24,000 Savannah Quadrangle map sheet is in error here (Map 2). As the 1855 overlay on Map 19 shows, there were at least three sizable islands in this area at that time. The one farthest upstream appears to have already been almost joined to the South Carolina bank in 1855 through the silting in of a preexisting channel. This silted channel appears to have been partially blocked at its upstream end by a structure identified as Union Causeway. A land plat in the files of the surveyor-general of Georgia indicates that this channel was open on May 12, 1760. A copy of this survey plat is included here as Map 20. A colonial precursor of the Union Causeway is suggested on this 1760 plat in the form of the words "Mr. Wright's Causeway" at the upper edge. Three islets devoid of vegetation symbolization are shown between "Mr. Wright's Causway" and the Barnwell Island marked "46 acres." A study of the USGS Quadrangle mentioned above indicates that this condition was not acknowledged when the state boundary information was drawn although the presence of the other downstream Barnwell islands was.

An even earlier survey plat shows these islands as they were perceived in 1733 (Map 21). This is the plat depicting a survey of 2,060 acres of South Carolina land granted to "James Oglethorpe, Esqr. for the use of the Trustees of Georgia." This plat was certified on January 20, 1733, by William Stobo, deputy surveyor of South Carolina. Although the Barnwell islands shown are incomplete and not a portion of the surveyed tract, they are recognizable. An islet is shown upstream from two much larger islands, apparently occupying the position of the three islets on the 1760 plat described above. The two large Barnwell islands are incompletely outlined in the 1733 plat but seem to coincide with the two shown on the 1760 plat (Map 20). On the 1733 plat, the caption "The N. East Branch of Savannah River" is written so as to extend along the channel between the Barnwell islands and the northern or South Carolina shore of the river. This South Carolina survey of 1733 shows the Barnwell islands as islands in the Savannah River and thus within the territorial limits of Georgia as described in her royal charter. This is consistent with the information provided on the 1760 plat, where "Savannah River" is boldly lettered along the northern or South Carolina riverbank. The fact that the islands were not included in the adjacent tract granted by South Car-

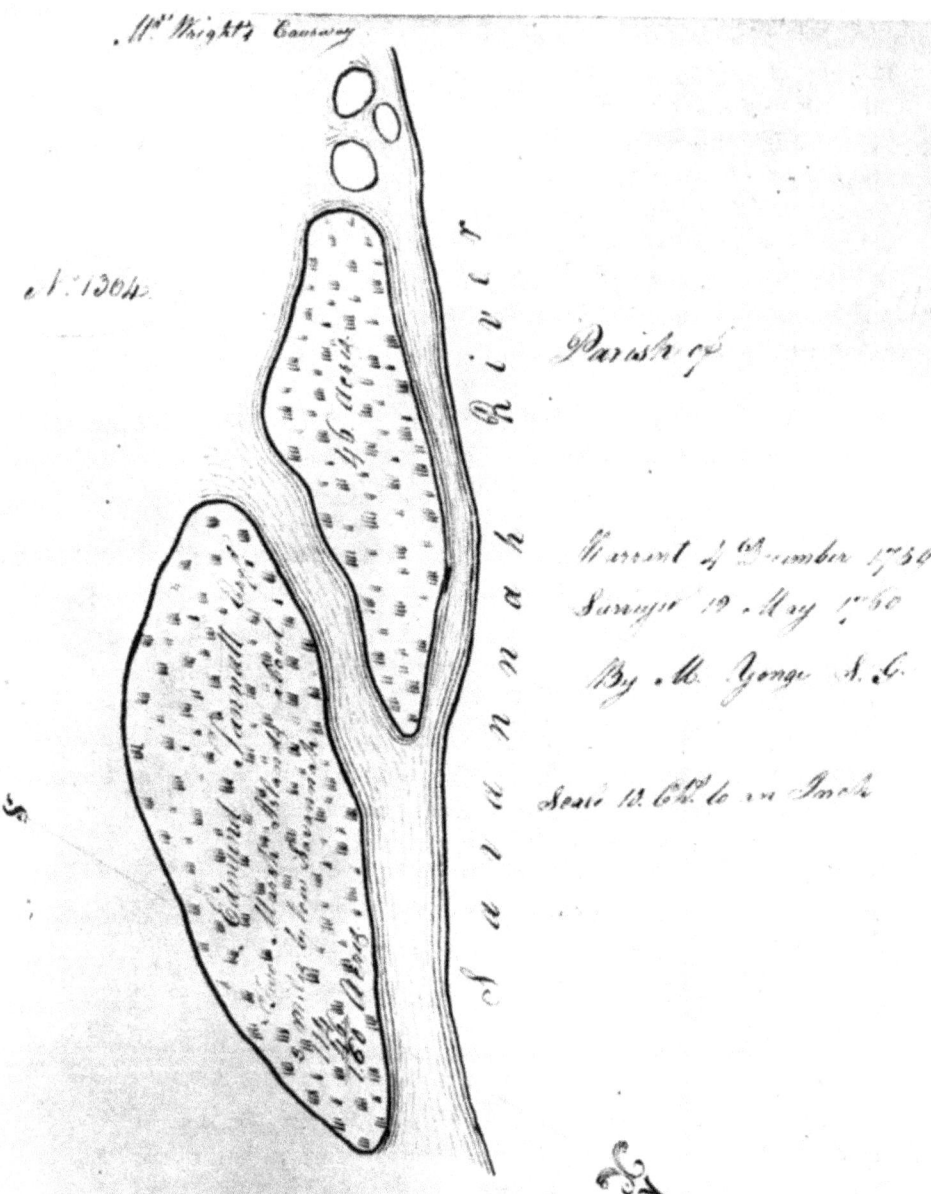

20. Plat of two marsh islands about 3 miles below Savannah, surveyed May 12, 1760 by H. Yonge S.G. for Edmund Tannatt Esqr. This 1760 land survey plat shows the Barnwell islands area in that year. The islands were granted by Georgia to Tannatt. (Photograph of original supplied through the courtesy of the Georgia Surveyor General Department.)

olina further supports the contention that the unnamed Barnwell islands were considered to be within Georgia in 1733.

A South Carolina plat depicting the Barnwell area in 1813 lends confirmation to the conclusions reached regarding the 1733 and 1760 plats (Map 22). The 1813 plat indicates that the Barnwell islands were granted to Archibald Smith and surveyed on March 24, 1813. According to the surveyor's description accompanying the plat, the Barnwell islands were perceived as "being three marsh Islands on Said River [Savannah] lying between Fort Jackson in the State of Georgia and Lands of the Said Archibald Smith." A small house symbol drawn on the South Carolina bank of the river is identified as "Smith's Settlement." A short distance upstream a double line of dots is marked "New Road to Charleston." In the widest portion of the river opposite Fort Jackson the caption "Savannah River or Back River" is included. Closer to the South Carolina shore is the caption "Part of Savannah River." Between the farthest upstream Barnwell Island and the Carolina bank the word "Creek" appears. The same term is placed in the channel between the two largest Barnwell islands. Also of significance is the indication of a "Small Island" close to the upstream end of the farthest upstream Barnwell Island and close to the terminus of the "New Road to Charleston." It would seem reasonable to assume that "Mr. Wright's Causway" had been either renamed "New Road to Charleston" or that the early causeway had been replaced by a new structure.

This 1813 plat indicates clearly that the "Three marsh Islands . . . lying between Fort Jackson in the State of Georgia, and Lands of . . . Archibald Smith" were recognized as islands in the Savannah River at that time. Significantly, three large islands are shown where there had been only two in 1760. A "16 acre" island is shown to have formed downstream from the largest of the two Barnwell islands shown in 1760. The third may have accumulated from the deposition of material eroded from the larger two upstream. This condition is suggested by the areal data provided by the surveyors in 1760 and 1813. In the earliest plat, the islands are shown as being 46 and 114 acres in area. In 1813 the smaller upstream island is recorded as 42 acres and the larger as 104 acres. If these figures are accurate, it would indicate that the two original Barnwell islands had lost material amounting to 14 acres in the fifty-three-year period between the surveys. This is very close to the sixteen-acre figure presented for the new third island in

21. Plat of 2,060 acres of land granted to James Oglethorpe, Esqr., for the use of the Trustees of Georgia, certified January 20, 1733/4. Although unnamed the Barnwell islands are partially shown on this South Carolina plat. The fact that they were not included in the grant would appear to be tacit

acknowledgment that the islands were Georgia territory. The placement of the name "Savannah River" tends to support this conclusion. (Photograph of original in Records of the Surveyor General, supplied through the courtesy of the Department of Archives and History of South Carolina.)

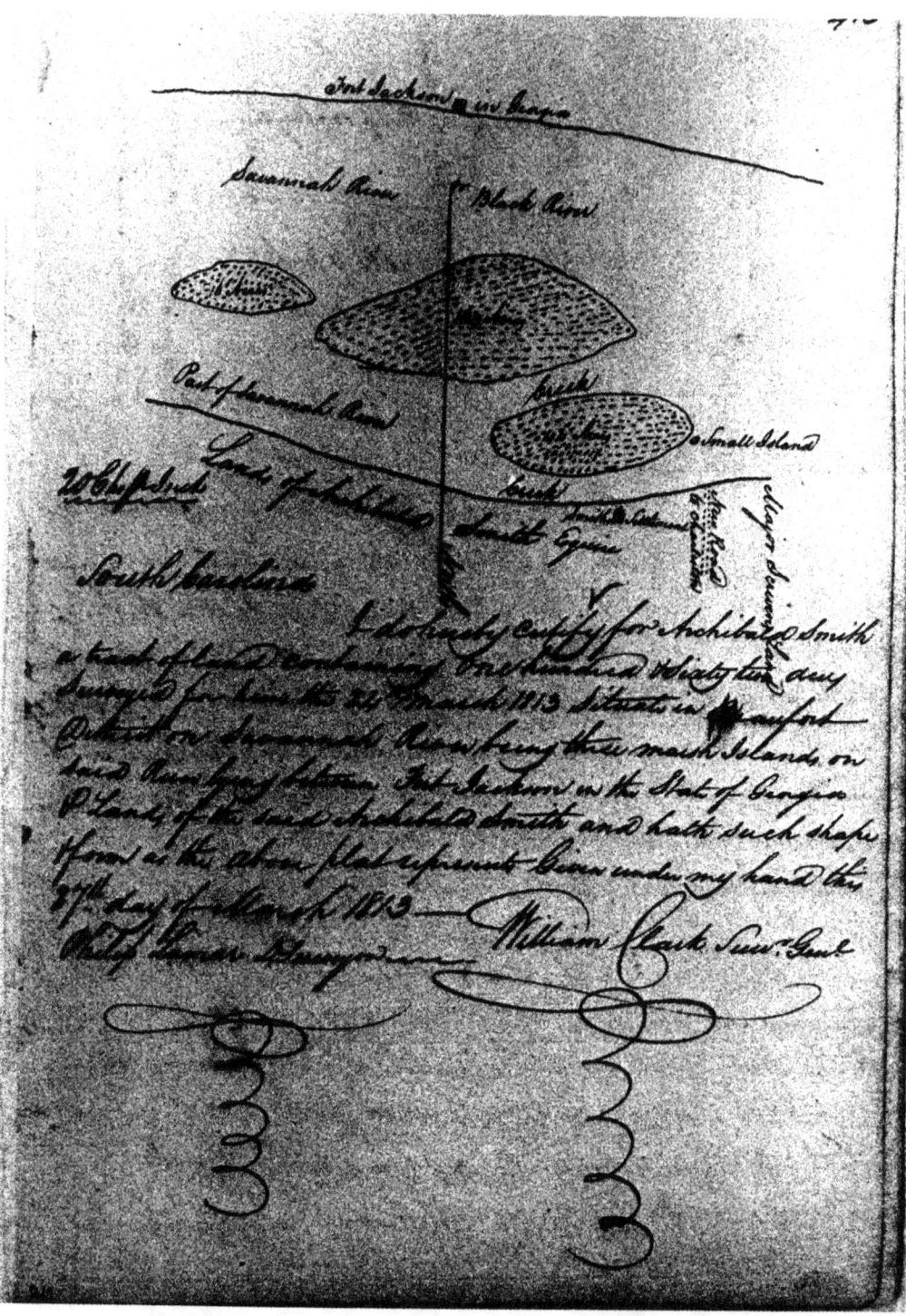

22. Plat showing three marsh islands granted to Archibald Smith, surveyed March 24, 1813. By the time this plat was made the original two Barnwell islands had increased to three. (Photograph of original in Recorded State Plats, Charleston Series, vol. 37, p. 413, Records of the Surveyor General, supplied through the courtesy of the Department of Archives and History of South Carolina.)

1813. It might further be speculated that the remaining two acres of the third island were contributed by replenishing sediments eroded from the three islets shown near "Mr. Wright's Causway" in 1760, which were also transported downstream.

The extremely detailed and refined survey and maps prepared by Lieutenant John Mackay in 1833 confirm these configurations (Map 14B) as does the 1855 Coast Survey chart (Map 16). There can be little doubt that a large area of the fast land now contiguous to the South Carolina shore opposite Fort Jackson is made up of the Barnwell islands unequivocally shown on the survey plats as having been in the Savannah River before and after the Treaty of Beaufort was signed in 1787. Table 1 summarizes the way the Barnwell islands are shown on maps during the more than a century from 1733 to 1902. From this and other evidence, it seems reasonable to conclude that the third Barnwell Island developed downstream of the original two during the period between 1794 and 1813.[1]

In summary, it can be seen that a stream of the Savannah River flowed between all three Barnwell islands including the one immediately adjacent to the causeway. The process of siltation appeared to have nearly joined the latter upstream island to the South Carolina shoreline by 1855. In earlier decades, including the period when the Beaufort Convention was signed, however, it was shown unequivocally as an island surrounded by Savannah River water.

Downstream from the Barnwell islands area the river flows in a large curving channel between present-day Elba Island and the South Carolina shore. This stretch of river is the portion of the main navigation channel now known as the Bight Channel. As can be observed on Map 19, some shoreline retreat has taken place along the Carolina bank of the Bight Channel since the 1850s. Elba Island has also been enlarged considerably through the incorporation of some marshy islands that were in the original Bight Channel in 1855. The largest of these incorporated marsh islands was known as Spirit Island. Spirit Island was joined to Elba Island by a number of dams and other structures built by the Corps of Engineers in the 1880s and 1890s. Several of these island- and channel-altering structures are indicated on "Index Map of Savannah River, Georgia Showing Works Constructed from 1804 to 1896" (Map 18). Any attempt to discover the true location of the Georgia–South Carolina boundary through this stretch of

TABLE 1
Barnwell Islands
Cartographic Analysis Summary

Date	Map	No. of Islands*	Comments
1733	Plat of South Carolina Grant to Oglethorpe	2L1S	Islands partially shown, channel between islands and shore shown as "Savannah River." Back River named "The Northeast Branch of Savannah River." No Wright River cut. No causeway.
ca. 1740	A Map of the County of Savannah	1L	No detail, a single elongated island shown.
ca. 1740	British Museum King George III's Topographical Collection CXXII.65	1L	No detail, a single elongated island shown.
1751	A Plan of the Inlets and Rivers of Savannah and Warsaw . . . Henry Yonge	2L	Two large, well-shaped islands, captioned "Marsh" with vegetation symbols. Channels indicated as "narrow places in the River Savannah, which if stoped up would probably open the main Chanel." Back River captioned "No. branch of Savannah River," area generally shoaling.
1752	A Map of Savannah River . . . Surveyed by William Noble of Brahm . . .	2L	Two large, well-shaped islands, no detail, area generally shoaling.
1757	South Carolina and a Part of Georgia . . . William De Brahm	2L	Two large, well-shaped islands, no detail, area generally shoaling.
1760	Plat of Georgia Grant to Edmund Tannatt Esqr. by Henry Yonge	2L3S	Two large, well-shaped islands with three tiny islets upstream, caption on largest "Two Marsh Islands about 3 miles below Savannah" 114 + 46 = 160 acres. Vegetation symbols on both islands, "46 acres" on smaller upstream island, "Mr. Wright's Causway" written upstream of islets, "Savannah River" written on north bank adjacent to islands.
1773	A Map of the Province of South Carolina . . . James Cook	2	"Rochester Ferry" shown just upstream. "Back Marsh" shown on area downstream.

Barnwell Islands—*Continued*

Date	Map	No. of Islands*	Comments
ca. 1775	Anonymous Map in Germain Papers, Clements Library	2L	Two large islands, largest downstream, probably marsh symbolization.
1775	An Accurate Map of North and South Carolina . . . by Henry Mouzon and Others	2	Very similar to James Cook's 1773 map.
1779	Siege De Savannah—several from French Archives and Ozanne Collection	2L	Two large islands captioned "Marais impraticables." Largest downstream, vegetation coloring and symbolization.
1780	Sketch of the Northern Frontiers of Georgia . . . by Archibald Campbell	2L	Downstream island slightly larger, suggestion of Wrights Cut opposite Elba Island not named. Road to river shown, no ferry indicated.
1780	The Coast Rivers and Inlets of the Province of Georgia, Surveyed by Joseph Avery and Others . . . by J. F. W. Des Barres	2L	Downstream island larger, both in stippled area, vegetation symbolization present.
[1779–80]	Untitled Map of Georgia–South Carolina Coasts with inset "Plan of the Siege of Savannah . . . Surveyed by John Wilson A, Engineer"	2	Upstream island larger, no detail.
1780	A Map of South Carolina and a Part of Georgia . . . by Stuart and De Brahm	2	Downstream island larger, in stippled shoaling area, "Rochester Ferry" shown.
1794	A New Chart of the Coast of North America . . . Exhibiting the Coast of Georgia etc. by Captain N. Holland	2	Downstream island larger, in stippled shoaling area, "Rochester Ferry" indicated.
1795	Plats of South Carolina Grant to Hezekiah Roberts	2L2S	Largest island 110 acres downstream, upstream 90 acres. Upstream end of small and downstream end of large are islets separated by "creeks." Large island marked "The second island in the mouth of Back River." "Five Fathom Hole" shown south of large island. Tip of "Hutchinsons Island" indicated.

176   Concluding Observations

Barnwell Islands—*Continued*

Date	Map	No. of Islands*	Comments
1813	Plats of South Carolina Grant to Archibald Smith	3L1S	Upstream island 42 acres, middle island 104 acres, downstream island 16 acres. "Small Island" shown at upstream end of 42-acre island. "New Road to Charleston" indicated. "Smiths Settlement" indicated. "Fort Jackson in Georgia" shown. Water between north shore and 42-acre island "Creek," water between 42-acre island and 104-acre island "Creek," downstream between 16-acre island and north shore "Part of Savannah River," between islands and Ft. Jackson "Savannah River or Back River."
1816	. . . Plan of the County of Chatham . . . by John McKinnon	3L	Upstream largest, "Causeway and Union [illeg.] to Charleston" terminates near upstream end of largest island. "Scrivens" and "Smiths," "Five Fathom Hole," and "Fort Jackson," "Ship Channel" shown to north of "4 mile point" on Elba Island. "South Channel" on south side of Elba.
1818	Map of the State of Georgia . . . Eleazer Early	3L	Shapes elongated, "Union Road Causeway 3 Miles," "Wrights Cut" and "Wrights River" form "Buck Island" downstream to unnamed Mud River.
1820	Map of Beaufort and District . . . surveyed by Charles Vignoles and Henry Ravenel	3L	Middle Island largest. "Union Causeway Turnpike" unnamed. Wright Cut shown. "Wrights River," "Elba Island" named, vegetation suggested.
1821	State of Georgia Chart of the River Savannah Surveyed by Captain J. Le Conte	2L1S	Barnwell area distorted. Upstream island largest. Vegetation suggested.
1823	Plat annexed to agreement between John Screven, Sam M. Bond and Archibald Smith	3L	Middle island largest. All three indicated as "Smith's Land." Water between islands and north shore "Boundary Creek," "Union Ferry Road," "Smith's Settlement."

Barnwell Islands—*Continued*

Date	Map	No. of Islands*	Comments
1825	Chart of Savannah River done from actual surveys . . . John McKinnon	1L	Suggests that upstream island has accreted. Middle island "Marsh Island," "Ferry Land," "Union Road to Charleston 3¼ miles to High Land," "Major Screvens," "Fort Jackson," "Five Fathom Hole" depths in main river.
1825	Beaufort District Surveyed by C. Vignolas and H. Ravenel 1820 Improved for Mills Atlas 1825	3L	Middle island largest, "Union Causeway Turnpike," "Wright River" and cut "Cook's Cut" vegetation symbols.
1833	Chart of Part of the Savannah River . . . Surveyed and Drawn by Lt. John Mackay . . .	3L	Middle Island largest and marked "Marsh Uncultivated," "Marsh" on others. Upstream Island nearly accreted to shore channel suggested by dotted line. "Road to Charleston," "Screven's Ferry," Ft. Jackson, Smith's, Barnwell's, and Proctor's shown. "Line of Greatest Velocity" and depth soundings.
1847	Map of the State of Georgia . . . Published by William G. Bonner	3L	Inadequate scale for details.
1848	Chart of a Portion of the Savannah River . . . by M. L. S. Smith	2L	Upstream island only suggested by indentation in shoreline. Middle Island largest upstream end has rice plantation symbols. "Ferry Road," "Line of greatest depth of water," small islet on Ft. Jackson side. Letter *a* in *Carolina* printed on relic upstream island.
1850	Plan and Resurvey of Tracts of Land the Property of Dr. James P. Screven . . . Richard H. Bacon, Surveyor	3L	Middle Island largest, named "Barnwell's Island, Capt. Barnwell's Island, and Barnwell's Island." "Ferry Road" and "Landing" narrow channel at upstream island. "Savannah Back River" shown north of two largest, "Wrights Creek" and "Wrights Cut."
1851	Sketch E No. 4 . . . Savannah River . . . Lt. J. N. Maffitt . . .	2L3S	Upstream island not shown. Three tiny islets on south. No landing etc. Ft. Jackson shown.

178 Concluding Observations

Barnwell Islands—*Continued*

Date	Map	No. of Islands*	Comments
1852	Map of Savannah River . . . By Henry L. Whiting	3L3S	Upstream island marsh with channel probably dry at low tide. Middle island diked for rice with four buildings on north side. Downstream island marsh. Three marsh islets in shoaling area on south side "Union Causeway."
1855	Preliminary Chart of Savannah River	3L3S	Very similar to Whiting's 1852 survey. Depths shown in channel north and south of Middle Island.
1862	Map Accompanying Report of Major O. T. Beard	3L3S	Upstream island captioned "Dr. Daniel's Island Rice Plantation." Middle island "Barnwell's Island Rice Plantation." Others marsh symbols. Islet between "Barnwell's" and Fort Jackson has "New Fort." "Sunken vessel" nearby. 24 x 700 foot raft.
1866	Topography of Part of Savannah River by H. L. Marindin	—	Shows details of "Battery Barnwell," "Battery Tatnall," "Fort Jackson," "Fort Lee," and some obstructions in river.
1865–66	Hydrography of Savannah River . . . Surveyed by C. O. Boutelle	3L3S	Upstream island has channel behind. Partial obstruction closing channel between upstream island and middle island "Barnwell's Island." Depths shown in channels between middle and downstream island and north shore. Obstructions in all channels downstream.
1867	Savannah River and Wassaw Sound	2L4S	Upstream island only suggested by indentations. Pier partially closing channel between it and middle island. Depths shown in channels. No detail on islands or bank.
1867	Rabbitt Island . . . Plat surveyed by Muller and Bruyn	1L1S	Upstream island named "Rabbit Island," middle island "Hog Island," downstream island "Long Island," small islet "Naval Battery." Continuous channel on north side shown.

Barnwell Islands—*Continued*

Date	Map	No. of Islands*	Comments
1867	Hog Island Plantation plat surveyed by Muller and Bruyn	1L1S	Shows properties on middle island, Jno. S. Barnwell, Leila Barnwell, A. L. Barnwell. "Naval Battery" small islet to south.
1874	Savannah River Vicinity of Ft. Jackson, Georgia	2L3S	Upstream island not shown, suggested by indentations apparently diked. Middle island "Barnwell Island," diked buildings on south and north sides, small circular revetment. Downstream island diked on east end two buildings. Revetments at Ft. Tatnall site. Elongated marsh islet to east of downstream island. Pilings and obstructions in all channels. Depths abundant.
1875	Chatham County . . . Charles G. Platen	3L3S	Upstream island separated from shore by narrow channel. Middle island "Smiths Island" has a dam or pier connecting to upstream island. Pattern of dikes or ditches on upstream and middle island. Downstream island has four buildings "Ft. Tatnall."
1883	Progress Sheet No. 3 Showing Works Constructed between Barnwell Island and Long Island . . .	2L4S	Upstream island suggested by indentation. Middle island "Barnwell Island," Downstream island "Barnwell No. 2," elongated islet "Barnwell No. 3." Dams No. 5, 11½, No. 15 dated 1883. Depths in channels.
1886	Tybee Roads Savannah River . . . Chart 440	3L3S	Upstream island has narrow channel. Symbolization for cultivated land, dam connecting to middle island "Barnwell Island." Cultivated and dikes, dam connecting to downstream island "Barnwell No. 2." Elongated islet "Barnwell No. 3" dam or pier toward Elba. Depths indicated all channels except narrow.

Barnwell Islands—*Continued*

Date	Map	No. of Islands*	Comments
1887	Chart of the Savannah River . . . from the head of Isla Island to the Sea	3L2S	Upstream island has narrow channel. Middle island "Barnwell Island," downstream "Barnwell No. 2," elongated islet "Barnwell No. 3," Dams No. 5, 11½, 15 shown. Proposed dam to tie "Barnwell No. 3" and Dam 15 to north shore.
1887	Chart of the Savannah River . . . by First Lt. Carter . . .	2L3S	Upstream island shown as part of shore. Middle island "Barnwell Island No. 1," downstream "Barnwell Island No. 2," elongated islet "Barnwell Island No. 3," Dams "No. 5 1883," No. 11½ 1883," "No. 15 1883." Planetable positions "Blue" "Blackberry" "Island" "Island No. 2." No depths to north.
1895	Tybee Roads Savannah River . . . Chart 440	3L2S	Upstream island narrow channel, cultivated symbolization. Dam to middle island "Barnwell Island," cultivated and diked dam to downstream island "Barnwell No. 2," dam to "Barnwell No. 3" with dam toward Elba and training wall extending to spur dams near mouth of Wrights Cut. Depths in channels except narrow.
1896	Map of Savannah Harbor . . . Showing Works Constructed . . .	2L4S	Upstream merged with shore. Dam No. 3 connecting to middle island "Barnwell Island No. 1," dam No. 2 connecting to downstream island "Barnwell Island No. 2," dam No. 1 connecting to elongated islet "Barnwell No. 3," No. 15 extends toward Elba, "Barnwell Island Training Wall" extends downstream to spur dams at shore.
1898	Tybee Roads Savannah River . . . Chart 440	3L2S	Upstream island narrow channel. Dam to middle island "Barnwell Island," dam to downstream island "Barnwell Island No. 2," dam to elongated islet dam toward Elba, training wall toward spur dams near mouth of Wright's Cut.

Barnwell Islands—*Continued*

Date	Map	No. of Islands*	Comments
1902	Tybee Roads Savannah River ... Chart 440	3L2S	Very similar to 1898. Depths in channels changed.

*Capital letter L indicates large and S indicates small. Thus the 1733 plat of a South Carolina grant to Oglethorpe showed two large islands and one small island or islet in the Barnwell islands area.

the river must take into account these post-1855 alterations in riverbank and island morphology.

Downstream from the Bight Channel the main navigation channel is now named Upper Flats Range. In 1855 this was a very broad flow with a hazardous shoaling area in its center (see Maps 18 and 19). The construction of an elaborate system of training walls and dams during the 1880s and 1890s drastically narrowed the channel through the Upper Flats to make it one of the most truly man-made courses of the lower Savannah River. The exact character and location of these morphological changes must be considered in any attempt to fix the true location of the states' boundary in this portion of the river.

Just abreast of the channel hazard known as Horseshoe Shoal was the entrance to a northerly flowing distributary channel or branch of the Savannah River. This channel is shown as Mud River on the 1855 overlay of Map 19. It is even more clearly shown on Map 16, which is a redrawn copy of the U.S. Coast Survey's 1855 chart of the Savannah River. In 1855, Mud River appears as a broad but shallow channel that joined a large tidal creek known as Wright River near the northern tip of Jones Island, a large, triangular-shaped marsh island.

A comparison of the 1855 and 1976 configurations on Map 19 shows that the upper Mud River branch of the Savannah River was largely obliterated by the Corps of Engineers Upper Flats navigation channel narrowing projects of the late nineteenth century outlined on Map 18. Other post-1855 evidence indicates that the navigability of Mud River channel already had begun to deteriorate through siltation in the 1860s and the channel probably was open only at tidal stages higher than those used as data for charting. This evidence indicates that Jones Island may have existed as a tidal island during the period immediately preceding the narrowing of the Upper Flats navigation channel of the main Savannah in the early 1880s. The U.S.

Coast Survey chart, titled "Coast Chart No. 55 Coast of South Carolina and Georgia From Hunting Island to Ossabaw Island Including Port Royal Sound and Savannah River . . . ," published in 1873, is typical of this evidence. On it Mud River can be discerned as a very narrow and incomplete feature in the marshland opposite the lower end of Elba Island. As indicated on the face of the chart, "Mean Low Water" is the plane of reference used for the soundings shown. Although not explicitly stated, it is probable that some similar low water datum was used for portraying topography on the chart. If this was the case (and logic suggests that it was), it is highly likely that Mud River continued to exist as a fairly broad expanse during periods of high water. The inclusion of the name "Jones I." on the 1873 chart lends some limited support to this thesis. This interpretation, however, is based on a large component of inference. Further research into the exact character of the Mud River distributary of the Savannah River during the decade of the 1870s and the period immediately preceding the Corps of Engineers constructions in the Upper Flats area will be required in any effort to fix the true location of the states' boundary in the vicinity of Jones Island. For the more than a century and one-quarter from Georgia's founding through the publication of the 1855 Coast Survey chart of the Savannah River and the Civil War, there seems to be no question as to the clear evidence for a Mud River branch of the Savannah and the existence of a Jones Island. Much of this evidence has been discussed in preceding parts of this study. One of the most persuasive items in this body of evidence not included in those earlier discussions is the survey plat of Jones Island made in 1768 by James Brown, the deputy surveyor. This plat is reproduced here as Map 23.

When viewing this plat it is helpful to place it on its side so that "No. 348" is at the right-hand edge. In this position north is more nearly at the upper edge of the plat and comparison with other maps becomes easier. The plat was prepared as part of a grant of "800 Acres Marsh Land" from the colony of Georgia to "Noble Jones Esquire."[2] The easternmost tip of Elba Island is shown but not named; rather, it is labeled "The Point of an Island Granted Jas. Whitefield." East of Elba, portions of Bird and Long islands are indicated. To the east of Jones Island a portion of unnamed land occupies the position of present-day Turtle Island.

The available evidence indicates that Turtle Island did not become

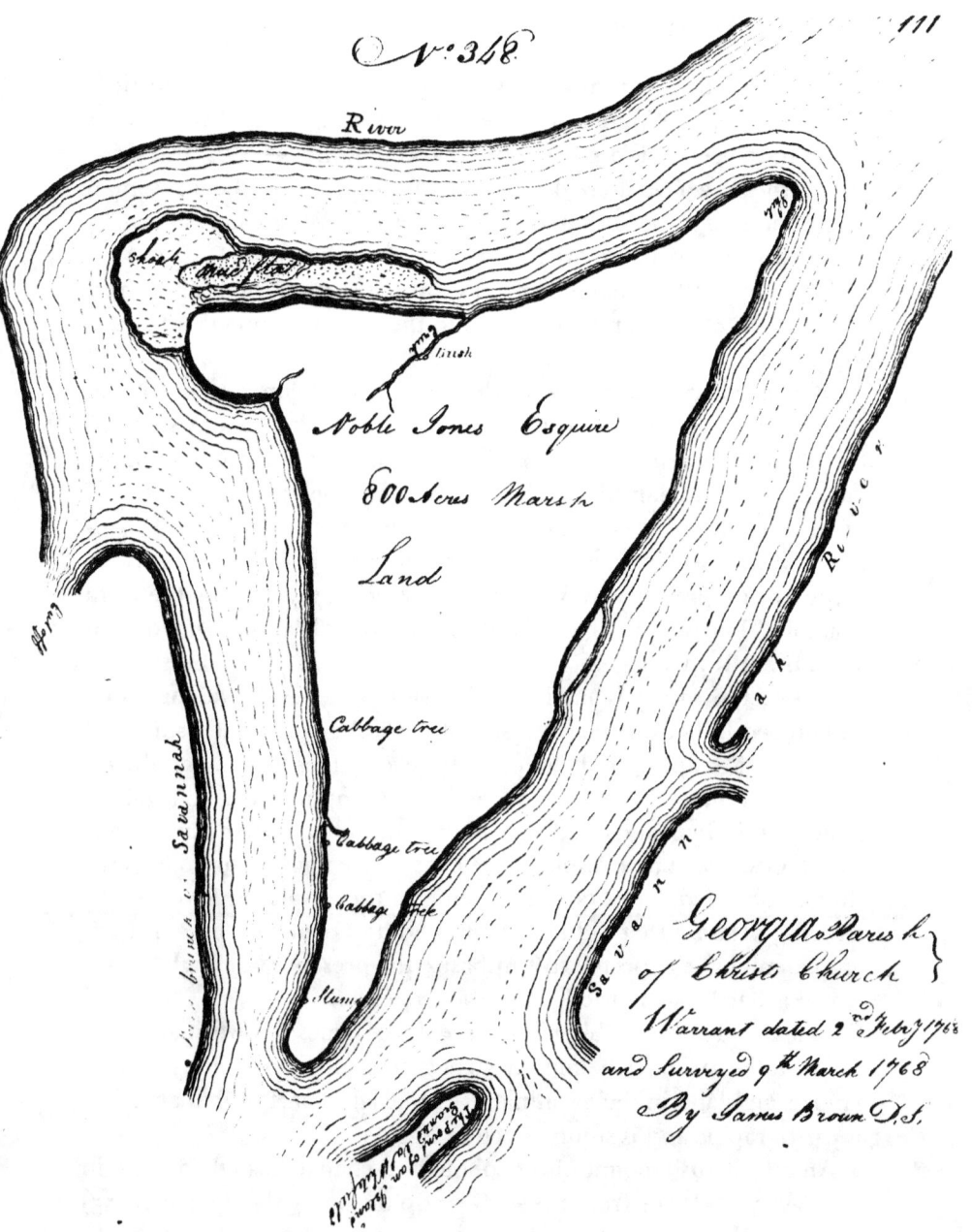

23. Plat of Noble Jones, Esqr.'s 800 acres marsh land, surveyed March 9, 1768. If this plat is rotated so that the Savannah River is along the bottom, the distinctive triangular shape of Jones Island is easy to make out. The waterway named "North branch of Savannah River" coincides with Mud River and Wright River as shown on nineteenth-century maps. (Photograph of original supplied through the courtesy of the Georgia Surveyor General Department.)

184   Concluding Observations

an island until a man-made cut joined the waters of the two tidal creeks known as Wright River and New River. At least three named "cuts" have been indicated over the years across the neck of land separating these two tidal creeks. Cooks Cut appears on the 1773 map published under the authorship of James Cook. Walls Cut is shown on the Eleazer Early map of 1818 and Mills Atlas Beaufort District Map of 1825. In 1838 the name Norton's Cut appears on the Wilkes chart of the area. Most later charts down to the present name this feature Walls Cut.

Of particular significance on this 1768 plat of Jones Island is the treatment and naming of the Savannah River in this area. A study of the plat can leave no doubt that Jones Island was construed as an island in the Savannah River. The flow passing along the northwest and northeast sides of the island is identified as "North branch of Savannah River." The presence of a smaller contributing flow from the west representing present-day Wright River is acknowledged by the term "Cut off." The flow along the south side of Jones Island is named "S-a-v-a-n-n-a-h R-i-v-e-r."

Before too much is made of this single piece of evidence, one should recall that this plat is just that—a survey plat, not a surveyed topographic map. Both the deputy surveyor James Brown and the influential grantee Noble Jones were doubtless aware that the legal climate of the time suggested that islands in the Savannah River were within Georgia. The plat may have exaggerated geographic elements that emphasized Jones Island as being in the Savannah River at the expense of those that did not. Thus a South Carolina source, for example, might be expected to emphasize the presence of Wright River, which is hardly acknowledged in the 1768 plat.

In spite of the possible bias in the 1768 James Brown plat, there seems to be an overwhelmingly strong case for identifying Jones Island as an island in the Savannah River. A large part of that evidence is cartographic and is summarized in Table 2.

An enormous amount of morphological change has taken place in the Savannah River from the eastern tip of Jones Island (as of 1855) to the northern tip of Tybee Island. Of particular interest and significance in this dynamic area is the feature known variously as the Oyster Bed or Oyster Bed Island. In many respects, Oyster Bed typifies the dynamism that makes it exceedingly difficult to make firm and sweeping statements concerning the island and riverbank configura-

TABLE 2
Jones Island–Mud River
Cartographic Analysis Summary

Date	Map	Island Shown?	Comments
ca. 1740	A Map of the County of Savannah	yes	Shows Jones Island very clearly with excellent shape; clearly an island in Savannah River.
ca. 1740	British Museum King George III's Topographical Collection CXXII.65	yes	Shows Jones Island very clearly, excellent triangular shape and vegetation; clearly an island in Savannah River.
ca. 1740	British Museum King George III's Topographical Collection CXXII.66	yes	Shows Jones Island very clearly as an island in Savannah River.
1748	Eman: Bowen a New Map of Georgia . . .	yes	Shows Jones Island very prominently within dotted line boundary.
1751	A Plan of the Inlets and Rivers of Savannah and Warsaw . . . Henry Yonge	partial	Does not show the whole of Jones Island. Does indicate the southern shoreline and the flow channel around. Recommends blocking upstream entrance to Mud River to "open the main channel."
1752	A Map of Savannah River . . . Surveyed by William Noble of Brahm . . .	partial	Does not show whole island. Shows southern shore and deep reaching Mud River channels. "Savannah River north branch" appears along south shore of Jones Island.
1757	South Carolina and a Part of Georgia . . . William De Brahm	partial	Suggests presence of Jones Island by showing southern shoreline and Mud River channels indenting.
1768	Plat of Georgia Grant of "800 Acres Marsh Land" to Noble Jones Esquire by James Brown	yes	Clearly shown Jones Island a triangular shape with longest side along south fronting "Sa-v-a-n-n-a-h Ri-v-e-r" Mud River to N.W. and N.E. of island marked "North branch of Savannah River." Tip of Elba Island marked "The point of an Island Granted Jas. Whitefield." Bird Island and Long Island shores indicated. No question that this was an island in the Savannah River.

Concluding Observations

Jones Island—Mud River—*Continued*

Date	Map	Island Shown?	Comments
1773	A Map of the Province of South Carolina . . . James Cook	yes	Shows Jones Island as a large elongate triangle in the Savannah River. "Black River" written on flow to north and east which joins.
ca. 1775	Anonymous Map in Germain Papers, Clements Library	partial	Suggests Jones Island but does not show complete Mud River.
1775	An Accurate Map of North and South Carolina . . . by Henry Mouzon and others	yes	Shows an elongated triangular island.
1779	Siege De Savannah . . . Ozanne Collection	no	Shows tapering entrance to Mud River.
1780	Sketch of the Northern Frontiers of Georgia . . . by Archibald Campbell	partial	Suggests presence of Jones Island by indentations for Mud River but is incomplete.
1780	The Coast and Rivers of Georgia by Avery–Des Barres	partial	Suggests presence of Jones Island by indentations for Mud River. Possible later versions show completed Mud River with light lines.
1780	South Carolina and Part of Georgia by Stuart–De Brahm	yes	Jones Island clearly shown as a large, triangular shape created by an unnamed branch of Savannah and Black River flowing from north.
1794	A New Chart of the Coast of North Carolina . . . Exhibiting the Coast of Georgia etc. by Captain N. Holland	yes	Jones Island clearly shown as a large, triangular shape formed by an unnamed branch of Savannah River and Black River on north.
1818	Map of the State of Georgia . . . Eleazer Early	yes	Jones Island clearly shown as a large, triangular shape formed by branch of Savannah River. "Walls Cut" is shown.
1820	Map of Beaufort and District . . . surveyed by Charles Vignoles and Henry Ravenel	yes	Shows and names Jones Island. Mud River unnamed. Wrights River named to west of Mud River. Venus Point and Cunningham Point named. Cooks and Walls Cuts shown.
1821	State of Georgia Map of the River Savannah Surveyed by Captain Le Conte	partial	Suggests but does not show Jones Island.

Jones Island–Mud River—*Continued*

Date	Map	Island Shown?	Comments
1825	Map of Beaufort and District . . . surveyed by C. Vignoles and H. Ravenel 1820 improved for Mills Atlas 1825	yes	Shows and names Jones Island as an island in the Savannah River. Two smaller islands upstream from Mud River entrance. Walls Cut and Cooks Cut are shown. Turtle Island named.
1837	Savannah River from Its Mouth . . . Blunt–Le Conte	partial	Shows Jones Island's southern shore. Only name "Jones Island" appears. A small island shown in entrance to Mud River.
1838	Chart of Southern Coast from Tybee Bar . . . Charles Wilkes	partial	Shows eastern side of Jones Island. Name is included. Walls Cut is named "Norton's Cut."
1847	Map of the State of Georgia . . . Published by William G. Bonner	yes	Shows Jones Island unnamed but good triangular-shape, waterways unnamed.
1852	Map of Savannah River from Ft. Pulaski to Four Mile Point by Henry L. Whiting	yes	This is an excellent large-scale manuscript (1:10,000). Jones Island is shown and clearly named. Two small islands near the entrance to Mud River are shown accreting to the upstream end of the island. Mud River is not named. Norton's Cut is shown. Horseshoe Shoal is shown just upstream from Mud River entrance.
1855	Preliminary Chart of Savannah River	yes	Jones Island clearly shown as an island in the Savannah. Mud River not named, shown with a pattern of stippling. No depth soundings are shown in Mud River. The shoaling islands upstream of the Mud River entrance are shown as also "Horse Shoe Shoal."
1858	Plat for A. Smith Barnwell 5,825 acres Beaufort District	partial	Shows "Mud River" and western side of "Jones or Cabbage" Island. Wrights River named to west.
1861	Sketch of the Atlantic Coast . . . From Savannah River to St. Mary's River	yes	Shows and names Jones Island. Mud River clearly shown but not named. Venus Point named. Two small islands at entrance to Mud River.

Concluding Observations

Jones Island—Mud River—Continued

Date	Map	Island Shown?	Comments
1862	Map of Tybee and Vicinity by Col. Risa and Lt. Wilson	yes	Jones Island and Mud River clearly shown and named. "Batry Vulcan" and "Venus Point" named. Two small islands shown near mouth of Mud River.
1867	Savannah River and Wassaw Sound	yes	Jones Island and Mud River clearly shown and named. Two small islands near mouth of Mud River. Back River named between Jones Island and Turtle Island. Wright River not shown.
1874	Part of Savannah River by John De Wolf	no	Shows only unnamed southern side of Jones Island. Venus Point beacon shown. Mouth of Mud River shown but unnamed. Wright's River prominently shown between Jones and Turtle islands. Island shown at eastern point of Jones.
1875	Hydrography of the Savannah River from Duck Island	no	Jones Island named but not fully shown on map. "Venus Point Beacon (1874)" shown but no wing dams.
1875	Chatham County . . . Charles G. Platen	yes	Jones Island and Mud River clearly shown and named. Two small islands shown at mouth. Platen attributes to Coast Survey. Towers shown on south side. Wright River named as far as Cook's Cut. Along north and east side Jones River, Back River appears.
1876	Savannah River and Wassaw Sound . . . Chart 440	no	Jones Island named but Mud River no longer a continuous feature, width diminished. Two small islands appear to have accreted to fastland.
1879	Chart of Savannah River, Georgia, from Barnwell Island to Tybee Roads	no	Jones Island named. Mud River unnamed and discontinuous. Venus Point and Beacons 3 and 4 shown, island shown at eastern tip. Present and proposed channels shown. No wing dams shown.

Jones Island–Mud River—*Continued*

Date	Map	Island Shown?	Comments
1886	Tybee Roads Savannah River ... Chart 440	no	Jones Island named. Mud River unnamed and discontinuous. Beacons shown along south side, topography between 1852 and 1874, hydrography between 1860 and 1875, wing dams shown.
1887	Chart of the Savannah River, Georgia from the Head of Isla Island ...	no	Jones Island named. Lower end of Mud River shown, unnamed. No indication of upper Mud River. Numbered wing dams shown in place.
1895	Tybee Roads Savannah River ... Chart 440	no	Jones Island named. Mud River unnamed and discontinuous. Beacons shown along south side, topography between 1852 and 1874, hydrography between 1860 and 1875, wing dams shown.
1896	Map of Savannah Harbor Georgia Showing Works Constructed and Condition of Channel Improvement June 30, 1896	no	Only shows south side of named Jones Island. "Jones Island spur dams," "North Elba Island Training Wall," and "North Long Island Training Wall" all shown; no mouth of Mud River.
1898	Tybee Roads Savannah River ... Chart 440	no	Same as 1895.
1902	Tybee Roads Savannah River ... Chart 440	yes	Mud River Cut shown with water depths. Relic of old Mud River mouth shown; spur dams, wing dams, and training walls shown. Hydrography between 1860 and 1900 flashing white light near small island at east tip of Jones Island.

tions of the lower Savannah. As pointed out earlier, this area is in the delta of a large and sometimes violent river at the margin of a large and often stormy tidal sea. The islands and banks formed here have been in a state of flux since the post-Pleistocene era and continue in a state of flux today. Added to the natural forces creating this flux has been the increasingly sophisticated technology of channel improvement that has been applied by a host of engineers from the postcolonial period to the present day.

An analysis of a large number of maps that show the lowermost area of the Savannah River through the period of Georgia's first century and a quarter of existence reveals that the Oyster Bed was probably a changing, inconstant feature even before man began to take a direct role in channel modification in the area. As indicated in Table 3, the earliest surveys and maps of the area between Cockspur Island and Jones and Turtle islands consistently show an island at the approximate position of Oyster Bed and another close to Turtle. If this cartographic evidence is valid, it appears that two islands existed north of Cockspur during Georgia's first three decades. They were last shown on De Brahm's published map of 1757. If one allows for the lag between De Brahm's field observations and the publication of the engraved map in London, the terminal date for the existence of Oyster Bed as an island shown on maps and charts might be placed at 1752. If this is the case, and it appears to be, the question of what happened to the island becomes a challenge. In suggesting a reasonable answer or cause for the disappearance of this island in 1752, one must again stress the incredibly dynamic nature of the area concerned. Thus it seems reasonable to suggest that the Oyster Bed fell victim to a natural disaster. The summer of 1752 was characterized by a very hot drought that was ended in September by a hurricane that totally devastated Charleston a bit farther up the coast.[3] If that hurricane struck the lower Savannah with even a fraction of the ferocity delivered in South Carolina, both Oyster Bed and its unnamed sister island nearer to Turtle Island may have been swept away to become shoals. The available evidence suggests that the eye of the storm passed between Charleston and Savannah, thus supporting this hypothesis.

A further consideration of Table 3 suggests that by the 1780s Oyster Bed was once again attracting a degree of attention exceeding that paid to other shoals and shallow areas in the vicinity. This condition is further emphasized by the specialized symbolization applied to the Oyster Bed by such surveyors as John Le Conte in 1821 and Charles Wilkes in 1838. Special attention was also paid to the Oyster Bed by the workers of the U.S. Coast Survey and can be observed on the 1855 Preliminary Chart (Maps 16 and 19).

In 1855 the Oyster Bed area was prominently shown as an extensive area of shoals and oyster beds that were probably exposed much

TABLE 3
Oyster Bed Island Area
Cartographic Analysis Summary

Date	Map	Island Shown?	Comments
ca. 1729 [1776]	Plan of the River and Sound of Dawfoskee in South Carolina by John Gascoigne	yes?	Gascoigne made his surveys here in 1729. This published chart is based on them. May have had problems due to weather. Shows "The Peeper" as continuous with marsh and thus no south channel. Small island to north is probably Cockspur, not Oyster Bed. Mentions oyster banks in the Passage from the north end of Tybee to the Savannah River.
ca. 1740	A Map of the County of Savannah	yes?	Shows Cockspur with name "Peep." A large, unvegetated island shown to north may represent the Oyster Bed but unnamed.
ca. 1740	British Museum King George III's Topographical Collection CXXII.65	yes	Shows Cockspur unnamed and small unnamed islands to north. Several other small islets to west of Cockspur.
1751	A Plan of the Inlets and Rivers of Savannah and Warsaw . . . Henry Yonge	yes	Cockspur Island named and shown as vegetated with tree and grass symbols. "Drum Bank" shown to north with small area vegetated. This is a small island in position of Oyster Bed. A similar feature near Turtle Island also.
1752	A Map of Savannah River . . . Surveyed by William Noble of Brahm . . .	yes	Shows Cockspur and Drum Bank with small island similar to Yonge's, also island near Turtle Island.
1757	South Carolina and a Part of Georgia . . . William De Brahm	yes	Small island shown north of Cockspur in area of Oyster Bed, similar island shown near Turtle Island.
1762	Map of Coxspur Island by William De Brahm	no	Drawn for Governor to show fortification on Cockspur. "Sand Banck" shown to north of "North Channal." No island shown at Oyster Bed.

Oyster Bed Island Area—*Continued*

Date	Map	Island Shown?	Comments
ca. 1765	Chart of the Savannah Sound by William De Brahm	no	Shows Cockspur with Fort George. "Oyster Banks" shown to northeast and a long shoal to the north marked "Shoal dry at low water."
1773	[Chart of Entrance to Savannah River, Public Record Office] by William Lyford	no	The channel south of Cockspur is main channel. Oyster Bed not shown.
1773	A Map of the Province of South Carolina . . . James Cook	no	Cockspur named but shown as part of Tybee Shoal, shown by stippling to north but not named. Black Oyster Bank named but no island shown.
ca. 1775	Anonymous Map in Germain Papers, Clements Library	no	Cockspur Island named. Elongated shoal to north in area of Oyster Bed unnamed. Small island shown near Turtle Island unnamed.
1775	An Accurate Map of North and South Carolina . . . by Henry Mouzon and Others	no	Cockspur shown as part of Wilmington Island. Long shoal shown by stippling in area of Oyster Bed not named.
1779–80	Plan of the Siege of Savannah by John Wilson	no	Cockspur shown but not named. No shoal or island shown in position of Oyster Bed.
1780	Sketch of the Northern Frontiers of Georgia . . . by Archibald Campbell	no	Cockspur shown and named and elongated shoal in Oyster Bed area.
1780	A Map of South Carolina and a Part of Georgia . . . by Stuart and De Brahm	yes	Cockspur shown with small islands to north in area of Oyster Bed. "Black Oyster Bank" named near Turtle Island, small islet also shown.
1780	The Coast Rivers and Inlets of the Province of Georgia, Surveyed by Joseph Avery and Others . . . by J. F. W. Des Barres	yes	A very small islet shown just off northern shore of unnamed Cockspur Island. A larger islet shown near Turtle Island. Stippled shoals shown north of Cockspur.
1794	A New Chart of the Coast of North America . . . Exhibiting the Coast of Georgia etc. by Captain N. Holland	no	Cockspur shown with stippled shoal in area of Oyster Bed. Black Oyster Bed shown but no island.
1818	Plat of South Carolina Grant to Archibald Smith	no	Cockspur shown but no shoals or islands to north.

Concluding Observations 193

Oyster Bed Island Area—*Continued*

Date	Map	Island Shown?	Comments
1820	Map of Beaufort and District . . . surveyed by Charles Vignoles and Henry Ravenel	no	Manuscript original for Mills Atlas Beaufort District Map. Nothing shown in Oyster Bed area. Mills Atlas shows an island as result of engraver's error.
1821	State of Georgia Chart of the River Savannah Surveyed by Captain J. Le Conte	no	Cockspur shown with triangular shoal area to north stippled. "Northern" and "Southern" channels shown.
1822	Chart of the Mouth of Savannah River by Captain John Le Conte	no	"Cock-spur Island" shown. Oyster Bed unnamed but prominent as a shoal or hazard area outlined by tiny x-shaped symbols with a cross symbol within. This may indicate wreck and is repeated farther east. North and south channels shown by isobaths.
1822	Savannah River chart in Blunt's *American Coast Pilot*	no	Cockspur Island shown and named. North and south channels shown by lines and soundings. North is deepest. Large stippled shoal area in position of Oyster Bed. North channel passes south of it.
1825	Beaufort District Surveyed by C. Vignoles and H. Ravenel 1820 Improved for Mills Atlas 1825	no	Cockspur Island shown with small island to north midway to Turtle Island. Incorrect due to engraver's error.
1831	Cockspur Island and the Adjacent Channels . . . surveyed and drawn by R. E. Lee	no	Shows "North" and "South" Channels either side of Cockspur Island with "6' below lowwater level" isolines. Oyster Bed area indicated by stippling and small +-shaped symbols and named "White Oyster Bed." A beacon symbol on southern side near 6-foot depth line.
1838	Chart of Southern Coast from Tybee Bar . . . Charles Wilkes	yes?	Cockspur Island shown with plan of Fort Pulaski and other buildings. Oyster Bed area occupied by an irregular area of dense symbolization probably indicating a very prominent shoal. A "Squ. Beacon" shown on southwest side.

Concluding Observations

Oyster Bed Island Area—*Continued*

Date	Map	Island Shown?	Comments
1852	Map of Savannah River from Ft. Pulaski to Four Mile Point	yes?	Cockspur Island shown with Fort Pulaski and buildings, etc. Oyster Bed shown by two symbol patterns but not named. Square Beacon shown on southwest. Symbolization very heavy similar to Wilkes. Upstream side drawn with closely spaced dots.
1855	Preliminary Chart of Savannah River	yes?	Oyster Bed not named but has a very dense symbolization. An area of shoals and shallows extends to tip of Jones Island. Topography from 1851–52.
1861	Sketch of the Atlantic Coast . . . From Savannah River to St. Marys River	yes	Oyster Bed not named but shown in full unbroken outline. Shoals to north and west shown.
1861	Sketch of the Atlantic Coast . . . from Savannah River to St. Marys River	yes	Oyster Bed shown as unnamed island.
1863	Map of Wassaw Sound and Vicinity . . . by William L. Dennis	no	Area of Oyster Bed outlined by closely spaced dots. "Square Beacon" shown. Three "wrecks" shown near beacon. Upstream a short distance "Oyster Beacon (destroyed)."
1867	Savannah River and Wassaw Sound	no	Oyster Bed shown as a shoal with less than 1 foot water at low tide. Beacon shown at upstream end.
1871	Sketch Showing Examination of the North Channel, Savannah River, Opposite Fort Pulaski . . . By Captain William Ludlow	no	Oyster Bed area outlined with closely spaced dots. Name "Oyster Bed" prominently shown. Beacon shown by symbol and range line to Tybee Light.
1873	Coast of South Carolina and Georgia . . . Chart 55	no	Oyster Bed area shown as a shoal with less than one foot of water at mean low water. Beacon on upstream side.
1874	Entrance to Savannah River Georgia Surveyed by William E. McClintock	yes	Oyster Bed area outlined with closely spaced dots. Large area along northwest side shown in marsh vegetation symbol. Caption "Sand and Shell Banks." "Oyster Bank Lt. Ho." shown.

Concluding Observations 195

Oyster Bed Island Area—*Continued*

Date	Map	Island Shown?	Comments
1875	Chatham County . . . Charles G. Platen	no	Oyster Bed area outlined by dots and beacon shown on upstream side. Tybee Knoll Light Vessel shown downstream.
1879	Chart of the Savannah River Georgia, from Barnwell Island to Tybee Roads	no	Shows Oyster Bed area stippled as shoal. Beacon on upstream side. Old and new Channels around Oyster Bed are shown.
1881	Red Light Channel and Oyster shoals Mouth of Savannah River	no	Shows southern portion of Oyster Bed area outlined by dotted line. "Quarantine Station" and another building symbol shown as well as "Red Light." Azimuth lines from Red Light to other features such as Tybee Light and Venus Point Beacon included.
1880	Tybee Roads Savannah River . . . Chart 440	yes	"Oyster Bed" clearly outlined. Symbols show location of "Quarantine" and "Custom Ho. Quarters." "Beacon" position shown by symbol and described "Red." Training wall shown extending to shoal about ¾ mile northwest. Dashed lines extend to east marked "Jetty (constructing)." Thalweg shown by dashed line passes very close.
1887	Chart of the Savannah River, Georgia, from Cross Tides to the Sea . . .	yes	"Oyster Bed" named and clearly outlined. "Quarantine" layout shown on northwest side. Training wall No. 31 shown and marked "Unfinished 1885." Beacon symbol on upstream side.
1887	Chart of the Savannah River, Georgia, from the Head of Isla Island . . .	yes	"Oyster Beds" clearly outlined and stippled. Training wall shown (No. 31) extending toward northwest. No beacon shown. Line of main navigation channel between Oyster Bed and Cockspur indicated.
1889	Hydrographical Survey of Savannah River, Georgia made 1889 . . . General Sketch showing location of Tide Gauges and of Gauged Cross Sections	yes?	Oyster Bed area outlined in dots not named. Two training walls shown extending northwest and east.

Oyster Bed Island Area—*Continued*

Date	Map	Island Shown?	Comments
1890	Tybee Roads and Wassaw Sound Georgia Chart to Accompany Report on Oyster Survey [USGS Bulletin No. 19, 1891]	yes	Oyster Bed area outlined. Large area of shoals to east marked "Oyster Beds." "Quarantine," "Custom Ho Quarters," and "Beacon-Red" shown by symbols. Training wall to northwest shown as well as jetty under construction to east. Thalweg shown by dashed line.
1893	Map showing the area to be dredged between Oyster Bed and Cockspur Island	yes	Shows Oyster Bed area outlined in fine dashed line with northwestern portion as a small island. Building and two probable pier structures shown on small island. "Dam No. 31" shown extending to northwest. "Red Light" and small building symbol on south near channel.
1895	Tybee Roads, Savannah River . . . Chart 440	yes	Oyster Bed area clearly shown with solid line. Caption "Oyster Beds" extends through shallows to east. Symbols marked "Quarantine," "Custom Ho. Quarters," and "Light Red." Two training walls shown. Thalweg shown as dashed line.
1896	Chart Showing Entrance to Savannah River, Georgia . . .	yes	Oyster Bed not named but delineated by dotted line. Small area at northwest edge enclosed by solid line corresponds with location of quarantine station. Quarantine pier shown on Cockspur. Two training walls and "Red Light" are shown. Thalweg indicated by dashed line marked "Least Channel Depth 19.0 feet at Mean Low Water."
1898	Tybee Roads, Savannah River . . . Chart 440	yes	Oyster Bed area outlined and shaded. Caption "Oyster Beds" in shallows to east. Dark shaded or black small area on northwest side marked "Quarantine." Symbols marked "Custom Ho. Quarters" and "Light-Red." Two training walls shown. Thalweg shown by dashed line.

Oyster Bed Island Area—*Continued*

Date	Map	Island Shown?	Comments
1902	Tybee Roads, Savannah River ... Chart 440	yes	Oyster Bed area outlined and shaded. Caption "Oyster Beds" extends over shallows to east. Very small kidney-shaped area on northwest side shown as island with caption "Quarantine." "Custom Quarters," and "Light F. R." shown. Northwest training wall shown completed to Turtle Island. Both jetties to east shown completed. Training wall and dams shown at Horseshoe Shoal. Main navigation channel shown with dashed line.

of the time. Exactly when Oyster Bed's reemergence qualified it for full status as an island is difficult to determine. The period after 1855 was dramatically punctuated by the Civil War and the siege of Fort Pulaski on Cockspur Island in 1862. A thorough review of the wartime activities in the vicinity of the Oyster Bed would be extremely valuable but space will not allow it here. For example, a number of ships were sunk in the vicinity to block the deep-water ship channel nearby. An 1863 manuscript survey by William Dennis of the U.S. Coast Survey titled "Map of Wassaw Sound and Vicinity Georgia" shows three "wrecks" very close to the southern limit of the Oyster Bed. Two beacons located between the Oyster Bed and Cockspur are marked "destroyed." These wrecks, if allowed to remain, might well have led to accelerated accretion in the area of the Oyster Bed. Dennis's 1863 manuscript used an outline of small dots to indicate the Oyster Bed; a chart published in 1867 used a "Mean Low Water" isobath to accomplish this task. This was the U.S. Coast Survey chart titled "Savannah River and Wassaw Sound," scale 1:40,000. On this finished chart, which incorporated work by Dennis, Oyster Bed is indicated as an area with less than one foot of depth at mean low water. Deep water was located close to its northern, southern, and western sides with a long, shallow tongue stretching to the east. At very low water much or all of the Oyster Bed was exposed in the post–Civil War period. Also, wrecks and other obstructions could be counted upon to contribute to siltation and eventual accretion if allowed to remain contiguous with the bed. Like some soggy Phoenix, the Oyster Bed seemed poised to rise again in the war's aftermath.

Lieutenant O. M. Carter's detailed essay, "History of Past Work—Improvement of Savannah River and Harbor," was quoted at length in Part III and should be consulted for a review of the U.S. Army Corps of Engineers' post–Civil War activities in the lower reaches of the river. Among several projects, he mentioned the dredging of the channel to the north of the Oyster Beds in 1869 and the undertaking of a major channel-deepening scheme in 1873 that included continued dredging adjacent to the Oyster Beds.

In 1874 a detailed topographic survey of the area at a scale of 1:5,000 was prepared by the U.S. Coast Survey under the direction of Charles Hosmer. Hosmer's large-scale chart provides an excellent view of conditions at the Oyster Bed north of Cockspur Island in April 1874. The shape of the shoal area of the bed is similar to that outlined by William Ludlow in 1871. Unlike Ludlow, whose main concern was the bathymetry of the dredged channel to the north of the bed, Hosmer included a number of topographic details. Of particular concern to this discussion is the fact that a portion of the northwest side of the bed is shown with a vegetation symbol covering an area of about 750 feet in length. In the unvegetated areas that were presumably still subject to frequent inundation, the caption "Sand and Shell Banks" provides an excellent verbal description of the Oyster Bed. Also shown are "Oyster Bank Lt. Ho" and a "Stake with 2 Barrels" obviously occupying the Oyster Bed to help provide for safe navigation. Thus it appears that sometime prior to 1874 the Oyster Bed had again emerged as an island with a large area suitable for the growth of a vegetative cover. It would appear that sedimentation and accretion were actively proceeding in this immediate area at this time. The two "Beacons" shown in the waters between Cockspur Island and Oyster Bed Island are indicated as being located on small islands with drawn shorelines indicating elevations above the datum.

In the next few years the newly reemerged Oyster Bed Island was to attract major attention and become the site of operations for an agency of the Savannah city government. This was the activity undertaken by the Board of Sanitary Commissioiners, whose responsibility included all matters dealing with public health in Savannah and its port. The inspection and quarantine of ships arriving was a major concern of the board.

Concluding Observations 199

On April 23, 1877, at a special meeting, the Savannah health officer brought several important matters to the board's attention. Among these was the question of how best to dispose of ballast from ships being disinfected. The health officer was directed to communicate with the commissioners of pilotage with respect to the best mode of ballast disposal. The health officer reported that they decided "that the ballast of all vessels from infected ports should be deposited in the Savannah River at the point designated by the Commissioners of Pilotage. In the North Channel, to the north of Oyster Shell Bed, opposite Cockspur Island, as far east as the eastern end of the Oyster Shell Bed" (John F. Wheaton, *Report of John F. Wheaton, Mayor of the City of Savannah, for the Year Ending December 31, 1877*, p. 78). The Corps of Engineers had earlier decided to abandon their dredging efforts north of the Oyster Bed in favor of a channel along its south side, where it remains today.

The health officer carried out these directions and was able to report that "all vessels from infected ports were detained at quarantine from ten to forty days after arrival, their ballast deposited in the North Channel, and they were thoroughly cleansed and disinfected before being permitted to come to the city" (ibid., p. 79). Thus two important facts are revealed concerning the nature of the area between Cockspur and Turtle islands. First, the "Oyster Shell Bed" is used as a reference point and, second, ballast is dumped in the abandoned North Channel between the Oyster Bed and Turtle Island. Significantly, the area was still designated as something other than an island at this date. One is prompted to speculate that the violent storm that devastated Tybee Island in 1874 also lowered the Oyster Bed once again to the status of a shoal. In view of Oyster Bed's past vulnerability to heavy weather, such a conclusion seems warranted.

The disposition of ballast as a concern in the area of public health is seldom thought of at the present time. In the nineteenth century, however, it was a serious matter, as illustrated in the following extract from the Savannah health officer's report:

> Dr. Habersham, Health Officer, made a report of having boarded and inspected the Norwegian bark Navedis, on the 5th of August at the Atlantic and Gulf Railroad wharf, . . . and finding her with foul ballast, part of which ballast having been discharged and spread out on the wharf. This ballast consisting of wet sand, with which rotten wheat was mixed, was reported by the Health Officer to be unsanitary, and it was

advised by him that the bark be remanded to the Quarantine Station for discharge of ballast, and disinfection at that point. [John F. Wheaton, *Report of John F. Wheaton, Mayor of the City of Savannah, for the Year Ending December 31, 1879*, p. 69]

The lower quarantine station for Savannah was well established and flourishing opposite Cockspur Island in the area of the Oyster Bed in 1879, when the city surveyor reported:

The breakwater for the protection of the quarantine buildings, which was in process of construction at the date of my last report has been completed. The plan has been somewhat modified in the following particulars: Instead of two rows of piles with a backing of plank on the seaward side, the backing has been omitted, and a third row of piles driven. Each row of piles has been thoroughly braced and capped, and a footway laid for conveying stone ballast from the wharf, to and along the breakwater for its protection. [Ibid., pp. 47–48]

In reporting his activities in the following year, 1880, the Savannah health officer again drew attention to the subject of ballast disposal: "Special attention has been directed to ballast from infected or suspected ports. No sand or mixed ballast has been allowed to be brought to the city, and until late in the month of November, even stone ballast brought from such ports was discharged at Quarantine Station. The discharge of ballast is considered absolutely necessary to the thorough cleansing of a vessel, as the timbers cannot be reached without so doing." [John F. Wheaton, *Report of John F. Wheaton, Mayor of the City of Savannah, for the Year Ending December 31, 1880*, pp. 69–70]

Although it was reportedly hard to reach during stormy weather, the quarantine station building and wharf on the Oyster Bed were described as being in "very good condition, the foundations of these having been much improved by the deposit of ballast" (ibid., p. 70).

The severe hurricane that struck on August 27, 1881, devastated the quarantine station. The portion of the Savannah mayor's report dealing with this calamity gives a very good description of the facility that had been built on the Oyster Bed a few years before:

QUARANTINE

The buildings at the Quarantine Station were destroyed, or so badly damaged by the hurricane in August last, as to be unsafe for further occupancy, and useless. The Wharf structure, except the original piling, the water tank, boats, furniture, provisions, disinfectants, etc., were entirely swept away by the force of the wind and sea. The Spanish bark, Marietta, abandoned by her officers and crew at the Quarantine Wharf, was dismasted, capsized and wrecked near the Quarantine Station. The lives of the Quarantine officer and assistants were in great jeopardy, and saved by their clinging to the timbers under the roof of the hospital building, and sustaining themselves there until the storm abated.

The Wharf has been rebuilt in an improved manner, and a contract made for rebuilding the hospital and dwelling for the Quarantine officer on a plan which it is believed will be secure in future. The work is now in progress, and it is expected will be completed early in February next.

New boats, furniture, and fixtures generally, have been purchased, and temporary quarters provided for the Quarantine officer, on Tybee Island, until the Station is again ready for occupancy. The cost of rebuilding, the purchase of boats, furniture, etc., and of stores and property, to replace those destroyed by the storm, will amount to $3,576.76, of which sum $2,000 have been expended. The quarantine of all vessels from infected ports has been strictly maintained and the regulations prescribed by the Sanitary Commissioners rigidly enforced. [John F. Wheaton, *Report of John F. Wheaton, Mayor of the City of Savannah, for the Year Ending December 31, 1881*, pp. 23–24]

No time was lost in building new facilities at the Oyster Bed site abreast of Cockspur Island. According to Mayor John Wheaton, they were convenient and decidedly more comfortable than the old quarters. Even more important, they were believed to be secure and safe against future storms.

Mayor Wheaton employed the term "island" in his 1882 report of the rebuilding effort at the Oyster Bed. The ballast dumped to protect the quarantine station foundations probably had aided in the area's emergence as an island in the few years immediately preceding the hurricane of 1881.

Construction details on an additional wharf built at the quarantine station in 1882 are worthy of quotation here:

QUARANTINE STATION

Proposals for building an additional wharf and a tramway to connect with breakwater in rear of the quarantine building was received, under resolution of Council, February 28th, authorizing the work. The contract was awarded to Mr. Francis M. Jones for the sum of $2,700.

The new wharf was built fifty feet west of the old, and is one hundred feet in length. It consists of three rows of twelve by twelve inch piles, thirty feet long. Each pile is covered with yellow metal from high water mark to a point two feet below the bed of the river. The braces and caps are of the same size as the piles. The joists are four by twelve inches, with six by twelve inch joists, at intervals of ten feet, the whole covered with three-inch planks.

Eleven fender piles, protected with yellow metal as a defense against worms, are driven along the wharf front and securely bolted to the piles and horizontal braces. The tramway is one hundred and ——— feet in length, and consists of two rows of piles, with diagonal braces. It was not thought necessary to protect more than half the tramway piles or up to the shore line at low water. The string-pieces forming the tramway have iron rails, it being designed to use a car for the transportation of rock and sand ballast from the vessels to the breakwater. This has not yet been done, however, and the work is being performed with wheelbarrows.

The accumulation of stone at the breakwater during the year has been considerable, giving additional security to the buildings. [Rufus E. Lester, *Annual Report of Rufus E. Lester, Mayor of the City of Savannah, for the Year Ending December 31st, 1883*, pp. 81–82]

By 1885, the work of the U.S. Corps of Engineers was perceived as creating a new problem at the quarantine station. This was shoaling, as explained in the health officer's report of that year:

It is reported to me by pilots of Savannah, who have taken the soundings, that the entrance to the quarantine anchorage has shoaled full eighteen (18) inches during the past year. This has resulted in consequence of closure of the Savannah River outlet by jetty there placed for improvement of channel of Savannah River. I call attention to this statement that city authorities may take such action as will ensure ballast wharves in the vicinity of the present station when those now in use prove unavailable. [Rufus E. Lester, *Annual Report of Rufus E. Lester, Mayor of the City of Savannah, for the Year Ending December 31, 1885*, p. 90]

By the following year, Savannah's health officer, Dr. J. T. McFarland, was obliged to report that the entrance of the quarantine anchorage was slowly but surely filling up. Vessels drawing twelve feet could not enter the quarantine ground at less than three-quarters floodtide. McFarland vigorously urged that the city authorities increase and improve the wharfing facilities at the station to avoid excessive delays to shipping bound for Savannah.

By 1887 the continued functioning of a quarantine facility at the Oyster Bed was in serious doubt. In his report for 1887, Savannah's mayor reported:

THE QUARANTINE

The quarantine expenses have been $5,444.06; $2,362.50 of this amount has been expended for dredging, driving mooring piling and repairing wharves.

The receipts have been $4,881.38 for boarding fees and fumigating vessels. The works constructed by the United States government in pursuance of its plan to deepen the main channel of the river is causing shoaling at the quarantine wharves so rapidly that in a very short time they will become useless and the station as a place for unballasting will have to be abandoned. Dredging has been tried, but its effects are so temporary as to discourage the hope of overcoming the difficulty by such means.

It is barely possible, however, that the station can be made to serve its purposes for another season. [Rufus E. Lester, *Annual Report of Rufus E. Lester, Mayor of the City of Savannah, for the Year Ending December 31st, 1887*, p. 14]

The bare possibility was not realized, and the Oyster Bed site was abandoned.

In 1889 the new quarantine facilities at Long Island were flourishing. Among other innovations included was a "steam hoister" that allowed ballast to be off-loaded for twenty cents per ton. Much of the rock ballast was sold by the city to sink the mats, which formed the jetties in the river. The old residence of the quarantine officer situated at the Oyster Bed Station was reported to be in good repair. It was, however, noted that "on account of the removal of ballast surrounding it, the water from the river now flows underneath it at high tide" (John Schwarz, *Annual Report of John Schwarz, Mayor of the City of Savannah, for the Year Ending December 31st, 1889*, p. 209). From this time onward the character of the area of the Oyster Bed would be largely determined by the Corps of Engineers as they struggled to control the forces of nature at play near the Savannah's mouth.

NOTES

1. For a discussion of the evolution of the third Barnwell Island, see Louis De Vorsey, Jr., "Dating the Emergence of a Savannah River Island: An Hypothesis in Forensic Historical Geography," *Environmental Review* 4 (1980): 6–19.

2. Noble Jones petitioned Georgia's executive for a grant of "an Island of Marsh lying below an Island heretofore Granted James Whitfield and above the Black Oyster Bank and bounded northerly by the North Branch of Savan-

nah River" on February 2, 1768 (Candler, ed., *Colonial Records of Georgia*, 10:400).

3. For a quoted eyewitness account of the event in South Carolina, see Louis De Vorsey, Jr., *De Brahm's Report of the General Survey in the Southern District of North America*, p. 13.

EPILOGUE

THIS EXAMINATION of Georgia's historical boundary line with South Carolina in the lower Savannah River was first organized as a research report to the attorney general of Georgia. In due course a copy of that research report was delivered to the attorney general of South Carolina in exchange for research reports compiled by experts working for that state. This exchange guaranteed that the main elements of historical geographic evidence in each state's case were available for study and analysis long before a trial was held in the spring of 1981.

Because of its length and comprehensive nature, my report was released to South Carolina in two separate portions, one covering the eighteenth-century material and one including the nineteenth-century and later material. The first material released comprised the work covered in Parts I and II of this book. After this had been studied by South Carolina attorneys and expert consultants, I was required to testify under oath regarding its contents and my opinions concerning the boundary dispute. This testimony took the form of a deposition that occupied the day of August 21, 1978, and was held at the Georgia Judicial Building in Atlanta. On that occasion I was interrogated by a South Carolina assistant attorney general who was accompanied by four additional attorneys from that state. The typewritten transcript of that deposition filled 107 pages and became available for analysis and use in cross-examinations during the trial in 1981.

Shortly after that deposition session I departed for a year in England on a research fellowship that had been awarded by the American Council of Learned Societies. My research during that year focused on the early exploration and charting of the Gulf Stream and had no direct bearing on the Georgia–South Carolina boundary dispute.

In due course, however, the remaining portions of my boundary research report were exchanged with South Carolina. On July 24, 1980, a second deposition was taken to cover the matters included in Parts III and IV of this book. This deposition session extended through a long day and resulted in 238 typewritten transcript pages of questions and answers. The attorney retained by South Carolina to take this deposition had not, however, completed his examination and a date was set for a third session.

This final pretrial interrogation took place in the now-familiar conference room of the Georgia Judicial Building on September 4, 1980. On this occasion a further 166 typewritten pages were required to transcribe the South Carolina attorney's questions and my responses. All of my deposition testimony was under oath and available for analysis by the South Carolinians along with my full report text and maps. Their skillful cross-examination of my direct testimony during the courtroom hearings of the following year frequently took the form of trying to show inconsistencies between the testimony and my earlier deposition statements.

Pretrial written briefs outlined the positions of the two states in considerable detail. These were addressed to the special master, Judge Walter E. Hoffman, and insured that he would be familiar with the major issues in advance of the formal hearing that opened in the U.S. District Court in Atlanta on the morning of April 27, 1981. During that week Georgia presented its case-in-chief supported by the testimony of its witnesses and experts and a mass of documentary and cartographic evidence.

On the afternoon of Monday, April 27, I took the witness stand and was placed under oath. I remained there, while the court was in session, until the afternoon of Thursday, April 30, 1981. The attorney representing Georgia conducted my direct examination, which consisted of a continuing series of questions based on most of the documents and maps discussed in this book. This process continued until the afternoon of Wednesday, April 29. At that point the South Carolina lawyer, who had interrogated me in Atlanta at the two deposition sessions in 1980, began his cross-examination. This continued through the afternoon of the next day, when I was excused and another Georgia witness took the stand.

After a two-week recess, the trial moved to Columbia, South Carolina. There, in the federal court building, South Carolina presented its case and witnesses from May 18 until May 28, 1981. Three expert witnesses, Dr. William P. Cumming, Dr. Arthur H. Robinson, and Dr.

Harry R. Merrens, were called to give testimony in the historical and cartographic areas that I had covered in Atlanta two weeks before. They too were intensively cross-examined by the attorney representing Georgia. As had been the case in Atlanta, masses of documentary and cartographic evidence accompanied their testimony. Predictably the South Carolina experts proffered interpretations of the maps and documents that differed, sometimes radically, from those that I had provided in Atlanta.

Final arguments and rebuttal testimony in the case were heard by Judge Hoffman in Atlanta from June 8 to June 10, 1981. In this phase only Dr. Robinson and I were called upon to give testimony on the historical maps and historical geographic issues in the case. As before, we were closely cross-examined by counsel for the disputing states as we developed our different views as to where the boundary should be.

During the summer and early autumn, attorneys for Georgia and South Carolina provided Judge Hoffman with detailed written posttrial briefs. In general these lengthy briefs emphasized the evidence and testimony that were deemed supportive of one state while derogating or ignoring evidence and testimony favorable to the other.

On October 1, 1981, the lawyers representing Georgia and South Carolina journeyed to Norfolk, Virginia, for one last day of oral argument before Judge Hoffman in the District Court there. At that time, the special master also assumed custody of the hundreds of map exhibits, photographs, and documents that had been entered as evidence. At the time of writing, Judge Hoffman is considering the evidence and testimony. Sometime in early 1982 he is expected to state his findings and opinions on the issues raised by Georgia's complaint in a formal report and recommendation to the Supreme Court of the United States.

Both states will then be given an opportunity to submit written exceptions to the special master's report. Finally, the justices of the Supreme Court will schedule and hear oral arguments by representatives from each state. After due consideration, a decision by the nation's highest tribunal may at last end this 250-year-old boundary dispute in the lower Savannah River.

LOUIS DE VORSEY, JR.

Athens, Georgia
November 12, 1981

BIBLIOGRAPHY

BOOKS AND ARTICLES

Anderson, Edward C. *Report of Edward C. Anderson, Mayor of the City of Savannah, for the Year Ending September 30, 1867, to Which is Added the Treasurer's Report.* Savannah, Ga.: C. E. O'Sullivan, 1867.

Blunt, E. M. *American Coast Pilot.* 10th ed. New York: E. M. Blunt, 1822 and 1826.

Bryant, Pat, comp. *Calendar of Georgia–South Carolina Boundary Papers in the State Archives Building.* Atlanta: Surveyor General Department, 1977.

Burnett, Edmund C., ed. *Letters of Members of the Continental Congress.* Vol 8, January 1, 1785–July 25, 1789. Washington, D.C.: Carnegie Institution, 1936.

Calendar of State Papers, Colonial Series, America and West Indies. Vol. 42, 1735–36. London: Her Majesty's Stationery Office, 1953.

Candler, Allen D., ed. *The Colonial Records of the State of Georgia.* Vol. 1, 1732–52, Charter of the Colony and Journal of the Proceedings of the Trustees. Atlanta, Ga.: Franklin Printing and Publishing Co., Geo. W. Harrison, State Printer, 1904.

———. *The Colonial Records of the State of Georgia.* Vol. 6, October 12, 1742–October 30, 1754, Proceedings of the President and Assistants. Atlanta: Franklin Printing and Publishing Co., George W. Harrison, State Printer, 1906.

———. *The Colonial Records of the State of Georgia.* Vol. 10, January 6, 1767–December 5, 1769, Proceedings and Minutes of the Governor and Council. Atlanta: Franklin-Turner Co., 1907.

Carter, Oberlin M. "History of Past Work—Improvement of Savannah River and Harbor." In U.S., Congress, House, 50th Cong., 2d sess., *Executive Document 1*, pt. 2, vol. 2, pp. 1012–30. Washington, D.C.: U.S. Government Printing Office, 1888.

———. "Improvement of Rivers and Harbors in Eastern Georgia. Report of Capt. O. M. Carter, Corps of Engineers, Officer in Charge, for the Fiscal Year Ending June 30, 1896, with other Documents Relating to the Works." In U.S., Congress, House, 54th Cong., 2d sess., *House Document*

2, pp. 1211–1303. Washington, D.C.: U.S. Government Printing Office, 1896.

———. "Modified Project of Improvement of Harbor at Savannah, Ga." In U.S., Congress, House, 53d Cong., 3d sess. *Executive Document 115*, pp. 2–5. Washington, D.C.: U.S. Government Printing Office, 1895.

———. "Project of Lieutenant O. M. Carter, Corps of Engineers." In U.S., Congress, House, 51st Cong., 2d sess., *Executive Document 1*, pt. 2, vol. 2, pp. 1259–1548. Washington, D.C.: U.S. Government Printing Office, 1891.

———. "Survey for Steamboat Channel, Seven Feet Deep at Mean Low Water, between Beaufort, S.C., and Savannah, Ga." In U.S., Congress, House, 53d Cong., 3d sess., *Executive Document 295*, pp. 1–7. Washington, D.C.: U.S. Government Printing Office, 1895.

Chief of Engineers. "Report from the Chief Engineer." In U.S., Congress, Senate, 24th Cong., 2d sess. *Senate Document 1*, pp. 190–212. Washington, D.C.: Printed by Gales and Seaton, 1837.

Clark, William Bell, ed. *Naval Documents of the American Revolution*. Vol. 4. Washington, D.C.: Division of Naval History, U.S. Government Printing Office, 1969.

Communication to His Excellency Governor Cobb, on the Boundary between South-Carolina and Georgia; by the Attorney-General of South-Carolina. Charleston: Steam Power Press of Walker & James, 1853.

Coulter, E. Merton, ed. *The Journal of Peter Gordon, 1732–1735*. Athens: University of Georgia Press, 1963.

Crabtree, William; Wellman, F. H.; and Hunter, William J. "Report on Examination of Dam between Hutchinson's and Fig Island, April 2, 1830." In U.S., Congress, House, 21st Cong., 1st sess., *Executive Document 106*, p. 59. Washington, D.C.: U.S. Government Printing Office, 1830.

Cumming, William P. *The Southeast in Early Maps*. Chapel Hill: University of North Carolina Press, 1962.

Daniell, Dr. William C. "Correspondence and Reports Concerning Savannah River Improvements, 1827–30." In U.S., Congress, House, 21st Cong., 1st sess. *Executive Document 106*, pp. 1–59. Washington, D.C.: U.S. Government Printing Office, 1831.

De Vorsey, Louis, Jr. "Dating the Emergence of a Savannah River Island: An Hypothesis in Forensic Historical Geography." *Environmental Review* 4 (1980):6–19.

———. "William Gerard De Brahm, Surveyor-General and Man of Science in Royal Georgia." *Bulletin of the Georgia Academy of Science* 34 (1976): 204–9.

———, ed. *De Brahm's Report of the General Survey in the Southern District of North America*. Columbia: University of South Carolina Press, 1971.

Easterby, J. H., ed. *The Journal of the Commons House of Assembly, November 10, 1736–June 7, 1739. The Colonial Records of South Carolina*. Columbia: Historical Commission of South Carolina, 1951.

Engineer Department. "Report from, November 15, 1835." In U.S., Con-

gress, Senate, 24th Cong., 1st sess., *Senate Document 1*, pp. 107–8. Washington, D.C.: U.S. Government Printing Office, 1836.
Furlong, Lawrence. *The American Coast Pilot.* Newburyport: Edmund M. Blunt, 1798.
Gamble, Thomas. *A History of the City Government of Savannah, Georgia, from 1790 to 1901.* Savannah: City Council, 1902.
Georgia Committee on Internal Improvement. "Report on Proposed Improvement of the Navigation of the Savannah River . . . December 9, 1835." In U.S., Congress, Senate, 24th Cong., 2d sess., *Senate Document 1*, pp. 276–77. Washington, D.C.: U.S. Government Printing Office, 1836.
Gillmore, Q. A. *Official Report to the United States Engineer Department of the Siege and Reduction of Fort Pulaski, Georgia, February, March, and April, 1862.* New York: D. Van Nostrand, 1862.
Granger, Mary L. *Savannah Harbor: Its Origin and Development, 1733–1890.* Savannah: U.S. Army Engineer District, Savannah Corps of Engineers, 1968.
Hawes, Lilla M., ed. "Proceedings of the President and Assistants in Council of Georgia, 1749–1751." *Georgia Historical Quarterly* 35 (1951): 323–50.
Henry, J. P. "Report to Secretary of Navy Respecting the Harbor of Savannah, November 12, 1828." In U.S., Congress, Senate, 20th Cong., 2d sess., *Senate Document 28*, pp. 8–15. Washington, D.C.: U.S. Government Printing Office, 1829.
Historical Manuscripts Commission. *Manuscripts of the Earl of Egmont.* Vol. 2, 1734–38. London: His Majesty's Stationery Office, 1923.
Jones, Charles C. *The Siege of Savannah in 1779, as Described in Two Contemporaneous Journals.* Albany, N.Y.: J. Munsell, 1874.
Journals of the American Congress: From 1774 to 1788. Vol. 4. Washington, D.C.: Way and Gideon, 1823.
Journals of Congress: Containing Their Proceedings from November 4, 1785, to November 3, 1786. Vol. 11. Philadelphia: Folwell's Press, 1801.
Knight, Lucien Lamar, ed., and Candler, Allen D., comp. *The Colonial Records of the State of Georgia.* Vol. 26, 1750–52, Original Papers, Trustees, President and Assistants and Others. New York: AMS Press, 1970.
Lane, Mills, ed. *General Oglethorpe's Georgia: Colonial Letters, 1733–43.* Vol. 1. Savannah: The Beehive Press, 1975.
Leowald, Klaus G.; Starika, Beverly; and Taylor, Paul S., eds. and trans. "Johann Martin Bolzius Answers a Questionnaire on Carolina and Georgia." Reprinted from the *William and Mary Quarterly*, 3d ser., vols. 14 and 15. The Georgia Salzburger Society, n.d.
Lester, Rufus E. *Annual Report of Rufus E. Lester, Mayor of the City of Savannah, for the Year Ending December 31st, 1883. To Which Is Added the Treasurer's Report, Reports of Different Departments of the City Government, and Cotton and Other Statistics of the Port of Savannah.* Savannah: George N. Nichols, 1884.
———. *Annual Report of Rufus E. Lester, Mayor of the City of Savannah, for the Year Ending December 31st, 1885. To Which Is Added the Treasurer's Report,*

Reports of Different Departments of the City Government, and Cotton and Other Statistics of the Port of Savannah. Savannah: Morning News Steam Power House, 1886.

———. *Annual Report of Rufus E. Lester, Mayor of the City of Savannah, for the Year Ending December 31st, 1888. To Which is Added the Treasurer's Report, Reports of Different Departments of the City Government, and Cotton and Other Statistics of the Port of Savannah.* Savannah: George N. Nichols, 1888.

Lonsdale, Richard, ed. *Atlas of North Carolina.* Chapel Hill: University of North Carolina Press, 1967.

M'Call, Hugh. *The History of Georgia, Containing Brief Sketches of the Most Remarkable Events, Up to the Present Day.* 2 vols. Savannah: Seymour and Williams, 1811–16.

McCulloch, Hugh. "Letter from the Secretary of the Treasury, in Answer to a Resolution of the House of 16th Instant, Relative to Obstructions in Savannah River." In U.S., Congress, House, 40th Cong., 2d sess., *Executive Document 123*, pp. 1–8. Washington, D.C.: U.S. Government Printing Office, 1868.

Mackay, Captain John. "Improvement of Savannah River, December 6, 1839." In U.S., Congress, Senate, 26th Cong., 1st sess., *Senate Document 58*, pp. 144–46. Washington, D.C.: U.S. Government Printing Office, 1840.

Mansfield, Joseph K. F. "Report of the Progress Made in the Improvement of the Navigation of the Savannah River, from the City of Savannah to its Mouth, to the Year Ending the 30th of September, 1836, Inclusive." In U.S., Congress, Senate, 24th Cong., 2d sess., *Senate Document 1*, pp. 273–77. Washington, D.C.: U.S. Government Printing Office, 1837.

Marbury, Horatio, and Crawford, William H. *Digest of the Laws of the State of Georgia.* Savannah: Seymour, Woolhopter and Stephens, 1802.

Parker, Mattie Erma Edwards, ed. *North Carolina Charters and Constitutions 1578–1698.* Raleigh: Carolina Charter Tercentenary Commission, 1963.

Patterson, C. P. "Letter to George S. Boutwell, Secretary of the Treasury, January 25, 1870." In U.S., Congress, House, 41st Cong., 2d sess., *House Executive Document 153*, pp. 2–3. Washington, D.C.: U.S. Government Printing Office, 1871.

Popple, Henry. *A Map of the British Empire in America with the French and Spanish Settlements Adjacent Thereto.* Introductory notes by William P. Cumming and Helen Wallis. Lympne Castle, Kent: Harry Margary, 1972.

Reese, Trevor R., ed. *Our First Visit in America: Early Reports from the Colony of Georgia, 1732–1740.* Savannah: The Beehive Press, 1974.

———. *The Most Delightful Country of the Universe.* Savannah: The Beehive Press, 1972.

Report of the Committee Appointed to Examine into the Proceedings of the People of Georgia with Respect to the Province of South Carolina, and the Disputes Subsisting between the Two Colonies. Charles-Town: Lewis Timothy, 1736.

Rhodes, Ralph F. *The Hydraulics of a Tidal River as Illustrated by Savannah Harbor, Georgia.* Savannah: U.S. Army Engineer District, Savannah Corps of Engineers, 1949.

Savannah Chamber of Commerce. "Memorial of . . . Praying the Removal of Obstructions to the Navigation of the Savannah River, January 3, 1846." In U.S., Congress, Senate, 29th Cong., 1st sess., *Senate Document 36*, pp. 1–5. Washington, D.C.: Ritchie and Heiss, 1846.

Saye, Albert B., ed. *Georgia's Charter of 1732*. Athens: University of Georgia Press, 1942.

Sears, Clifton B.; Bixby, W. H.; and Symons, Thomas W. "Report of Board of Engineers on Project for Improvement of Savannah Harbor and Steamboat Channel from Beaufort, S.C., to Savannah, Ga." In Annual Reports of the War Department for the Fiscal Year ended June 30, 1900. *Report of the Chief of Engineers*, pt. 3, pp. 1922–27. Washington, D.C.: U.S. Government Printing Office, 1900.

Schwarz, John. *Annual Report of John Schwarz, Mayor of the City of Savannah, for the Year Ending December 31st, 1889. To Which Is Added the Treasurer's Report and Reports of the Different Departments*. Savannah: George N. Nichols, 1890.

Sholes, A. E. *Chronological History of Savannah*. Savannah: Morning News Press, 1900.

Smith, Lieutenant M. L. "Report and Plan of November 6, 1849." In U.S., Congress, Senate, 31st Cong., 1st sess., *Executive Document 19*, pp. 1–9. Washington, D.C.: U.S. Government Printing Office, 1851.

South Carolina v. Georgia et al., Supreme Court, October 1876 (93 U.S. 4).

Topographic Bureau. "Report for 1839." In U.S., Congress, Senate, 26th Cong., 1st sess., *Senate Document 58*, pp. 51–58. Washington, D.C.: U.S. Government Printing Office, 1840.

United States v. 450 Acres of Land Known as Barnwell Island, and E. B. Pinckney et al. Amicus Curiae Brief for Appellant, State of Georgia. n.d.

Ward, John E. *Report of John E. Ward, Mayor of the City of Savannah, for the Year Ending October 31st, 1854*. Savannah: Purse's Print, 1854.

Watkins, Robert, and Watkins, George. *Digest of the Laws of the State of Georgia*. Philadelphia: R. Aitken, 1800.

Wheaton, John F. *Report of John F. Wheaton, Mayor of the City of Savannah, for the Year Ending December 31, 1877, To Which Is Added the Treasurer's Report and Reports of the Different Departments*. Savannah: George N. Nichols, 1878.

———. *Report of John F. Wheaton, Mayor of the City of Savannah, for the Year Ending December 31, 1879, To Which Is Added the Treasurer's Report, and Reports of the Different Departments*. Savannah: Morning News Steam Printing House, 1880.

———. *Report of John F. Wheaton, Mayor of the City of Savannah, for the Year Ending December 31, 1880, To Which Is Added the Treasurer's Report, and Reports of the Different Departments*. Savannah: George N. Nichols, 1881.

Wright, James. "Report of Sir James Wright on the Condition of the Province of Georgia, on 20th Sept. 1773." *Collections of the Georgia Historical Society*. Vol. 3. Savannah: Morning News Office, 1873.

MANUSCRIPTS

Alexander, B. S. Letter to I. K. Tefft, February 25, 1845. Keith Read Manuscript Collection, University of Georgia Libraries, Special Collections, Athens, Ga.

Georgia–South Carolina Boundary File. Georgia Surveyor General Department, Atlanta, Ga.

Gilmer, J. F.; Bache, A. D.; and Bowman, A. H. "Report of the Commissioners on the Improvement of the Savannah River." Record Group 23, National Archives, Washington, D.C.

Port of Savannah Commissioners of Pilotage, Minutes, Collection No. 963, Georgia Historical Society, Savannah, Ga.

NEWSPAPERS

Georgia Republican and State Intelligencer
Savannah Daily Morning News
Savannah Morning News
Washington Post

INDEX

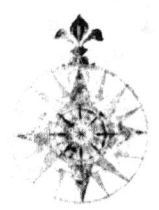

Abert, J. J., 113
Alexander, Barton S., 75
The Alexander Hamilton, 88
Altamaha River, 28, 29, 36
American Coast Pilot, 46, 89, 100–101
Anderson, Edward C., 122
The Anne, 59
Arnold, Richard D., 117, 120
The Atlantic Neptune, 41
Avery, Joseph, 41
Avery–Des Barres Chart, 46, 77
Azilia, Margravate of, 26, 27

Bache, Alexander Dallas, 83, 120–21
Back River, 90. *See also* Savannah River
Bailey, Thomas N., 140
Bargy, (engineer), 93
Barnwell islands, 1–4, 15–16; proposal to close channel between, 69; progress sheet shows works constructed, 140; increase in number, 169, 173; Cartographic Analysis Summary (Table 1), 174–81
Beaufain, Hector, 56
Beaufort Convention. *See* Beaufort Treaty
Belmont Plantation, S.C., 9
Bethesda Orphanage, 151
Bird Island, 3

Bloody Point, 46, 57
Blunt, Edmund M., 100
Board of Trade, British, 32
Bolton, Arthur K., 8, 12
Bolzius, Johann Martin, 63
Bowman, A. H., 116
Braddock, David Cutler, 73
Breakwater, submerged, 146
Broad River, 38
Broughton, Elijah, 112–13
Brown, James, 182
Brownfield, John, 58
Bull, John, 34
Busbee, George, 2, 10, 11
Butler, Pierce, 35

The Caesar, 73
Campbell, James, 85
Carter, Oberlin M., 127–33, 140, 142, 143, 198
Causton, Thomas, 29
Causway, Mr. Wright's, 169, 173
Chatham County State of Georgia, 138
Civil War, 122
Clinton, Henry, 38
Coast Survey of the U.S., 85
Coastal Zone Management Act, 2–3
Cobb, Howell, 50
Cockspur Island, 3, 13, 46, 66, 151
Colonial Charter of Georgia, 1, 13, 23, 38
Columbian Museum, 88
Colver, Stephen, 87–88, 113

215

216   Index

Commissioners of Pilotage for the Port of Savannah, 85, 87, 88, 90, 97
Cooks Cut, 184
Corps of Engineers, U.S. Army, 1, 14, 101
Crabtree, William, Jr., 98
Crombie, Alexander, 57
Cross Tides channel, 90–91
Cross Tides Dam, 142, 147
Culver, Stephen. *See* Colver, Stephen
Cumming, William P., 24, 36
Cunningham, David, 69

Daniell, William C., 91, 92, 94–97
Daufuskie Island, 46
Davis, Jefferson, 120
De Brahm, William Gerard, 63, 64, 66, 83, 190
Dennis, William, 197
Des Barres, Joseph Frederick Wallet, 41
Dredge, 85–86

East Florida, 28
Ebenezer, Ga., 63
Edwards, Edward B., 10–11
Egmont, Earl of, 31
Elba Island, 3, 138
Elbert, Samuel, 33
Engineer Department Report for 1834, 105
Engineers, U.S. Army. *See* Corps of Engineers
Eppley, F. M., 137
Estaing, Count Jean Baptiste d', 80
Eveleigh, Samuel, 55

Few, William, 31, 32, 34
Fig Island channel, 69, 91, 94
Fisher, T. H., 140
Flood: in 1871, 154; in 1878, 154; in 1888, 156
Ford, Gerald, 2
Fort George, 66, 75

Fort Greene, 151
Fort Jackson, 3
Fort Moore, 30
Fort Pulaski, 3–4, 104
Freshet, 153, 156. *See also* Yazoo
Furlong, Lawrence, 46, 89

Gamble, Thomas, 90
Gascoigne, John, 55
Gazette of the State of Georgia, 49
George II (king of England), 13
George III (king of England), 64
Georgia (Confederate ram), 122
Georgia Commission on Internal Improvement, 110
Georgia Legislature: "An Act for regulating trade, . . . and also an impost in the tonnage of Shipping," 41, 47, 84
Georgia Port Authority, 5
Georgia Republican and State Intelligencer, 150
Georgia v. South Carolina (1922), 14
Georgia v. South Carolina (1947), 12–19
Gercopely, Frances J., 159n
Gibbet Island. *See* Elba Island
Gill, (chief engineer), 93
Gillette, Cassius E., 159n
Gillmore, Quincy A., 130, 133, 137, 140; submits project for channel, 129; prepares chart of Savannah River, 139; describes Mud River and Jones Island, 144–45
Gilmer, J. F., 116, 120
Gordon, Peter, 58
Granger, Mary L., 77, 122
Guerro, C. (surveyor), 137

Habersham, James, 35, 69–74, 83
Habersham, Joseph C., 199
Halley, Edmund, 24
Henry, J. P., 98–99
Hilton Head Island, 11, 15, 40, 55, 68
History of the City Government of Savannah from 1790 to 1901, 90

Hoffman, Walter E., 19
Hosmer, Charles, 137, 138, 198
Houston, John, 34, 35
Houston, William, 33, 34
Howell, William, 6
Humphries, A. A., 133
Hunter, William J., 98
Hurricane damage, 150–51
Hutchinson Island, 13, 32, 40; considered part of Georgia, 56; proposal to join with Fig Island, 69; flooded, 150–51
The Hydraulics of a Tidal River as Illustrated by Savannah Harbor, Georgia, 83–84

Ingham, Benjamin, 62–63
Isundiga River. *See* Savannah River

Jenkins's Ear, War of, 28
Jones, Charles C., 80
Jones Island, 1–3, 15, 40; a neck of land in S.C., 80; condition of in Civil War, 144–45; survey and grant of, 182–84; Cartographic Analysis Summary of (Table 2), 185–89

Kean, John, 34
Kennard, J. S., 126
Keowee River, 13, 27, 28, 34, 36, 38–40
Kilbury, William, 54

Law Enforcement Demarcation Line, 10
Lazaretto Creek, 46
LeConte, John, 47, 101, 190
Lighter Aboard Ship Handling (LASH), 5
Lords Commissioners of Trade and Plantations, 24
Lords Proprietors of Carolina, 26
Luck Island, 27
Ludlow, William, 137, 198
Lyford, William, 75

McClintock, William E., 137
McIntosh, Lachlan, 35
Mackay, John, 104, 111, 113, 173
McKinnon, John, 88
Mansfield, Joseph K., 76, 104, 110
Martineau, John, 91
Mathews, George, 35
Milledgeville (gun boat), 122
Montgomerie, Sir Robert, 26
Moore, Francis, 62
Morris and Cumming, Messrs, 123
Mouzon, Henry, 36, 38
Mud River, 40, 69, 144; Cartographic Analysis Summary (Table 2), 185–89
Myers, Bacon, 57

Naval Depot, 91
Navy, U.S. Agent in Savannah, 98
New Windsor, 29, 57
Newton, John, 157–58n

Oconee County, S.C., 27, 49
Ogeechee (Confederate ram), 122
Oglethorpe, James Edward: establishes posts south of St. Marys River, 28; promulgates laws, 29; rejects South Carolina's opinion on navigation rights, 30; describes Savannah, 54; describes Savannah River mouth, 55; directs construction of lighthouse, 56; on boatmen at Tybee Island, 58
Overstreet, William B., 8–9
Oyster Banks, 66, 92
Oyster Bed Island, 1, 3–4, 6, 15–17; Cartographic Analysis Summary (Table 3), 191–97; condition in 1874, 198; site for quarantine station, 199; ballast dumped near, 199; hurricane damages, 200–201; quarantine station rebuilt at, 201–2; quarantine station abandoned, 203

Patterson, Carlile P., 137–38; de-

Patterson (*continued*)
  scribes post–Civil War condition of Savannah River, 127
Pearson, Captain (of *Snow Mary*), 72
Pennyworth Island, 15, 166
Penrose, John, 72
Pickens, Andrew, 35
Pilotage. *See* Commissioners of Pilotage
Pinckney, Charles Cotesworth, 34–35
Platen, Charles G., 138
The Polly, 85
Popple, Alured, 24
Popple, Henry, 24, 27
Prevost, August, 80
Purrysburg, Ga., 63

Quarantine station, 200, 201–2, 202–3

Rhodes, Ralph F., 83–84
Rice, (dredge supervisor), 85
Richardson, Elliot L., 2
Rochambeau, Count Jean Baptiste de, 38
Rocky River, 38
The Rose, 80
Ryan, Andrew J., III, 11

Saint Marys River, 28, 36
Saint Mathias River, 27
Savannah, Ga., 33, 58, 116–17
Savannah Chamber of Commerce, 112
Savannah Harbor, 48, 83–84, 141
Savannah Morning News, 151, 155–56
Savannah Old Town, 29, 57. *See also* New Windsor
Savannah River, 28, 30, 63; estuary, 9; most northern stream, 15, 26, 29, 69, 74; bar, 40, 46; obstructions listed, 99; charts of, 121–22, 138–41; entrance, 137; flooding, 155–56; flow around Barnwell islands, 173
Savannah River improvement, commission on, 117–20
Savannah River mouth, 18, 53, 54
Savannah River pilots, 15–16, 100
Savannah Sound, 64
Saxon, James B., Jr., 11
Saye, Albert B., 23
Sayer and Bennet (map publishers), 36
Scranton, William, 85
Seaward boundary, lateral, 2–5
Seneca River. *See* Keowee River
Shepherd, Peter, 57
Sherburne, Jonathan W., 92
Smith, Archibald, 169
Smith, M. L., 113, 116
Smith's Island, 139
Smith's Settlement, 169
The Snow Mary, 72
South Carolina, 16, 29, 50n, 57, 129
Special Master. *See* Hoffman, Walter E.
Stevens, Ebenezer, 85
Stouf, Isadore, 86–87
Supreme Court of the U.S., 12, 129, 163

Taft, Alonzo, 133
Tanner, Joe D., 9
Territorial Sea, 18–20
Throop, Captain (harbor master), 88
Treaty of Beaufort, 1; establishes boundary, 13; concerning islands, 15; first printed version, 35; first article quoted, 40; and Georgia's right to collect port tax, 47; newspaper summary, 49; no map to accompany, 53; involved to halt river project, 105–10
Trench's Island, 46, 55. *See also* Hilton Head Island
Trustees for establishing the Colony of Georgia, 28, 31, 54, 58, 69

Tugaloo River, 12, 27, 28, 33, 36, 38, 40
Tybee Island, 15, 40, 54, 58, 89, 154–55
Tybee Lighthouse, 46, 56
Tybee National Wildlife Refuge, 3

United States Constitution, 111
United States Geological Survey (USGS), 3, 4, 5–6, 8, 11–12, 14
United States v. Maine et al, 5

Vanderplank, Captain, 57
von Reck, Baron Georg Philipp Friedrich, 59

Waddell, James M., Jr., 6–8

Wallis, Helen, 24
Walton, George, 34
Ward, John E., 158n
Washington, George, 38
Washington Post, 11
Welles, Henry S., 128
Welman, F. H., 98
Whiting, W. H. C., 120
Wilkes, Charles, 100, 190
Wolf, John de, 138
Wright, Sir James, 74–76
Wright River, 40

Yamacraw Bluff, 55–56, 58, 59
Yazoo freshet, 113
Yonge, Henry, 47, 66, 68–69, 83

www.ingramcontent.com/pod-product-compliance
Lightning Source LLC
Chambersburg PA
CBHW051640230426
43669CB00013B/2384